The
of *The*

The Many Lives
of *The Twilight Zone*

Essays on the Television and Film Franchise

Edited by RON RIEKKI *and*
KEVIN J. WETMORE, JR.

McFarland & Company, Inc., Publishers
Jefferson, North Carolina

LIBRARY OF CONGRESS CATALOGUING-IN-PUBLICATION DATA

Names: Riekki, R. A., editor. | Wetmore, Kevin J., Jr., 1969– editor.
Title: The many lives of the Twilight Zone : essays on the television
and film franchise / edited by Ron Riekki and Kevin J. Wetmore, Jr..
Description: Jefferson, North Carolina : McFarland & Company, Inc., Publishers, 2022. |
Includes bibliographical references and index.
Identifiers: LCCN 2022038310 | ISBN 9781476681016 (paperback : acid free paper) ∞
ISBN 9781476644493 (ebook)
Subjects: LCSH: Twilight zone (Television program : 1959-1964) |
Twilight zone (Television program : 1985-1989) | Twilight zone
(Television program : 2019-2020) | Twilight zone (Motion picture) | BISAC:
PERFORMING ARTS / Television / Genres / Science Fiction, Fantasy & Horror
Classification: LCC PN1992.77.T87 M36 2022 | DDC 791.45/75—dc23/eng/20220902
LC record available at https://lccn.loc.gov/2022038310

BRITISH LIBRARY CATALOGUING DATA ARE AVAILABLE

ISBN (print) 978-1-4766-8101-6
ISBN (ebook) 978-1-4766-4449-3

Front cover image © 2022 Bruce Rolff/Shutterstock

Printed in the United States of America

*McFarland & Company, Inc., Publishers
Box 611, Jefferson, North Carolina 28640
www.mcfarlandpub.com*

Dedicated to Rod Serling,
who gave us entire universes
to imagine ourselves in.

Acknowledgments

The editors would like to thank the contributors first and foremost, who were able to engage the topic and create such interesting and wonderful writing in the middle of a global pandemic.

We would like to thank McFarland & Company, Inc., Publishers, and our editors.

Ron would like to thank Western Michigan University (where he earned his Ph.D.); the Graduate Theological Union, Brandeis University, and the University of Virginia (where he earned his MA, MFA, and second MFA, respectively); and Central Michigan University (where he earned his BS). Also, thank you to his parents for always encouraging his writing and reading. "For civilization to survive, the human race has to remain civilized."—Rod Serling, "The Shelter" (1961).

Kevin would like to thank Loyola Marymount University, the William H. Hannon Library and its staff, and especially Lacy, Kevin III, and Cordelia. Also, thanks to his parents who put up with a weird kid who wanted to stay up late and watch *The Twilight Zone*, beginning a lifelong love.

Table of Contents

vii

Part V. Staging the Zone

Preface

Ron Riekki

A cousin of mine would get high and do one of two things, both with extreme enthusiasm. The first thing he might do was put on old rock/punk music and give me a detailed recounting of the story of the song, its performers, that moment in history, so that he transformed into this wonderfully intense college professor if college professors swore more and weren't afraid to weave in a *lot* of their own opinion. It was oddly magical, listening to The Rolling Stones' "Cocksucker Blues" and having him passionately explain how the band was giving a grand fuck you to their label, Decca Records, in the same year my anti-college prof/cousin was born, sprinkling in details of "why that drum sound" and the specific brand of guitar played and who was drunk in the studio when this or that section was being recorded. Those academic-y rants turned me on to a whole list of artists I'd missed, being too caught up in contemporary albums and missing the work of the music industry's Beat Generation that was David Bowie, Iggy Pop, and Lou Reed, as well as a whole onslaught of Michigan bands I should have known but didn't, like the MC5, ? and the Mysterians, Sonic's Rendezvous Band, Sixto Rodriguez, and so many more.

The alternative thing my cousin would do was put on *The Twilight Zone*. The God-like respect he gave to Mick Jagger, Iggy, and Marvin Gaye, all got compiled down to one person: Rod Serling. The Mick/Iggy/Marvin rock star of television. God Serling. The sterling god of television writing.

Music and TV—this was my cousin's world, and he'd work to transform it to real meaning—not just as a way to pass time, but to instead consider the meaning of time itself, to question time, to question everything. It was a perfect program for pot and trivia-addicted intelligence. Jimmy would watch the show and be blown away, exploding at the end about the revelation we'd just witnessed, a sort of soft biblical transformation the viewer had gone through, a denouement he knew was coming from previous other multiple viewings, but which still surprised him for its craftsmanship. He loved to re-quote Serling's final words, whatever they were, all of them like a new and better (and simplified) Shakespeare, lines like "There was an old woman who lived in a room and like all of us was frightened of the dark" ("Nothing in the Dark," 1962), laughing about it in a way that I never fully understood. Jimmy found this extreme joy in how Serling would put things, the shock of Serling's words—"some men decided to turn the Earth into a graveyard" ("Deaths-Head Revisited," 1961)—so that my cousin would slap his knee, excited, a feeling like we'd just witnessed the epitome of cool, the characters in the story all frazzled and lost, and then this ultra-calm smoking strange-faced mortician appears, talking so oddly, so stoic and passionate at the same time, like he was part alien himself, saying things like "It has patterned itself after every dictator who has ever planted the ripping imprint of a boot on the pages of history since the beginning of time" ("The Obsolete Man," 1961).

"Jesus Christ!" my cousin would say. "Jesus Christ," standing suddenly and laughing extremely loudly, "Fucking *poetry*. How many shows you hear where they recite *fucking poetry*?" And he'd turn it off, and we'd sit there, this blank screen in front of us, its black mirror, and we'd think, me enjoying the sheer joy he had for the show. It's wonderful to see something someone else loves, to just observe perhaps why they love it so much, and to feel the glow coming off them. But, also, I loved the show too.

Then my cousin would start up another episode. We could go on and on like that, throughout the dull night in the dull towns where he always lived, towns that resembled *The Twilight Zone* towns, quaint and nothing and just waiting for something big to happen.

The show wasn't a "show." It wasn't the vacuity of *Entertainment Tonight* or *Dancing with the Stars*. There was substance. There was philosophy. Politics. Religion. The taboo subjects weren't taboo to Serling. He jumped right into the middle of their madness.

And that madness was shot in a style that seemed decades ahead of its time. From 1960 to 1963, *The Twilight Zone* earned six Primetime Emmy Award nominations for Outstanding Writing Achievement in Drama and Outstanding Achievement in Cinematography for Television. Writing and cinematography, that's what the show excelled at. Images I'll never forget.

I remember being home and stumbling on an episode on my little piece of crap TV, an episode entitled "It's a Good Life," with the visual of a dead gopher with three heads, an image I didn't see on the screen, but, more horrifically, saw in my mind. (If only contemporary horror films could understand the power of this cinematic move.) I didn't think that image could be topped, but it was with the climactic end of a man turned into a jack-in-the-box. I remember the chills when I saw that, chills that I still feel now, bodily, tingling through my brain down to my feet, when

I see that image. I have no idea why it affects me so much, but it did, and does. Others probably have different moments from different episodes, but for me, especially at that time, at that age, with such limited choices, such few programs I actually liked, such schlock that was so much a part of other shows, the emptiness of game shows and soap operas and talk shows, the pure lack of feeling when watching TV then, but then that image ricocheted, reverberated throughout my body. I loved it. I loved being frightened and challenged and just the sheer shock of, "Oh, this is what story can do. *Anything.*"

Submitted for Your Approval

*A Host and His Series and Their Remarkable
Afterlives—An Introduction*

KEVIN J. WETMORE, JR.

Its theme song is iconic and is sung or whistled to imply that things
have become strange. Its name is a metaphor for a weird, uncomfortable
situation. References to it abound in popular culture from pop songs to
Saturday Night Live sketches. *The Twilight Zone*, like the most sublime narratives or pop franchises in our culture, transcends itself as mere television program and instead has become a cultural presence. Its very name is
shorthand, its host easily recognizable: dark suit, cigarette in hand, standing off to one side offering insight and narration in a clipped baritone. In
a *Bloom County* cartoon from the eighties, as a character's life takes an
ironic twist he immediately begins looking around saying, "Rod?" *The
Twilight Zone* is simply iconic, in every sense of the word, as is its creator,
with whom it is firmly identified. The two are inseparable. Other writers may write for its multiple incarnations, other hosts may introduce us
to those about to visit the zone (looking at you, Forest Whitaker, Charles
Aidman, Robin Ward, and Jordan Peele), but Rod Serling is *The Twilight
Zone*.

Serling was born on December 25, 1924, in Syracuse, New York, the
second of two sons, to a Jewish grocer and butcher and his homemaker
wife. Growing up in Binghamton, New York, Serling was a class clown and
performer who later become a writer and editor of his high school newspaper. He was also an ardent radio listener, with a special passion for horror and fantasy anthology shows, a devoted fan of Arch Oboler, writer and
show runner of *Lights Out*, with whom we might later compare the adult
Serling.

The advent of the Second World War saw Serling enlist in the army
the morning after his high school graduation. His experiences in the war,

5

including seeing a great deal of destruction and many deaths of both friends and enemies, later shaped both his philosophy and writing.[1] He suffered nightmares from the war, and had he been born in later time, would have most likely been diagnosed with PTSD. After the war, Serling attended college, taking classes in literature, theater and broadcasting. He also met his wife Carol (Carolyn Louise Kramer) Serling, with whom he had two daughters. Serling began working in radio, but rapidly switched to the growing medium of television. His scripts began to garner attention and awards, with "Requiem for a Heavyweight" for the television series *Playhouse 90* in 1956 showing him to be a serious writer of great ability. In 1959, Serling wrote and produced a new series for CBS entitled *The Twilight Zone*, an anthology show with Serling as host that allowed him to write contemporary social criticism disguised in the genres of fantasy, science fiction, and horror. At a time neither was popular, Serling embraced racial equality and antiwar positions, presenting them in the series distanced through genre in a manner he thought viewers could accept, but still be given food for thought. He went on to produce other television series (including *Night Gallery*, another genre anthology show), teach, and write until his death in 1975 at the age of fifty, but nothing ever came close to *The Twilight Zone*.[2]

Nor did it need to. As a result of *The Twilight Zone*, Serling is larger than life. Can you name anyone else writing for television at the time who has inspired numerous biographies (some verging on hagiography) and portraits by those who knew him, including a biography by his daughter and a fiftieth anniversary retrospective co-edited by his widow. Only Gene Rodenberry, creator of *Star Trek*, comes close, and if we are honest, he is not nearly as loved or admired as Serling.

The Twilight Zone can be said to have produced two Serlings: Serling the writer and Serling the persona. He wrote ninety-two of 156 episodes, relying on genre writers such as Richard Matheson, Charles Beaumont, and William Clayton Johnson for episodes equaling the intelligence and quality that Serling himself produced. The level of writing and the devotion of *The Twilight Zone*'s fanbase has seen a number of episode scripts published in book form—Richard Matheson's, Earl Hamner's, Jerry Sohl's, and a ten-volume series of all ninety-two of Serling's teleplays entitled *As Timeless as Infinity: The Complete Twilight Zone Scripts of Rod Serling* (Matheson and Wiater; Hamner and Albarella; Sohl; Serling and Albarella). How many television series have had the majority of the teleplays published?

The show, however, is equally responsible for Serling the persona, as he introduced each episode in his inimitable way (although, if we are honest, it has actually been frequently imitated, both by comics and attempted, at least in form, if not style, by other show hosts). Serling did not introduce the idea of the host—radio anthology shows did that. Indeed, the closest analogy to Serling and *The Twilight Zone* on radio might be Arch Oboler and *Lights Out* (1936–1947), one of Serling's favorites, in which show runner and chief writer also served as host and was singularly associated with it. It was his duties as host that established Serling the persona, and was also singular in the iconic nature of *The Twilight Zone*. Even the episodes he did not write bore the stamp of Serling, not least of which because his was the voice and face that introduced, as well as being the last thing we heard on each episode. Serling's narration framed every episode, making them all his in a sense. He was *The Twilight Zone*, or at least our one and only guide to it.

In terms of hosting, *The Twilight Zone*, as noted above, was not the first, just arguably the best. For example, *Science Fiction Theatre* (1955–1957), another science-fiction anthology television program, influenced Serling and his imitators, and was hosted by Truman Bradley. With *The Twilight Zone*, however, the floodgates opened, and hosted genre anthology shows followed for the next several decades: *Thriller* (1960–1962), hosted by Boris Karloff (with the signature line, "As sure as my name's Boris Karloff, this one's a thriller," like *The Twilight Zone* investing each episode with the host's persona and reputation as much as the episode itself), *Way Out* (1961), hosted by Roald Dahl, *The Outer Limits* (1963–1965, genre show, but hostless, interestingly), and Serling's own *Night Gallery* (1969, 1970–1973), his follow-up to *The Twilight Zone*, which he also hosted.

The eighties saw a number of Serling imitators: *Darkroom* (1981–1982), hosted by James Coburn, *The Hitchhiker* (1983–1991) hosted by the eponymous character, played first by Nicholas Campbell, then Page Fletcher, *Tales from the Darkside* (1983–1988) with George Romero and Richard Rubinstein producing a hostless anthology series, and Steven Spielberg's *Amazing Stories* (1985–1987)—Spielberg also served as producer on *The Twilight Zone: The Movie* and his first professional directing experience was for Rod Serling on the set of *Night Gallery* (1969). The eighties also saw the first rebirth of *The Twilight Zone* on television.

Despite the tragic accident on the set of *Twilight Zone: The Movie* (1983) and its unenthusiastic reception by critics and audiences,[3] CBS, which had purchased the rights to *The Twilight Zone* from Serling in 1964, decided to revive the series, starting the transformation from single series into a franchise and cultural phenomenon. This second series lasted from 1985 to 1989 with two hosts: Charles Aidman (1985–87) and Robin Ward (1988–89). Although Aidman had performed in a few episodes of the original series, and both brought the required gravitas to the role of narrator, neither one was Rod Serling. A third series followed in 2002–2003, hosted by Forest Whitaker, and Jordan Peele produced and hosted the fourth incarnation beginning in 2019 and still in production as of this writing. In sixty years, Serling's "little show" has spawned three more series and a film and inspired dozens of other series. Again, only Roddenberry's *Star Trek* franchise can boast a family tree bigger than this from a simple television program in the sixties.

The Twilight Zone is more than a screen presence, however. Both a comic book series and a magazine bearing the name continued Serling's project and legacy from the early sixties through the late eighties. Gold Key Comics published *The Twilight Zone* comic book from 1962 to 1979 for a total of ninety-one issues. The comic was "hosted" by the likeness of Rod Serling, who introduced both stories adapted from episodes, as well as stories original to the comic. Even in two dimensions and four colors, *The Twilight Zone* needed the presence of Serling to work.

Similarly, Serling's presence ran throughout *The Twilight Zone Magazine*. Beginning in 1981 and with T.E.D. Klein as editor, *The Twilight Zone Magazine* (also known as *Rod Serling's The Twilight Zone Magazine*) ran articles about *The Twilight Zone* and its contributors, offered a multi-part *The Twilight Zone* episode guide, included a teleplay from the original series in each issue, all alongside original fiction by major genre writers (many of whom are still active today and who credit Klein and *The Twilight Zone Magazine* as being one of the best markets for short story writers). (Full disclosure: I still have my complete run of the 'zine—it was truly great for a teen horror and sci-fi fan!) Sadly, it only ran through June of 1989 before ceasing publication. Still, despite premiering six years after Serling's death, it was responsible for helping the careers of many rising horror, fantasy, and science-fiction authors, promoting *The Twilight Zone* to a new generation of fans, and sharing information about the show and its producers to those interested in learning more about the program. The magazine was both product of and promoter of the growing *The Twilight Zone* fanbase.

The Twilight Zone was a radio series on BBC Radio 4 from 2002 to 2012. Stacy Keach served as narrator, taking the role of Serling, and numerous British and American actors appeared on the series, which both updated the original episodes, making them contemporary for performance on radio and also adding new scripts, for a total of 176 episodes. *The Twilight Zone* is also a popular pinball machine released in 1993 by Midway, which used images and sounds from the series as part of the game. Lastly, the show inspired a ride at the Disney Theme Parks in Anaheim, Orlando, Tokyo, and Paris—*The Twilight Zone Tower of Terror*. The ride consists of a mock hotel in which characters had vanished supernaturally from an elevator. Riders then are strapped into an elevator car, *The*

Twilight Zone opening with Serling's narration is played, and then they are repeatedly lifted at great acceleration and dropped in freefall.

It is not inappropriate that Serling's vision makes its way into comic books, pinball machines, and theme park rides. *The Twilight Zone* is not just a dimension of sight, sound, and mind, it also represents a dimension of transition into adulthood for many. Many of us, including several contributors to this volume, discovered *The Twilight Zone* in reruns in childhood. Similarly, in some cases, we were told to turn off the television, as Brandon Grafius notes in his essay, as the subject matter was not suitable for children, an experience several of the contributors have also had.[4] Yet, we returned to this series again and again, finding in it adult narratives that children could understand and conversely stories told using elements familiar to us: spaceships, aliens, monsters, clowns, yet serving a purpose greater than the other stories we had encountered using these same tropes. To become a fan of *The Twilight Zone* is a step into adulthood in which one can still hold on to childlike delights and the joys of make-believe for a higher purpose.

The present volume is divided into five sections, each containing a number of essays that explore a variety of aspects of Serling's show and its epiphenomena. The first part offers essays examining the major ideas, themes, and philosophies of the original series. In "Middle Ground: *The Twilight Zone* as Social Criticism" Valerie L. Guyant argues certain episodes have enduring appeal as they focus on "enduring, nearly universal, concerns and fears," and this is done through the story of "a central male character who is struggling in a situation where he seems at odds with those around him, misunderstood, and unable to fit into a socially acceptable role." Through a reading of several such episodes, Guyant concludes the enduring *The Twilight Zone* themes are the need to refuse to conform and the need to face (and overcome) the fear of death.

Brandon R. Grafius considers the theological worldview of *The Twilight Zone*, finding manifestations of the divine in episodes in which God is portrayed as a character, a divine being has been sent by God or enforces the rules which God has mandated, and in the presence of a universal mechanism for "just desserts"—divine justice (not to mention ironic justice) being a recurring theme in the series. In "Rod Serling and the Ambiguity of Being," Kevin Bolinger reminds us, conversely, that rather than being dogmatic about anything, Serling "reveled in ambiguity and moral relativism" and that as a writer and philosopher, Serling has much in common with the early French postmodernists. Employing episodes in which Serling explored consciousness through artificial intelligence, Bolinger finds that *The Twilight Zone* often explored issues of consciousness, self-awareness, and existential loneliness, but offered no firm answers about our unknowable fellow beings, who may or may not be encountering us in the same way we are them. Similarly, Alexander E. Hooke proposes an affinity between postmodernism and Serling, arguing in "The Twilight of Humanism" that the series posits human absurdity and ambivalence towards sociocultural assertions of human superiority drive the series forward, pointing towards an end of traditional humanism as defined from the renaissance through late modernism. Hooke sees Serling's episodes undermining rationality and unity (in all senses of the word), positing a cosmos in which meaning and human activity are both rendered moot.

In "The Strange Zone of Speculative Rhetoric," Jimmy Butts agrees, observing, "*The Twilight Zone*, in particular, reasons with and against the world as though something otherwise might be considered." Arguing that speculative fiction is its own kind of rhetoric, designed to combine the real and unreal for the purposes of argument, Butts sees *The Twilight Zone* as a space of potential persuasion, of seeing the world otherwise, and, therefore, we may consider the series a model of "plausibility experimentation," in which the rhetoric allows us to reshape the world.

Molly A. Schneider reminds us that "the bomb" was not a popular nor appropriate topic for popular television dramas during the Cold War, yet Serling was able again and again to "scold humanity for its own self-destructive actions." Several episodes feature the after-effects of nuclear war, events that lead to nuclear war, and the repeated likelihood of human aggression, malice, and just plain incompetence that indicate the foolishness of ultimate weapons. Schneider gives a close reading of "The Shelter" (an episode Michael Meyerhofer also explores in great detail in the next section). Not that conventional weapons were much better. Concluding the first section, Elsa M. Carruthers and Paul Popiel consider conventional warfare and Serling's own experiences as made manifest in the series. "*The Twilight Zone* Goes to War!" offers insight and close readings into specific episodes that echo what Serling went through in the Pacific.

The second section, "Remember that one episode?" contains four essays offering close readings of specific episodes, mining them for multiple perspectives, meanings, and influences on subsequent narratives. Erin Giannini examines the shifts and changes between the original episode of "It's a Good Life" and the remade version directed by Joe Dante for *Twilight Zone: The Movie*. Dawn Keetley considers the classic episode "Stopover in a Quiet Town" and how it frames and echoes the trope of the evil child in subsequent horror cinema. In "Grief, Loss, and the Unknown: The Hauntological Phantasm of Richard Matheson's *The Twilight Zone*" Melissa A. Kaufler specifically looks at the episodes written by Richard Matheson, considering them from a hauntological perspective and the idea that they deconstruct time. Lastly, like Schneider in the previous section, Michael Meyerhofer finds great meaning in the classic third episode of the third season: "The Shelter." In "'It's simply out of my hands': Human Nature as Illustrated in *The Twilight Zone*'s 'The Shelter,'" he offers an analysis of the episode in question in the context of the Milgram Experiment and Stanford Prison Experiment, considering how all three demonstrate the rapid erosion of civility and mutual care and respect. Meyerhofer examines the episode's cautionary tale of the need to strengthen our communal humanity or face the end of humanity in a metaphoric as well as literal sense.

In the third section, "*The Twilight Zone* in the Eighties," volume coeditor Kevin J. Wetmore, Jr., examines how both the accident on set and John Landis' two scripted sections of *Twilight Zone: The Movie* resulted in elements of metacinema that actually damaged the perception and reception of the entire film. The deaths of three performers, the necessary changes in the script due to scenes not filmed before the accident, and the audience's knowledge of all of this reframe Landis' segment, resulting in a rather non–Serlingesque story and ending. Similarly, the Landis-written and directed wraparound narrative, "Something Scary," attempts to create a metanarrative of the *Twilight Zone* but descends into something closer to Landis' previous comedies (most notably *An American Werewolf in London*), rather than Serling's *The Twilight Zone*.

Missing from the original series was often traditional monsters, which finally showed up in the eighties reboot of *The Twilight Zone*. In "Twilight of the Vampires: *The Twilight Zone*, Vampires, America, and War," Simon Bacon gives close readings of two episodes from this incarnation of *The Twilight Zone*: "Monster!" and "Red Snow." After contextualizing the episodes in eighties vampire cinema, he looks at how each episode employs the vampire in different social critiques, exploring the legacy of the Vietnam War and the ongoing concerns of the Cold War.

"If You Dream It, They Will Film It" tells the firsthand account of Paul Chitlik and his writing partner first pitching the episode "Aqua Vita" to the new *Twilight Zone* in the eighties, and subsequently becoming a story editor for the series. Similarly, David Bennett Carren shares the diary of the shoot and the afterlives of his script for *The Twilight Zone* reboot entitled "If She Dies." Both writers present unique, behind-the-scenes insights into how *The Twilight Zone* was produced and created in the eighties, and how their affiliation with the show affected their subsequent careers.

"Comparative Zones" is the title of the fourth section, with two essays placing *The Twilight Zone* in contrast and comparison with other texts, including a movie and the most recent incarnation of the series. In "Strange Realities: *Twilight Zone*–sploitation in *Encounter with the Unknown*" Nicholas Diak analyzes the presence of Serling's voice in the

1973 film *Encounter with the Unknown*, positing that "*Encounter with the Unknown*, by leveraging distinctive and iconic attributes of *The Twilight Zone*, specifically Serling's narrations and visual cues, becomes both a multiplicity and an exploitation film derivative of the original *Twilight Zone* series." A confluence of echoes between series and film, some intentional, some coincidental, is also framed by Diak's comparison with specific episodes from the original series.

Arguing against legacy, and critiquing the dearth of *The Twilight Zone* scholarship, while suggesting that edited academic collections (such as this one) provide "an idiosyncratic narrative paradigm" that focuses on random, author-generated subjects providing an artificial and incomplete history of the franchise, David Melbye, author of *Irony in The Twilight Zone: How the Series Critiqued Postwar American Culture*, compares the first season of the Jordan Peele–created reboot of the show with the original series. After a thorough grounding in the cinematic and televisual contexts of both series, and as with Wetmore and *Twilight Zone: The Movie*, Melbye finds the new series strays from Serling's approach and, because of its complex artificiality that "seems forced," the new series does not function in context as well as the original.

The final section, "Staging the Zone," considers two moments of adaptation that also serve as examples of participatory culture and the recycling of the original series for new cultural creations. While Mark Scott Zicree has detailed the many attempts to adapt *The Twilight Zone* for live theater, many listed by William C. Boles in his essay in this collection, one of the more successful ones was a British production adapted from the series by American playwright Anne Washburn. Boles presents a history of the play and production, from Washburn's process in selecting episodes to dramatize to the critical reception of the show after it opens. Boles' focus is on the narrative and political choices of the playwright, finding in it echoes of the rhetoric of Donald Trump, which made the production a financial, but not necessarily a critical success.

In our last essay, Steve Krahnke and Michael Aronson document an experiment at the Media School of Indiana University in 2016. The school collectively worked to create three reimagined episodes of the original series: "The Shelter," "The Monsters Are Due on Maple Street," and "Will the Real Martian Please Stand Up?" Calling their project *21st Century Twilight Zone*, the Media School sought to employ Serling's scripts as educational tools to develop new versions of these stories. Krahnke and Aronson's purpose in detailing this experiment is "to describe the educational objectives of teaching with Serling's work and to describe the process of production as an integral part of storytelling. Our goal was not to improve on or copy Serling, but to use his work as an inspirational foundation to simulate realistic, collaborative, creatively successful production environments in an academic setting." The project can certainly serve as a model for future educational experiments based in Serling's work.

As the essays in this volume demonstrate, Serling's work is widely influential and his legacy only continues to grow. Several of the essays contained herein cite the critically and popularly acclaimed *Black Mirror* as yet another echo from the stories Serling brought to the television each week in a dimension not of sight or sound (though it was that, too), but of mind. Submitted for your approval—an anthology of essays by academics and artists analyzing this most enduring set of stories from a remarkable artist and philosopher.

NOTES

1. See Carruthers and Popiels' essay in this volume for more on Serling and the war. See Molly A. Schneider's essay for how this hatred of war also shaped Serling's approach to nuclear weapons.
2. Biographical information compiled from Engel; Parisi; Sander; Shadmi; Serling; Zicree, and Brode and Serling.
3. See Kevin J. Wetmore, Jr.'s, essay in this volume on *Twilight Zone: The Movie*, the accident, and the film's reception.
4. See my essay "Fanbase Press's Scariest 2020: Mr. Garrity and the Graves" for a detailed discussion of being scared by *The Twilight Zone* as a child (Fanbase Press.com, October 26, 2020).

WORKS CITED

Brode, Douglas, and Carol Serling. *Rod Serling and The Twilight Zone: The 50th Anniversary Tribute*. Barricade Books, 2009.
Engel, Joel. *Last Stop, the Twilight Zone: The Biography of Rod Serling*. Antenna Books, 2019.
Grams, Martin, Jr. *The Twilight Zone: Unlocking the Door to a Television Classic*. O T R Publishing, 2008.
Hamner, Earl, and Tony Albarella. *The Twilight Zone Scripts of Earl Hamner*. Cumberland House Publishing, 2003.
Matheson, Richard, and Stanley Wiater. *Richard Matheson's The Twilight Zone Scripts: Volume 1*. Edge Books, 2002.
_____. *Richard Matheson's The Twilight Zone Scripts: Volume 2*. Edge Books, 2002.
Parisi, Nicholas. *Rod Serling: His Life, Work, and Imagination*. University Press of Mississippi, 2018.
Rubin, Steven Jay. *The Twilight Zone Encyclopedia*. Chicago Review Press, 2017.
Sander, Gordon F. *Serling: The Rise and Twilight of TV's Last Angry Man*. Cornell University Press, 2012.
Serling, Anne. *As I Knew Him: My Dad, Rod Serling*. Citadel, 2013.
Serling, Rod, and Tony Albarella. *As Timeless as Infinity: The Complete Twilight Zone Scripts of Rod Serling*. 10 vols. Gauntlet, 2012.
_____. *The Best of Rod Serling's Twilight Zone Scripts*. Gauntlet, 2014.

Shadmi, Koren. *The Twilight Man: Rod Serling and the Birth of Television*. LifeDrawn, 2019.

Sohl, Jerry. *The Twilight Zone Scripts of Jerry Sohl*. Edited by Christopher Conlon. Bear-Manor, 2016.

Wetmore, Kevin J., Jr. "Fanbase Press's Scariest 2020: Mr. Garrity and the Graves," Fanbase Press.com (October 26, 2020).

Zicree, Mark Scott. *The Twilight Zone Companion*. 3rd ed. Silman-James Press, 2018.

PART I

A Dimension of Mind
Ideas, Philosophy, and the Original Series

Middle Ground

The Twilight Zone *as Social Criticism*

Valerie L. Guyant

Near the end of his life, Rod Serling said, of his own creative output, "I've pretty much spewed out everything I have to say, none of which has been particularly monumental. Nothing which will stand the test of time. The good writing, like wine, has to age well and my stuff has been—momentarily adequate" (qtd. in Lacy). Fans of *The Twilight Zone* are likely to disagree vehemently with this assessment but analyzing this and similar sentiments by Serling tells us a great deal about what he was hoping to achieve and whether continuing iterations of *The Twilight Zone* are achieving any of those goals.

Serling created *The Twilight Zone* during a time in network television history when sponsors held a great deal of sway over content, demanding writers make changes that may seem ludicrous, such as removing the word gas from a movie about Auschwitz or insisting that no one ask for a match if the sponsor sold lighters (Wallace). To avoid wrangling over content as much as possible, many writers engaged in pre-censorship, avoiding difficult subject matter because, as Serling put it "if you have the temerity to try to dramatize a theme that involves any particular social controversy currently extant then you're in deep trouble" (Wallace); however, doing so could lead a show to become "a lukewarm, vitiated, emasculated kind of show" (Wallace). Certainly, Serling was speaking from experience, as shown by the well documented events of trying to dramatize his teleplay "Noon on Doomsday" (1956). With the advent of *The Twilight Zone*, Serling had decided to act the self-professed "role of the tired conformist" (Wallace). It seems to be a role he did not play very well, as little of what he was doing can be considered an act of conforming.

Conforming was particularly difficult for Serling since he strongly believed that good television should be able to entertain while also acting as a vehicle for social criticisms and a means of commenting on the general human condition, human conflict, and human emotion (Serling, *Library of Congress*). By 1957, after the "Noon on Doomsday" debacle and frustrations with "The Arena" (1956) for *Studio One*, he had realized that drama was too controlled by sponsors and that he would best be able to accomplish his goals if he made his venue science fiction, utilizing robots in place of minorities (Serling, "About" 394) and the "fifth dimension, beyond that which is known to man" (*The Twilight Zone* season 1) to comment on the social issues and human conditions that were known to his audience but seldom examined. "A Martian," Serling noted, "can say things that a Republican or Democrat can't" (qtd. in Murray 97).

As George Clayton Johnson, a frequent writer for *The Twilight Zone*, noted, they crafted "Wisdom Fiction" for the series, a term originally coined by Theodore Sturgeon: stories with an "added touch of *strange* [that] included not only the seen but the unseen; not only the truth but the greater truth" (Johnson 52). The forms of greater truths they presented were varied, the reliance on an O. Henry style ending rampant, but *The Twilight Zone* often focused on generalized fears, especially isolation, conformity, and fears of aging or dying. In addition, many episodes highlighted societal and cultural fears of the time, reflecting on the recent past of World War II (1941–1945) and the Korean War (1950–1953), the initiation of the Cold War (1947–1991) and the advent of America's post-war consumer culture. Further, episodes often focused on fears that seem to, unfortunately, transcend time or place, such as fears of invasion by outsiders and fears of marginalized peoples (racial prejudice may have been exacerbated by the onset of the civil rights movement [1954–1968] but such fears were not new).

Interestingly, the episodes that now seem most likely to fall flat for viewers are those that have no depth beyond entertainment, such as "Mr. Denton on Doomsday" (1959) where, in the Old West, Al Denton is given a chance to be an expert shot again, but only for a day, "Elegy" (1960) where three astronauts are marooned on a cemetery planet and are granted their wish to be in their ship headed for home, "Mr. Dingle, the Strong" (1961) where a two-headed alien experiments on an unsuspecting, non-descript individual, giving him strength and then intelligence, or "The Whole Truth" (1961) where a used car salesman is forced to tell the truth as long as he owns a cursed car. In the end, he sells the vehicle to Nikita Khrushchev. Since the original series contained 156 episodes, it is no surprise that there were several episodes of this type that are definitely "momentarily adequate" as Serling assessed.

However, their entertainment value is one of the reasons that several of these episodes have been remodeled in the newer remakes, such as "A Kind of a Stopwatch" (1963) sharing clear similarities to "A Little Peace and Quiet" (1985) from *The Twilight Zone* (1985–1989) or "Living Doll" (1963) and "The Dummy" (1962) being precursors to "Mr. Motivation" (2002) in the short-lived 2002 revival. Of course, the conceit in each is easily adaptable to a new generation. The allure of being able to stop time increases as the speed of society increases, so one might expect that the newest revival of *The Twilight Zone* (2019) will eventually craft an entertaining approach to this idea as well, although it has not as yet. Of course, imagining that dolls and ventriloquist's dummies are sentient, and evil, is a recurring motif that has continued to be explored for entertainment, for example in *Goosebumps* stories, "The Puppet Show" episode of *Buffy the Vampire Slayer* (1997), and in *Annabelle* (2014).

Of more permanent appeal, as one might expect, are those episodes where Serling and other writers are presenting what one might consider enduring, nearly universal, concerns and fears. Perhaps two of the best-known original episodes fall into this category—"Time Enough at Last" (1959) and "Nightmare at 20,000 Feet" (1963)—as well as one that is less often cited on lists of best episodes, "The Obsolete Man" (1961). These episodes are spread throughout the original series: the eighth episode of the first season, the final episode of the second season, and the third episode of the fifth. While dealing with completely different surface subject matter, one common element is that each has a central male character who is struggling in a situation where he seems at odds with those around him, misunderstood, and unable to fit into a socially acceptable role.

In the case of "Time Enough at Last," Henry Bemis (Burgess Meredith) wants to read but is prevented from doing so at every turn by a job, a wife, and a life that prevent him from enjoying his passion. Nearly the entire episode shows Bemis trying to find a single moment to enjoy the printed page, while being threatened with the loss of his job and having his wife disfigure a book of poems as a preventative measure. Finally, he hides in a vault to escape long enough to read. In essence, he breaks from even an appearance of conformity to enjoy his passion, outside of social norms. That act saves his life when the city is hit with a bomb blast, leaving him alone. He teeters on the brink of suicide, adrift from the social expectations that have defined him and against which he has railed, until he realizes he has the time to assuage his craving, to embrace his individuality. Before he can do so, he mistakenly breaks his glasses, leaving him worse off than he was at the beginning of the episode. His last, mournful words are "There was time now. There was—was all the time I needed. It's not fair." The suggestion seems to be that conformity to society is preferable to isolation, that ignoring social convention can lead to isolation and despair, but that social demand is not fair to ask of any of us.

This same theme of a flawed social demand for conformity is promoted in "The Obsolete Man." As Serling's opening narration informs the viewer, Romney Wordsworth (also played by Burgess Meredith) is "a citizen of the State but will soon have to be eliminated, because he's built out of flesh and because he has a mind." The episode begins with Romney on trial for obsolescence because he is a librarian and books are no longer allowed in this totalitarian possible future. We learn during the episode that Wordsworth is also a skilled carpenter and could have secured a safe life by relinquishing his books and sublimating his love of knowledge. His refusal to do so is an important part of his unwillingness to conform to society he perceives as unfair, and which Serling's narrative voice reinforces as severely flawed. Also important is the means by which Wordsworth highlights the hypocrisy of a society that demands conformity. Before meeting his death, he forces the Chancellor to beg to survive "in the name of God," which proves his own obsolescence to a society that does not acknowledge religion. The episode ends with Serling proclaiming "Any state, any entity, any ideology which fails to recognize the worth, the dignity, the rights of Man, that state is obsolete." While this episode could easily be viewed exclusively as a condemnation of a nation that had recently gone through the Red Scare of McCarthyism (1950–1954), it also emphasizes the need of the individual to fight against pressure to conform in the larger social context, devoid of a specific historical moment.

That same need to fight against conformity can be seen in "Nightmare at 20,000 Feet," where Robert Wilson (William Shatner) is traveling home after having been in a sanitarium "where he spent the last six months recovering from a nervous breakdown." His fear of flying is so extreme that it led to the initial breakdown, putting him at odds with social expectations of the time as they pertained to a husband, father, and businessman. That fear of flying, as well as his fear of being considered outside the norm, lead him to question the existence of the gremlin he sees on the wing of the plane for some time. His history of not conforming to socially rational behavior leads his wife, the flight attendant, and the pilot to all doubt him, even attempting to sedate him to maintain the appearance of calm expected in society. As with Henry Bemis, Robert Wilson could have conformed. He could have taken the sedative and let himself be convinced that he was again experiencing a mental break caused by his fear of flying. Although it would have made him appear damaged, it would have been within already accepted social constraints. Instead of conforming, he could, like Romney Wordsworth, have accepted his death; however, unlike Wordsworth, he would not have made any impact on society and its mandates by doing so. Instead, he feigns conformity, thwarts authority represented by the sleeping police officer whose gun he steals, and saves everyone by shooting at the gremlin.

The episode ends with Wilson on a stretcher, in a straitjacket, with everyone clearly believing he has lost all hold on reality. If that were the entire ending, one might read this as reaffirming our need to adhere to social codes. Instead, the closing narration and close up of the damaged wing emphasizes that Wilson no longer has reason to fear the gremlin or people's perception of him. Rather, he will soon be vindicated, his place as a unique individual secured by tangible proof. We can read the gremlin on the wing as symbolic of a number of possible social issues that Serling was suggesting we should fight against, cementing the realization that all three of these episodes underscore the need of the individual to fight against the push to conform.

Several other, more lighthearted, episodes in the original series also emphasize the need not to conform, especially "Mr. Bevis" (1960) from season one and "Cavender is Coming" (1962) from season three. In each of these episodes, the main character is offered a life-changing opportunity through the auspices of a guardian angel. To take full advantage of the life changes, they must each also change their personalities, inhabiting a more traditionally accepted life and exhibiting a more culturally approved personality. Both Mr. Bevis (Orson Bean) and Agnes Grep (Carol Burnett) realize that their happiness is not dependent on being successful or on fitting in. Rather, their happiness is assured by the very uniqueness of personality that makes it difficult for them to conform.

Issues of conformity are a recurring issue brought up in the remakes as well, but with an important difference. Most notable are "Examination Day" (1985) and "Evergreen" (2002). In "Examination Day," Richard "Dickie" Jordan Jr. (David Mendenhall) celebrates his birthday and readies himself for a government mandated IQ test. He is excited and tries to reassure his parents that he will do well. This short episode ends with the parents being informed that Dickie has exceeded the intelligence level allowed and asking where they would like his body delivered. A similarly dark turn occurs in "Evergreen" where the Winslow family moves into a gated community called Evergreen, designed to help families deal with rebellious teens, such as their daughter Jenna Winslow (Amber Tamblyn). Jenna has tattoos and colored hair, likes rock music, and fails to conform to her parents or her society's expectations. Eventually, Jenna discovers that the Arcadia Military Academy that she is threatened with is the Arcadia Fertilizer Company. Her own sister, Jules, turns her in to the neighborhood watch, and the episode concludes with the parents planting a tree in their front yard and nurturing it with the fertilizer provided as the leader of the neighborhood watch says, "Let this tree be a reminder that there's something good in each and every one of us." While it is possible to view "Examination Day" as a scrutiny of governmental overreach and

"Evergreen" as a commentary on parenting, it is impossible to avoid the underlying commentary on conformity. Although produced nearly twenty years apart, these two episodes emphasize a similar message of conforming to a social structure as the only way to survive. In comparison to the earlier series, conformity is reinforced rather than warned against.

This alteration of theme from the original can also be seen in the most recent remake of "Nightmare at 20,000 Feet," now titled "Nightmare at 30,000 Feet" (2019) where the main character is now Justin Sanderson (Adam Scott), a journalist suffering from PTSD who learns the plane is in danger through a mysterious podcast. Justin trusts a fellow traveler, only to find his confidante is the one responsible for the crash. Justin is eventually beaten to death by the other passengers. The gist of the episode is that, if Justin had conformed, the crash would not have happened, the passengers would have been safe, and he would have survived. Sadly, this update, while maintaining a similarity of plot, presents an overall point that is antithetical to Serling's original as well. In a time when we would like to think we are becoming more socially responsive to differences, *The Twilight Zone* seems to be repeatedly enforcing how important it is to get along and fit in.

In addition to shows that emphasized issues of conformity, one of Serling's most abiding interests was episodes that investigated the universal fear of death. As early as episode two, "One for the Angels" (1959), Serling gives us Lew Bookman (Ed Wynn), who is so anxious to escape death that he makes a deal with Mr. Death (Murray Hamilton), which nearly leads to a young girl's death in his place until he realizes that saving another is more important. Of the dozens of episodes in the original series where death is mentioned, there are several where it is not only the focus of the plot but also part of the lesson to be learned. In "The Hitch-Hiker" (1960), Nan Adams (Inger Stevens) struggles desperately to avoid a man who seems to be following her, only to discover that he is the embodiment of death and that she herself has already died; in "The Purple Testament" (1960), Lt. Fitzgerald (William Reynolds) discovers he has the ability to see who will die in the next military skirmish, including himself, but not the ability to stop it; in "The Passersby" (1961), a Civil War sergeant exchanges dialogue with Lavinia Godwin (Joanne Linville) until they both realize they are already dead, declaring "Your life, it's kind of like a song. You play it right to the end, and when the notes are finished, and they die out, there's only silence." In "Nothing in the Dark" (1962), perhaps the most compelling of this group, Gladys Cooper (Wanda Dunn) has spent most of her adult life hiding from death until he (Robert Redford) appears at her door and gently takes her hand. As is true with many such episodes, the wisdom imparted at the end of the episode is that death itself is as much a part of life as living is, or "that there was nothing in the dark that wasn't there when the lights were on," as Serling's end narration states. Unlike conformity, which Serling inspires us to avoid, death, he tells us, is something we embrace when it comes.

These episodes continue to appeal, no matter how dated the cinematography or rudimentary the production quality, not because they have aged well, but because the underlying message, a message that we are not alone in our fears of death, continues to resonate. It is no surprise that every iteration of *The Twilight Zone* has addressed fears of death in some way, although not always with the same message. For instance, "Welcome to Winfield" (1986) shows us a town filled with people who have bargained with agents of death to not be "reclaimed"; "Dead Run" (1986) offers a truck driver who decides it will be his job to determine who deserves to go to Hell; and an updated version of "The Purple Testament" titled "Into the Light" (2003) allows Rachel Stark (Samantha Mathis) to see the glow of death on faces, but also to affect change during a school shooting. As with the issue of conformity, the lesson has changed in these newer episodes.

The continuing and recurring interest in these issues, from Serling's inception of *The Twilight Zone* to now, certainly suggest that he crafted a venue to allow for investigations of the human condition and human emotion. The enduring appeal of original episodes as well as the desire to remake aspects of them is a testament to the quality with which they presented those emotions.

This leaves us with the third component of what Serling considered great work: literature, television as a means of social commentary. Media in all its forms has been used as a means of creating and disseminating moral panics, at least since *Reefer Madness* (1936) insisted we should all fear the "new and deadly menace lurking behind closed doors … marijuana, the burning weed with its roots in hell." This use of media to craft panic is described by Stephen Cohen as the way in which society crafts deviance because:

> Societies appear to be subject, every now and then, to periods of moral panic. A condition, episode, person or group of persons emerges to become defined as a threat to societal values and interests; its nature is presented in a stylized and stereotypical fashion by the mass media; the moral barricades are manned by editors, bishops, politicians and other right-thinking people. [...] Sometimes the panic passes over and is forgotten, except in folklore and collective memory [1].

This spreading of moral panics can be seen in "The Card" (1987) where a woman signs up for a new credit card. It's clear from her husband's reaction that she has problems with managing her money and the company exacts a high charge for late payments, taking the family pets and then the children, and eventually her husband and her very existence. The last image of the episode is the credit card floating to the ground. The message is clear: those who misspend on revolving credit deserve to lose their entire existence. Equally clear, not everyone is likely to behave in this way; it is a moral flaw.

Serling could have easily fallen prey to this trap, as many in television and film, including the remakes, do, creating and perpetuating moral panics. The closest he comes is in his revisiting, numerous times, the ideas of alien invasion and sentient machines; both were staples of the science-fiction genre in the 1950s, so their use alone does not constitute enacting moral panics. First season episodes, especially "The Fever" (1960) and "A Thing About Machines" (1960) seem, on the surface at least, to be suggesting that machines are out to destroy us all; however, "A Thing About Machines" suggests in the closing narration that Bartlett Finchley (Richard Haydn) may have imagined being tormented by machines because he lacked human interaction and "The Fever" suggests that Franklin Gibbs (Everett Sloan) succumbs to manipulation because he is ill-tempered. Similarly, the couple who are apparently manipulated by a fortune telling machine in "Nick of Time" (1960) are eventually masters of their own fates, working together to break free of a negative cycle. Serling, then, does not suggest a moral panic about reliance on machines so much as a playful use of surreal forms of machinery to carry other moral lessons. The same is true of most of his uses of alien invasion, except for the principally humorous episodes such as "Hocus-Pocus and Frisby" (1962). The aliens are not a threat to societal values, nor are a specific person or type of person in most of these episodes. Rather, the point of an episode like "To Serve Man" (1962) is that our own hubris will prevent us from seeing a threat and "The Invaders" (1961) suggests that we may be a small part of a much larger universe.

Most importantly, *The Twilight Zone* highlighted the ways in which moral panics and those who believed in them were flawed and at fault in a handful of exceptional and important episodes. Serling often visited war as a vehicle for narrative in *The Twilight Zone*: "Judgment Night" (1959) where Carl Lanser relives the night he ordered his U-boat to fire on a passenger vessel without warning, materializing on the bridge of the vessel repeatedly throughout eternity; "A Quality of Mercy" (1961) where Second Lieutenant Katell finds himself inhabiting the life of Lieutenant Yamuri in the Imperial Japanese Army so he can understand why continuing to fight when a war is won is inhumane; and "The Encounter" (1964), perhaps the most uncomfortable of the three, where Fenton and Takamori both admit their individual guilts from the attack on Pearl Harbor, try to forgive each other and themselves, but finally succumb to the influence of the samurai sword that lays between them.[1] A moral-panic-laden episode might have relied on showing why viewers should fear and hate; instead each of these episodes poignantly showcased how fear of the Other leads to and perpetuates unwarranted violence.

Another excellent example where fear of an outsider leads to disaster is "The Gift" (1962). In this episode, an alien arrives in a small Mexican village. He lashes out when confronted by an angry villager and accidentally kills him. Only two individuals in the village are kind to him, a doctor and a young boy. The alien gives the boy a gift and tells him that the doctor will know how to use it. When he is cornered by the villagers and killed, they also destroy the gift, which was an explanation of how to cure all cancer. Again, the theme here is clear and highlighted in the closing moments. The doctor exclaims "We have not just killed a man; we have killed a dream," and Serling's end narration emphasizes "the subject: fear. The cure: a little more faith." Moral panic, implemented in issues of invasion and encroachment by others, would emphasize our need to fear. Serling emphasizes our need to do the opposite.

While these examples deal with war and with a foreign country, Serling also brought his thoughts about fear, scapegoating, and the danger they pose to our way of life into neighborhoods reminiscent of his viewers' own in "The Monsters Are Due on Maple Street" (1960) and "The Shelter" (1961). In both episodes, aliens are not at fault; the supernatural is not truly at fault. The average person's susceptibility to fear and willingness to use violence in the face of that fear is the integral failing of the human race. "The Shelter" is the more dated of the two, but the emotional point is still pertinent. Serling's opening narration warns us: "what you are about to watch is a nightmare. It is not meant to be prophetic, it need not happen, it's the fervent and urgent prayer of all men of good will that it never shall happen." Engulfed by fear of a possible nuclear attack, without bomb shelters of their own, the Stockton family's neighbors devolve into nativism, pent-up hostility, and violence. Serling's "fervent prayer" is that we might learn to not succumb to the moral panic that lead them there.

In comparison, "The Monsters Are Due on Maple Street" is less dated and continues to resonate so well that it has been remade in radio and graphic novel format, as well as during the 2003 reboot. In the original, unexplained electrical events in the neighborhood are frightening the adults when Tommy, a neighborhood boy, insists that aliens must have infiltrated the neighborhood. Although using extraterrestrials as the purported evildoers, it does not take much imagination to imagine viewers who might have been worried about Communist sympathizers at the time. The entire neighborhood turns on each other, seeking someone to blame, until one neighbor is dead of a gunshot, young Charlie is a target for possible violence, and another neighbor is suffering from cuts caused by a broken window. The 2003 remake is very close in plot, with the marked exception of the concern being terrorism rather than aliens.

In addition, the closing narration of the two episodes differs and that difference is important. In the original, Serling says:

> There are weapons that are simply thoughts, attitudes, prejudices to be found only in the minds of men. For the record, prejudices can kill and suspicion can destroy and a thoughtless, frightened search for a scapegoat has a fallout all of its own, for the children and the children yet unborn. And the pity of it is that these things cannot be confined to the Twilight Zone.

For the epilogue of the 2003 version, "The Monsters Are on Maple Street," Forest Whitaker warns us: "It isn't enough for a sole voice of reason to exist. In this time of uncertainty, we're so sure that villains lurk around every corner that we will create them ourselves if we can't find them; for while fear may keep us vigilant, it's also fear that tears us apart, a fear that sadly exists only too often, outside the Twilight Zone." Note that the original insists that prejudice and suspicion are unfounded weapons to be avoided; whereas, Whitaker suggests we should embrace a certain amount of fear, since it will keep us vigilant and that there are villains, even if we can't find them. Whitaker's version is using a subtle form of moral panic; we should fear the unseen villain, but not fear it so much that we replace vigilance with self-destruction. In each instance, Serling's warning narration attempts to dissolve moral panic and the narrative and plot of the remakes encourages that panic, albeit subtly more often than not.

The original The Twilight Zone episodes show Serling achieving all three of his goals: entertaining, highlighting the general human condition, and being "a vehicle of social criticism [through which he strove to] involve an audience, to show them wherein their guilt lies ... a universal guilt, which they should feel or at least in part understand" ("Conversations"). This is also how later iterations of The Twilight Zone most often fail. They are often entertaining. As noted, they occasionally highlight aspects of the human condition in ways that lead to a new perspective. They do not avoid moral panics in order to lead to the sense of understanding and catharsis that Serling's best episodes were able to.

It is difficult to say if this is a difference in production values, network involvement, or audience interest. Serling asserted that censoring writers and creators who are trying to comment on the human condition and critique society "begins a process of decay that ultimately leads to disaster" (Serling, "The Challenge" 133). "So long as men write what they think," Serling insisted, "then all the other freedoms may remain intact. It's then that writing becomes a weapon of truth, an act of conscience, an article of faith" ("The Challenge" 133). The original *The Twilight Zone*, under Serling's expert guidance, was wielded most often as a weapon of truth hidden beneath a veneer of imagination, and as a bastion against the moral panics that all too often inhabit even our best television. For those reasons, it is most definitely more than "momentarily adequate."

NOTE

1. See Carruthers and Popiel's essay on *The Twilight Zone* and war in this volume.

WORKS CITED

"The Card," *The Twilight Zone*, written by Michael Cassutt, directed by Bradford May, CBS, 1987.

"Cavender Is Coming," *The Twilight Zone*, written by Rod Serling, directed by Chris Nyby, Image Entertainment, 2011.

Cohen, Stephen. *Folk Devils and Moral Panics*. Routledge Press, 2002.

"Dead Run," *The Twilight Zone*, written by Alan Brennert, directed by Paul Tucker, CBS, 1986.

"The Dummy," *The Twilight Zone*, written by Rod Serling, directed by Abner Biberman, Image Entertainment, 2011.

"Elegy," *The Twilight Zone*, written by Charles Beaumont, directed by Douglas Heyes, Image Entertainment, 2010.

"The Encounter," *The Twilight Zone*, written by Martin Goldsmith, directed by Robert Butler, Image Entertainment, 2010.

"Evergreen," *The Twilight Zone*, written by Jill Blotevogel, directed by Allan Kroeker, United Paramount Network, 2002.

"Examination Day," *The Twilight Zone*, written by Philip DeGuere, Jr., directed by Paul Lynch, CBS, 1985.

"The Gift," *The Twilight Zone*, written by Rod Serling, directed by Allen H. Miner, Image Entertainment, 2011.

"The Hitch-Hiker," *The Twilight Zone*, written by Rod Serling, directed by Alvin Ganzer, Image Entertainment, 2011.

"Hocus-Pocus and Frisby," *The Twilight Zone*, written by Rod Serling, directed by Lamont Johnson, Image Entertainment, 2011.

"Into the Light," *The Twilight Zone*, written by Moira Kirland Dekker, directed by Lou Diamond Phillips, United Paramount Network, 2003.

"The Invaders," *The Twilight Zone*, written by Richard Matheson, directed by Douglas Heyes, Image Entertainment, 2011.

Johnson, George Clayton. "Horror Legend." *The Twilight and Other Zones: The Dark World of Richard Matheson*, edited by Stanley Wiater, Matthew R. Bradley, and Paul Stuve, Citadel Press Books, 2009, pp. 52–56.

"Judgment Night," *The Twilight Zone*, written by Rod Serling, directed by John Brahm, Image Entertainment, 2010.

"A Kind of a Stopwatch," *The Twilight Zone*, written by Rod Serling, Directed by John Rich, Image Entertainment, 2011.

Lacy, Susan, dir. *American Masters, Rod Serling: Submitted for Your Approval*, PBS, 29 November 1995. *YouTube*, uploaded by Aeolus 13 Umbra, 28 June 2015.

"A Little Piece and Quiet," *The Twilight Zone*, written by James Crocker, directed by Wes Craven, CBS, 1985.

"Living Doll," *The Twilight Zone*, written by Charles Beaumont, directed by Richard C. Sarafian, Image Entertainment, 2011.

"Mr. Bevis," *The Twilight Zone*, written by Rod Serling, directed by William Asher, Image Entertainment, 2010.

"Mr. Denton on Doomsday," *The Twilight Zone*, written by Rod Serling, directed by Allen Reisner, Image Entertainment, 2010.

"Mr. Dingle, the Strong," *The Twilight Zone*, written by Rod Serling, directed by John Brahm, Image Entertainment, 2010.

"Mr. Motivation," *The Twilight Zone*, written by Brent V. Friedman, directed by Deran Sarafian, United Paramount Network, 2002.

"The Monsters Are Due on Maple Street," *The Twilight Zone*, written by Rod Serling, directed by Ronald Winston, Image Entertainment, 2013.

"The Monsters Are on Maple Street," *The Twilight Zone*, written by Erin Maher and Kay Reindl, directed by Debbie Allen, United Paramount Network, 2003.

Murray, Brian. "The Enduring Legacy of *The Twilight Zone*." *The New Atlantis*, vol. 48, Winter 2016, pp. 90–112. *Academic Search Complete*. Accessed 3 June 2020.

"Nick of Time," *The Twilight Zone*, written by Richard Matheson, directed by Richard L. Bare, Image Entertainment, 2010.

"Nightmare at 30,000 Feet," *The Twilight Zone*, written by Marco Ramirez, directed by Greg Yaitanes, CBS All Access, 2019.

"Nightmare at 20,000 Feet," *The Twilight Zone*, written by Richard Matheson, directed by Richard Donner, MGM Studios, 1963.

"Nothing in the Dark," *The Twilight Zone*, written by George Clayton Johnson, directed by Lamont Johnson, Image Entertainment, 2011.

"The Obsolete Man," *The Twilight Zone*, written by Rod Serling, directed by Elliot Silverstein, Image Entertainment, 2011.

"One for the Angels," *The Twilight Zone*, written by Rod Serling, directed by Robert Parrish, Image Entertainment, 2010.

"The Passersby," *The Twilight Zone*, written by Rod Serling, directed by Elliot Silverstein, Image Entertainment, 2011.

"The Purple Testament," *The Twilight Zone*, written by Rod Serling, directed by Richard L. Bare, Image Entertainment, 2010.

"A Quality of Mercy," *The Twilight Zone*, written by Rod Serling, directed by Buzz Kulik, Image Entertainment, 2011.

Serling, Rod. "About Writing for Television." *Problems and Controversies in Television and Radio*, edited by Harry J. Skornia and Jack William Kitson. 1957. Pacific Books, 1968, pp. 377–395.

_____. "The Challenge of the Mass Media to the 20th-Century Writer." *The Quarterly Journal of the Library of Congress*, vol. 25, no. 2, 1968, pp. 130–133. *Academic Search Complete*. Accessed 20 May 2020.

_____. "Conversation with Rod Serling." *Library of Congress*, 1968, www.loc.gov.

"The Shelter," *The Twilight Zone*, written by Rod Serling, directed by Lamont Johnson, Image Entertainment, 2011.

"A Thing About Machines," *The Twilight Zone*, written by Rod Serling, directed by David Orrick McDearmon, Image Entertainment, 2010.

"Time Enough at Last," *The Twilight Zone*, written by Rod Serling, directed by John Brahm, Image Entertainment, 2010.

"To Serve Man," *The Twilight Zone*, written by Rod Serling, directed by Richard L. Bare, Image Entertainment, 2011.

Wallace, Mike. "The Mike Wallace Interview: Featuring Rod Serling," American Broadcasting Company, 22 September 1959. *YouTube*. Uploaded by Paul Eres, 29 Sep 2010, www.youtube.com.

"Welcome to Winfield," *The Twilight Zone*, written by Les Enloe, directed by Bruce Bilson, CBS, 1986.

"The Whole Truth," *The Twilight Zone*, written by Rod Serling, directed by James Sheldon, Image Entertainment, 2011.

Social Liberalism and Orthodox Theology

Ideas of God in The Twilight Zone

BRANDON R. GRAFIUS

The universe of the original *The Twilight Zone* series is large, multi-faceted, and frequently contradictory, due both to its structure as an anthology series and its nature as engaging in speculative scenarios. Even so, numerous patterns run between episodes, and many of the stories exhibit overlapping worldviews. This essay will explore the ways in which *The Twilight Zone* depicts God, either directly or (much more frequently) indirectly through the structures of its posited worlds.

This essay will focus on three types of *The Twilight Zone* episodes that seem to most directly speak to a theological worldview. In the first (relatively rare) type, God appears within the narrative, with a specific character serving as a stand-in for the divine. In the second type, God does not appear, but is instead represented by a being in the employment of the divine, such as an angel or Death. The third type, the "just desserts" model in which evil characters receive an ironically fitting punishment, seems the farthest removed from theology, as there is usually no direct reference to God; however, these episodes present a world that is organized around the concept of justice, indicating a divine hand which has created a universe where evil deeds are judged appropriately. Sometimes, the episodes make this connection directly. More often the cause lurks in the background as some unspecified mechanism of fate. But even when the cause is not explicitly stated, the results make it easy for viewers to slot the cause-and-effect nature of the scenario into comfortably pre-existing theological worldviews.

The Twilight Zone was a ground-breaking television series in many ways, functioning as a critique of the Cold War (Mortenson), domestic relations in the "traditional" American family (Laudadio), and American consumer culture (Brokaw). But the three-fold schema explored in this essay reveals a strand of theological traditionalism that underlies many episodes of the series. Though many of the episodes present powerful social critiques of post-war American society, they frequently also offer a worldview in which bad people are punished, and the divine plan keeps things running smoothly.

When God Makes an Appearance

With only a handful of exceptions, God doesn't appear in *The Twilight Zone* narratives. In places where God is depicted, it's most often through a character with God-like powers who serves as a stand-in for the divine. Two episodes, in particular, offer starkly different views of God. The first is a normative Christian portrayal of a benevolent God, but the second offers one of the more unsettling theological claims in the entirety of *The Twilight Zone*'s corpus.

The series' most positive portrayal of the divine is from the fifth season episode "The Old Man in the Cave." Set in a post-apocalyptic 1974, God is represented as a reclusive old man who lives in a cave outside of town, occasionally passing helpful advice along to his messenger. At first, the people ignore the old man's advice about where to plant their crops, leading to a dangerously poor harvest. The episode opens with the town waiting to receive advice regarding a recently discovered supply of canned food; the verdict they receive is not favorable. But when the "old man" is revealed to be a computer, the townspeople decide that all of the instructions they have received are a hoax, and decide to disregard the advice to stay away from the newly discovered food. The town pays for this decision with their lives. In this episode, the problem is located within humanity's capacity for doubt—the divine (as represented by the computer) is a benevolent force, one which seeks to help the townspeople avoid catastrophe. Their unwillingness to believe is their undoing.

In this episode, God is benevolent, and looks out for the people. The "old man in the cave" gives them detailed instructions as to how to grow nourishing food and how to avoid bad food. Mr. Goldsmith, as the intermediary between the village and the old man, plays the role of Moses, traveling up the mountainside to receive commandments. These commandments are proven reliable, and it is only when the people stop believing that they run into trouble. These connections are made explicit in the episode's (rather heavy-handed) closing speech, delivered by Mr. Goldsmith as he walks among the dead townsfolk. "When we talked about the ways men could die," he says, "we forgot the chief method of execution. We forgot faithlessness." The Old Man had "kept them alive," as Mr. Goldsmith reminded them, but this wasn't enough for them to trust in him. From the perspective of Christian history, a more orthodox theological position could hardly be imagined: trust and obey in the commandments of God, and live. Doubt leads to death.

A more chilling, and almost diametrically opposed, portrayal of God is found in the third season episode "It's a Good Life." Here, the stand-in for God is a young child, Anthony, who is inexplicably omnipotent. He uses his powers as one might expect a six year old would: he creates misshapen creatures to play with, changes the weather at his whim, and sends anyone who thinks bad thoughts about him to the "cornfield." (Where, exactly, the cornfield is located is left unspecified, but the concept recalls the New Testament idea of God sending people to the "outer darkness.") The town, cut off from the rest of the world, lives in fear of Anthony, and spends their entire lives trying to please him.

As an all-powerful being, Anthony is clearly a stand-in for God. But unlike the God of "The Old Man in the Cave," Anthony represents a capricious, self-absorbed God, who is only able to use his powers for selfish ends. The God of this episode has more in common with God as portrayed by the "New Atheists," such as Richard Dawkins or Christopher Hitchens, who find in the Bible's depiction of God an extremely unpleasant bully. It's a disquieting portrait of a deity who is only concerned with his self-gratification, and views humanity as existing simply to make him happy and serve as an audience for the nightly television shows he puts on. This God is not great, and the only reason the characters in this episode proclaim anything "good" is because they're hoping to save themselves from the fate of banishment to the cornfield. The God in this episode is not a benevolent protector of the people, but a spoiled, self-absorbed six year old. This episode stands as one of the few places where *The Twilight Zone* addresses questions of theology, but comes away with a pessimistic viewpoint, one which stands far outside of the mainstream of Christian thought. While it's not one to teach in Sunday School, it raises important questions, ones which darker corners of the Bible (such as the book of Job) have wrestled with as well.

The theodicy of the book of Job is an immense subject; the scholarly literature addressing this problem could fill numerous bookshelves. Based on the discussion between God and Satan (here in his role as one of God's helpers, not yet a full-fledged Devil figure) about Job's righteousness, it seems as if all of the horrible things that happen to Job, his family, his servants, and his livestock are all on account of God's vanity. And while Job is restored at the story's end (though that doesn't help his deceased children, servants, and animals), God comes out of the book looking rather petulant, like a deity who is less concerned with creating a just world than with berating humanity into submission. The bulk of the book is Job's time in the cornfield.[1]

Both "It's a Good Life" and the book of Job represent minority reports in their respective traditions. For the most part, God is portrayed as righteous and just.

The Divine Bureaucracy

In most cases, God doesn't appear directly in *The Twilight Zone*; however, in a number of episodes, a divine being serves as a representation of God, revealing the workings of the universe to the main character. In several episodes this role appears as an embodied Death; in others, it's a sort of divine butler who shepherds the main character through the afterlife. In others, it's the Devil, or some other representative of hell. But all of these figures imply an ordered universe, overseen by a God who controls events according to a divine plan. God is the chief executive of a well-ordered universe.

In "One for the Angels," salesman Lew Brookman learns receives a businesslike visit from Death, informing him that his time will be up at midnight tonight.[2] He manages to talk Death into an extension so he can pull off the perfect sales pitch; he's given his chance when he finds out that Death is scheduled to claim a young girl in Lew's apartment building that night. By enrapturing Death with his sales pitch, Lew causes Death to miss his appointment, and the girl's life is spared. Fairness and order rules in this universe. Everything runs according to a schedule, and even when that schedule is disrupted by Lew, Death has contingency rules to follow.

Death also shows up in "The Hitch-Hiker," one of the series' more unsettling episodes. A young woman is taking a cross-country drive, and keeps seeing the same hitchhiker thumbing for a ride. Of course, no one else can see him. She becomes more and more desperate to escape him. Finally she calls home, only to find that she died several days ago. The hitchhiker is then waiting for her in the backseat of her car. While the image of being pursued by death is certainly haunting, the deeper undertones of the episode actually offer the same sort of comfort as episodes such as "One for the Angels." This young woman isn't being punished, it's simply her time to go. Once she recognizes this, and realizes that this hitchhiker is a representative of Death, she is able to accept her fate.

In both of these episodes, Death serves the purpose of ensuring that the people get to the afterlife at their appointed time. In spite of Death's occasional creepiness, these episodes offer a relatively comforting portrait of a well-ordered world, a world in which God is in control of events on earth, and things operate according to plan.

In some episodes, the bureaucracy is infernal rather than divine. Even so, these depictions of the Devil and hell also present a world governed by divine order. The Devil has his part to play in the bureaucracy as well. In "Escape Clause," for example, hypochondriac Walter Bedeker encounters a Devil who fully comports to the contours of Christian theology, offering Walter an extended life in exchange for his soul. The presence of the Devil, who falls in line with post–Augustinian ways of understanding Satan as tempter,[3] suggests a universe that is ordered by a benevolent deity. For centuries, Christians of many types have taken an odd kind of comfort in the existence of the Devil; after all, if the Devil exists, then God must exist as well. The world depicted in "Escape Clause" is right next door to Puritan folk tales, or classic "deal with the Devil" films such as *The Devil and Daniel Webster* (William Dieterle; see Grafius, *Devil's Advocates*). While the Devil is a frightening figure, for many believers a universe in which the Devil exists is far preferable to a universe with no divine presence at all.

The Devil also appears in the second season episode "The Howling Man," which features a setup right out of *The Old Dark House*. American David Ellington, touring post–World War I Europe by foot, seeks shelter from a storm in an old castle. He finds the castle inhabited by a strange band of monks; further investigation leads to a prisoner held captive in the castle's basement. The prisoner turns out to be the Devil. By releasing him, David has unleashed Satan back on the world, and the conclusion implies that this leads directly to World War II. While in some ways offering a chilling meditation on how thin the line is that keeps evil at bay, the episode also works as an apologetic for God. If the great evils of the world only happen because Satan has been released from his captivity, then these evils aren't God's fault. God can still be the benevolent Old Man in the Cave, in spite of what we see all around us. And in a similar fashion to "The Old Man in the Cave," humanity would have been just fine if they would have listened to God's earthly representatives. The monks of this foreboding castle had Satan perfectly under control, until David freed him out of misguided compassion. David was told of the prisoner's identity, but couldn't bring himself to believe the monks' warnings. As a result, the evil of World War II falls on humanity.

In both "The Howling Man" and "The Old Man in the Cave," God is absolved of responsibility for the problems of the world, and these problems are instead blamed on humanity. In "Old Man," the townsfolk refused to listen to their prophet, and as a result died of food poisoning. In "Howling Man," David couldn't fathom that the monks truly had Satan locked up in a basement cell, so he freed the Prince of Darkness. In both cases, listening to the religious authorities would have led to a much better outcome. However, they also offer a hope for humanity, albeit one grounded in religious conservatism: a return to faith holds the potential for solving the world's evil, and this is a choice we're still able to make.

Just Desserts

Another frequent pattern of *The Twilight Zone* episodes involves the viewers following a villainous person of some form or another, perhaps a small-time crook, a con artist, an abusive husband, or someone whose evil is on a larger scale. By the end of the episode, this person will receive punishment in an ironic fashion, a punishment which fits his or her crimes. We might call this pattern "Just Desserts." In this strand of storytelling, viewers are presented with a universe in which the guilty are punished, usually in a manner befitting of their crimes.

This isn't a worldview that's unique to *The Twilight Zone*. It was common in the horror comics of the 1950s, as well as the many contemporary horror narratives that have taken their cue from these sources such as HBO's *Tales from the Crypt* series and the *Creepshow* films.[4] But moving farther back, it's also a worldview that is well-represented in the Bible, particularly in Deuteronomy and the Wisdom literature, such as the book of Proverbs.[5] In Proverbs, these are frequently framed as maxims that describe the way the world works: "Treasures gained by wickedness do not profit, but righteousness delivers from death," for example (10:2; all translations in this essay are from the New Revised Standard Version). However, there's an understanding that the world works in this way because God has created it so; the world's mechanisms of justice are part of God's plan for how everything should work out. Sometimes, God's hand in all of this is named explicitly, such as in Proverbs 10:3: "The LORD does not let the righteous go hungry, but he thwarts the craving of the wicked." But even when the name of God is absent, God's presence in the working of the world is implied. As biblical scholar William Brown puts it, "Creation's regularity allows for discerning observable patterns in which human actions have predictable consequences, and knowing these consequences leads to an informed life" (Brown, 17). Creation exists in regular rhythms and patterns, including days and seasons. These patterns also include predictable outcomes for behaviors.[6] By observing these patterns, we can understand the nature of God.

In the world of *The Twilight Zone*, and many horror narratives, this means that the bad guy is going to get what's coming to him or her. It's a simple formula, but one that engages viewers on multiple levels. We enjoy watching a fitting punishment unfold, we enjoy seeing justice meted out, and we can leave feeling as if the universe is fundamentally fair. However, we might also be left wondering what would happen if that fairness were turned back on us.

In the episode "What's in the Box," cab driver Joe Britt doesn't seem to do much besides watch TV and yell at his wife. Just in case he's not sleazy enough as a character, his wife also suspects that Joe's having an affair, and by the end of the episode her suspicions will prove to be correct. There's really not much that's redeeming about Joe. He just wants his wife to leave him alone so he can watch TV. But after a strange "repairman" shows up to fix his television, he's surprised that the only show that's on *is* his own life. First it's a fight he and his wife just had, then it's him carrying on his affair, and finally it's a vision of the future where he kills his wife. Joe finds himself helpless to change the channel, as the events of his future play out in front of his eyes. Joe is unable to keep himself from killing his wife, just as seen on TV, and winds up convicted of murder.

From the moment he steps onscreen, Joe is an unpleasant man. He's nasty to his wife and seems to have no ambition in life aside from watching his favorite TV shows. In the show's ironic twist, he's forced to watch his own life unfold on TV, and must passively observe as his fate plays out, helpless to make different choices or avoid his fate. Joe definitely got what was coming to him.

One of the more chilling examples of the just-desserts framework is "Deaths-Head Revisited." (On a personal note, I stumbled on this episode as a re-run when I was eight; it's one of the few times in my childhood I remember my mother telling me to turn something off because it wasn't appropriate for me. In this case, she was probably right.) It involves a creepy middle-aged man, Gunther, who is returning to Dachau to reminisce about his past as an SS officer. When he arrives at the ruins of the camp, he finds the grounds are inhabited by Alfred Becker, one of the former inmates whom Gunther remembers having murdered years ago. Becker reminds Gunther of all the torture he inflicted upon the captives, and refuses to accept Gunther's excuse that he was just following orders. Eventually, Becker leads his former tormentor to one of the barracks, which is stocked with a jury comprised of the ghosts of men whom Gunther had mistreated. They sentence him to experience the same things they experienced as inmates; as a result, Gunther falls to the ground, stricken by madness.

While most episodes of this type leave the theological implications unstated, this episode concludes with Becker explaining the divine justice that is at work. "This is not revenge," he tells the writhing Gunther. "This is justice. But this is only the beginning, Captain. Only the beginning. Your final judgment will come from God." In Becker's framing, the supernatural justice meted out by this undead jury is a partial justice. The real just desserts that Gunther will receive will come in the afterlife, when God will hold him to account. Even when grave injustices happen on this earth, including atrocities such as the Holocaust, this worldview asserts that God will enact a fair punishment on those responsible. Evil does not go unpunished, and the wicked are held accountable for their actions. Interestingly enough, both this episode and "The Howling Man" attempt to offer explanations for the Holocaust. In "The Howling Man," the hand of Satan is behind the terrible atrocities of the Nazis. In "Deaths-Head Revisited," humans are responsible, but will suffer the consequences of their choices.

Occasionally, episodes will blend these last two categories, presenting a portrait in which the divine bureaucracy is directly responsible for dispensing just desserts. An example is the first season episode "A Nice Place to Visit," in which a small-time thief named Rocky finds himself in the afterlife, where a helpful "guide" named Pip fulfills his every wish. For Rocky, he must be reaping the reward of some unknown good deeds, and has been granted a stay in paradise. But after a month of winning every hand of poker and sinking every billiard ball on the first shot, Rocky finds all the joy has been drained out of the activities that used to inject thrills into his life. It's only then when he realizes that his final destination is not the one he had assumed, and that he's instead been condemned to an eternity of empty loneliness. As in "Deaths-Head Revisited," this episode directly ties the ironic justice to a divine plan. Here, the afterlife has been structured in such a way as to ensure that people like Rocky get their just desserts. While we may not see it every day, the world is, in fact, structured to make sure that people end up with the consequences that fit their choices in life.

While many *Twilight Zone* episodes and horror narratives that use this pattern can be chilling to watch, with viewers experiencing a dawning sense of dread as we realize the inevitable consequences of the protagonist's actions, they also offer a strange sense of comfort. We leave these narratives having the inherent fairness of the world affirmed. Of course, the challenge is with our own insecurity—while most of us like to think of ourselves as living basically good lives, we also harbor frequent seeds of doubt. *What about those mistakes I've made, or those times when I haven't made the choices I know I should have? Are those enough to keep me out of the category of "good person"? What would my just desserts really be?*

Conclusion

Of course, not all of *The Twilight Zone* episodes are built on a foundation of theological orthodoxy. Episodes like "The After Hours" or "Five Characters in Search of an Exit" suggest that we could be living with a fundamental misunderstanding of the world and our role in it, a misunderstanding that would make all theology (and everything else we think we know about the world) irrelevant. To say the least, this isn't a comforting view of the world. These episodes are also ones where theological questions are pushed into the background, only implied by the existential questions which are the episode's main concern. When theology is in the foreground of *The Twilight Zone*, the answers tend to be rather traditional.

At its heart, theology is the discipline of taking our experience of the world and attempting to put it into a framework that makes sense. It's a way to take all of the individual data points of our lives and collate them into a story that explains everything in a meaningful way. Frequently, *The Twilight Zone* displays this same impulse, using extremely imaginative scenarios to demonstrate that even the anomalies of the world still function within the overall framework of a divine plan. It's a testament to the creativity of the series (as well as the flexibility of its format) that this impulse towards orthodox theology can exist side-by-side with the counter-cultural social critique for which the series is also known. Both aspects are an important part of the series, and the seeming contradictions that arise from their juxtaposition are part of what makes the series so consistently engaging and surprising, even after several decades.

Notes

1. I've explored this reading more fully in my monograph *Reading the Bible with Horror* (Lexington Books/Fortress Academic, 2019), 131–133 and notes. See also the intriguing article by Tod Linafelt, "The Wizard of Uz: Job, Dorothy, and the Limits of the Sublime," *Biblical Interpretation* 14.1–2 (2006): 94–109, or the commentary by J. Gerald Janzen, *Job* (Interpretation; A Bible Commentary for Teaching and Preaching; Westminster John Knox, 1997), 247–259, who argues that Job remains unconvinced by God's final speech.

2. As pointed out by Kevin J. Wetmore, Jr., in comments to an earlier version of this essay, the appearance of personified death brings to mind the tradition of Medieval morality plays, such as *Everyman* (late 15th century), in which Death frequently appears as a character. In these plays, and novels inspired by this tradition such as John Bunyan's *Pilgrim's Progress* (1678), the characters are frequently on a journey, and the plot is intended to provide instruction for the characters (and audience) regarding what is necessary for salvation. For a concise introduction, see Pamela M. King, "Morality Plays," pages 235–262 in *The Cambridge Companion to Medieval English Theatre* (eds. Richard Beadle and Alan J. Fletcher, 2nd ed., Cambridge University Press, 2008).

3. An in-depth exploration of the satan's historical development is Ryan E. Stokes, *The Satan: How God's Executioner Became the Enemy* (Grand Rapids: Eerdmans, 2019). For discussions of Satan in the American cultural landscape, an excellent resource is W. Scott Poole, *Satan in America: The Devil We Know* (Rowman & Littlefield, 2009).

4. For an introduction to the horror comics of the 1950s and the moral panic they induced, see David Hajou, *The Ten-Cent Plague: The Great Comic-Book Scare and How It Changed America* (Picador, 2008).

5. Most introductions to the Old Testament Wisdom will discuss this cause-and-effect relationship of actions and consequences; an example can be found in James L. Crenshaw,

Old Testament Wisdom: An Introduction (Revised and Enlarged; Westminster John Knox Press, 1998), 68–76.

    6. Of course, this worldview has serious limitations, most notably that the experience of human life is one in which the wicked do not, in fact, get punished regularly, and the righteous rewarded. The biblical authors were well aware of this problem, with the books of Job and Ecclesiastes offering specific challenges to it (Penchansky 2012). For many scholars, ideas of the afterlife emerged from the reality that justice is not always accomplished in this life (Nickelsburg 2006).

Works Cited

"The After Hours," *The Twilight Zone*, written by Rod Serling, directed by Douglas Heyes, Image Entertainment, 2013.

Brokaw, David. "The Purchasing Powerless: Postwar Consumption in *The Twilight Zone*." *History of Retail and Consumption* vol. 3, no. 1, 2017, pp. 38–52.

Brown, William P. *Wisdom's Wonder: Character, Creation, and Crisis in the Bible's Wisdom Literature*. Eerdmans, 2014.

Crenshaw, James L. *Old Testament Wisdom: An Introduction*. Revised and Enlarged. Westminster John Knox Press, 1998.

Dawkins, Richard. *The God Delusion*. Houghton Mifflin Harcourt, 2006.

"Deaths-Head Revisited," *The Twilight Zone*, written by Rod Serling, directed by Don Medford, Image Entertainment, 2013.

"Escape Clause," *The Twilight Zone*, written by Rod Serling, directed by Mitchell Leisen, Image Entertainment, 2013.

"Five Characters in Search of an Exit," *The Twilight Zone*, written by Rod Serling, directed by Lamont Johnson, Image Entertainment, 2013.

Grafius, Brandon R. *Devil's Advocates: The Witch*. Liverpool University Press/Auteur Publishing, 2020.

_____. *Reading the Bible with Horror*. Lexington Books/Fortress Academic, 2019.

Hajou, David. *The Ten-Cent Plague: The Great Comic-Book Scare and How It Changed America*. Picador, 2008.

"The Hitch-Hiker," *The Twilight Zone*, written by Rod Serling, directed by Alvin Ganzer, Image Entertainment, 2013.

Hitchens, Christopher. *God Is Not Great: How Religion Poisons Everything*. Little, Brown, and Company, 2008.

"The Howling Man," *The Twilight Zone*, written by Charles Beaumont, directed by Douglas Heyes, Image Entertainment, 2013.

"It's a Good Life," *The Twilight Zone*, written by Rod Serling, directed by James Sheldon, Image Entertainment, 2013.

Janzen, J. Gerald. *Job*. Westminster John Knox, 1997. Interpretation: A Bible Commentary for Teaching and Preaching.

King, Pamela M. "Morality Plays." *The Cambridge Companion to Medieval English Theatre*, edited by Richard Beadle and Alan J. Fletcher, 2nd ed., Cambridge University Press, 2008, pp. 235–262.

Laudadio, Nicholas C. "All Manner of Revolving Things: Musical Technology, Domestic Anxiety, and *The Twilight Zone*'s 'A Piano in the House' (1962)." *Science Fiction Film and Television* vol. 5, no. 2, 2012, 159–177.

Linafelt, Tod. "The Wizard of Uz: Job, Dorothy, and the Limits of the Sublime." *Biblical Interpretation* vol. 14, nos. 1–2, 2006, 94–109.

Mortenson, Erik. "A Journey into the Shadows: *The Twilight Zone*'s Visual Critique of the Cold War." *Science Fiction Film and Television* vol. 7, no. 1, 2014, 55–76.

"A Nice Place to Visit," *The Twilight Zone*, written by Charles Beaumont, directed by John Brahm, Image Entertainment, 2013.

Nickelsburg, George W.E. *Resurrection, Immortality, and Eternal Life in Intertestamental Judaism and Early Christianity*. Expanded Edition. Harvard University Press, 2006.

"The Old Man in the Cave," *The Twilight Zone*, written by Rod Serling, directed by Alan Crosland, Jr., Image Entertainment, 2013.

"One for the Angels," *The Twilight Zone*, written by Rod Serling, directed by Robert Parrish, Image Entertainment, 2013.

Penchansky, David. *Understanding Wisdom Literature: Conflict and Dissonance in the Hebrew Text*. Eerdmans, 2012.

Stokes, Ryan. *The Satan: How God's Executioner Became the Enemy*. Eerdmans, 2019.

Rod Serling and the Ambiguity of Being

Kevin Bolinger

Prior to the landmark series, *The Twilight Zone*, Rod Serling was already an award-winning playwright noted for his deep explorations into the psychology of character and examinations into human motivations. In the 1956 production of *Playhouse 90*, Serling's award-winning "Requiem for a Heavyweight" foreshadows much of his *The Twilight Zone* writings in that there is a clearly defined conflict between the characters' motivations and their somewhat self-destructive actions. Serling's illustrations of the ambiguity of existence are a hallmark of the more enduring episodes of *The Twilight Zone*. Perhaps nowhere does Serling more poignantly explore the human condition than through the episodes around robotic intelligence. Though nominally a series in the science-fiction genre, *The Twilight Zone* was essentially a dramatic inquiry into being human. There were indeed episodes where pontification on a particular moral position was evident in both the dramatization and the inevitably touching epilogues, such as "The Obsolete Man" (1961), Serling's critique of totalitarianism. More often, however, the viewer is left with less clarity about a moral choice or position with no satisfactory outcomes. "The Shelter" (1961), for instance, chronicles the choices made by a neighborhood of close-knit families and their reaction to impending disaster from a perceived nuclear attack. Neither the neighbors nor the doctor in his basement shelter react in a way that could be considered civilized or compassionate, but neither is Serling willing to proffer an alternative to what would have been civilized or compassionate. While it is not unusual that two people reading the same book or viewing the same story might have differing interpretations, leading them to opposite interpretations is a tricky bit of storytelling and the particular genius of Rod Serling. As a writer, he quite often leaves his viewers just short of the resolution, somewhere between the problem and the solution. It is with a similar constructed ambiguity that Serling tackles the intractable problem of consciousness in one of the first episodes produced for *The Twilight Zone*, "The Lonely" (1959). Some of *The Twilight Zone* episodes dealing with robotics ignore the problem of consciousness but others explore it in a way that debates the question of mechanical thought but do not provide definitive certainty on the robot's state of being.

The landscape of 1950s television was notoriously populated with saccharine melodramas, situation comedies, westerns, and police dramas. In one sense, this is not an ideal medium for a writer such as Serling, who reveled in ambiguity and moral relativism. In another sense, it is what brought notice and critical acclaim to some of his first teleplays, as they stood out as more adult and comprehensive treatments of the dramatic form. Much has been written about Serling's dissatisfaction with sponsors interfering with his scripts ostensibly to make them less offensive to viewers who might be less inclined to see the sponsor favorably (Zicree 14–15). This may be a motivation to move into the science-fiction genre where a current social issue, like the murder of Emmett Till (he wrote two scripts paralleling this injustice; both were subsequently neutered), could be more easily disguised. The risk he was taking was evident as the popular view of science fiction was that it was somewhat beneath the talents of a real writer. This is apparent in a 1959 interview with Mike Wallace (Zicree 3). Wallace asks Serling rhetorically whether he has, for the time being, given up on writing anything important. Avoiding sponsor interference might explain the sudden shift into a new and less respected genre, but not why he developed the iconic style of ambiguous endings and moral relativism.

While *The Twilight Zone* may predate the start of the formalized post-modernists movement by a few years, Serling was certainly embracing some of what would become the tenants of both the philosophical and literary branches of that movement. His ability to create narratives that were not only open to, but also actively promoted multiple interpretations and his desire to challenge ethical standards and moral certainty are certainly part and parcel of some of the postmodernist viewpoint. In the very best of *The Twilight Zone* episodes, viewers are left uncertain, and it is quite possible that Serling himself was uncertain, exploring this dissonance through the catharsis of writing. In "Walking Distance" (1959) and "A Stop at Willoughby" (1960), Serling seems to be exercising this cathartic muscle. Both detail an overworked middle-aged man with a desire to return to a simpler childlike existence. Both end, however, with an unsatisfying failure to do so. Serling wants to return to the Garden, before the knowledge of good and evil tainted his innocence, but as his characters realize, he must confront the challenges and uncertainty of life as it comes. Much of the critique of power hierarchies and capitalism put forward by the French postmodernists can be seen in these avatars for Serling in these episodes.

To get a sense of how this style differed from the prevailing narratives, consider the classic tale *Pinocchio*. In this well-known tale, Geppetto, the wood carver, wishes that his toy creation of a puppet boy could be transformed into a real boy, only to be confronted with something in between a boy and a puppet or a puppet with the consciousness of a boy. Inevitably, Pinocchio is granted humanity through a series of trials. This is a very common motif in storytelling. The hero must suffer some trials, battle their demons successfully and in the end is rewarded with what they most desire. Had Serling written Pinocchio, it would be more likely that the boy puppet would die, leaving the grieving Geppetto to reconcile if, though only made of wood, he was not a boy after all. In the original story Pinocchio is in a transitional state of being, between a boy and a puppet, eventually becoming a boy. In Serling's writings, characters are not only in transitional states but ambiguous states, neither one thing nor the other with no rewarding ending of regressing to or progressing to another state. The opening narration as well as the title indicate that this is where he is taking us. *The Twilight Zone* is a state between light and dark, between the summit of knowledge and the pit of fears, between science and superstition. The purpose of *The Twilight Zone* is not to get to the light from the dark, but to dwell between the light and the dark and discover how we manage to exist in the grey between. This is precisely how he examines consciousness through Artificial Intelligence (AI).

Throughout the five-year run of *The Twilight Zone* series, Serling returned many times to the subject of artificial intelligence, but his most critical examination of the subject was his first episode dealing with robots, "The Lonely." There were several other artificial intelligence episodes penned by Serling, such as "The Mighty Casey" (1960), "The Lateness of the Hour" (1960), "Uncle Simon" (1963) and "The Brain Center at Whipple's" (1964), but none of these had a phenomenological perspective as evident as "The Lonely." Both "The Mighty Casey" and "The Brain Center at Whipple's" examined the emerging issue of automation as a threat to human productivity and meaning; whereas, "The Lateness of the Hour" and "Uncle Simon" use AI as a plot device rather than a focal point for exploring consciousness. There are other episodes of *The Twilight Zone* that do explore artificial intelligence in a more substantive way, but which were not written by Serling, such as "I Sing the Body Electric" (1962). Later we will explore how different these interpretations are.

In the episode "The Lonely," a prisoner at some undetermined point in the future is sentenced to solitary confinement on an asteroid. The prisoner, Corry, played by Jack Warden, suffers from intolerable loneliness, having limited contact with supply ships only every few months. The captain of these supply runs, Allenby, played by veteran character actor John Dehner, takes pity on Corry and leaves him with a robot in the shape of a human female, Alicia, played by Jean Marsh. After initially reacting with hostility toward the robot, Corry accepts her companionship and ultimately falls in love with her. In the final scene, Corry is granted a pardon and allowed to return back to Earth, but cargo restrictions mean that he must leave Alicia behind. This presents us with the central question of the episode as Corry believes she is alive, whereas, Allenby considers Alicia to be simply a machine. The story ends with Allenby destroying Alicia and Corry trying to reconcile his feelings about the woman/machine he loved. Throughout the episode, Serling weaves in many ambiguities that leave the question of Alicia's status as truly conscious in doubt.

It is helpful to define our terms before we examine how Serling explored consciousness through AI. For instance, the word artificial could have a different definition depending on whether we mean replication or simulation. A simple allegory might be how we experience artificiality in food additives. As a child, assorted popsicles were a common staple in my freezer. The flavors were of a common variety: orange, grape, cherry, and so on. Invariably the last Popsicle in the box was the banana flavored. In comparison with the orange Popsicle, it was not just less tasty, but less like the thing it represented. The orange had a citrus tang, along with a scent that was easily recognizable as that of an orange. On the other hand, the banana Popsicle in no way resembled the actual taste of a banana. It was, however, recognizable as all other banana-flavored confection, as they all contain the same artificial flavor ingredient, and it was easily noted as a banana flavor. Banana gum, for instance, had the distinct flavor of all candies flavored similarly. One could recognize it as artificial banana flavor just because it had so often been experienced in other foods that were described as banana flavored. In this case, the banana flavor was a simulation for actual banana, not a replication.

This distinction between simulation and replication can best be illustrated between the arguments of philosopher John Searle and his Chinese box thought experiment and the famous physicist Alan Turing who developed the Turing test for AI. Searle argues that a computer works with algorithms that are entirely syntactic, lacking meaning. In his view, a computer algorithm must follow a set of rules to formulate a response, even if those rules allow for creation of new sets of rules or parameters that are needed to solve a problem (2–6). In Searle's Chinese box thought experiment, he imagined a room wherein a human operator sat with a large collection of

Chinese symbols and an English instruction book. The human operator (analogous to the operating system of a computer) does not speak or read Chinese. If a note is passed under the door from a Chinese-speaking person with a query, the operator can consult his English instruction book for the proper Chinese characters to formulate a reply. From the perspective of the Chinese speaker there is a native Chinese speaker in the room even though the operator at no time understood the question being asked nor the response given. The operator lacks meaning, possessing only a set of rules for response. The term for this is "weak AI," demonstrating more simulation than replication.

Turing, on the other hand, proposed that if a human interacting with a machine could not tell the difference between the responses of a machine and the responses of a human this would be evidence of strong AI, demonstrating more replication than simulation (439–440). In the mind of Turing, something that is sufficiently simulated is indistinguishable from something that is replicated. In this viewpoint, there is a blurry line between simulation and replication, not a hard dichotomy. The closer a simulation approaches perfection the nearer it also gets to replication. This is the blurry line that Serling explores in "The Lonely."

The term intelligence is just as confounding as the term artificial. If we use a simplistic notion of intelligence, being able to store and regurgitate facts, then, of course, machine intelligence has already surpassed human capacity. If the definition is problem solving, again, we are outmatched by the speed and precision of a calculator. No, there is something more than storage and computational capacity that defines intelligence. When we casually think of someone possessing a vast intellect it might be a person who possesses a vast amount of knowledge, but more often it would be someone like Einstein or Edison, Da Vinci or Galileo. It is not knowledge that defines them as intelligent, but rather creative capacity. They possess imagination and curiosity, engines that drive the creation of new knowledge and the ability not to just solve problems but to ask new questions. In order to imbue conscious thought into a mechanical brain, they must not merely be problem solvers, but problem creators; not just reacting to a set of commands, but rather initiating new commands of their own.

Another way of thinking of this is independent intention. Does Alicia, our female robot mentioned earlier, have curiosity, imagination, and intention? These kind of emotional qualia or inner states of being are not well demonstrated within the episode "The Lonely." In a brief moment with Corry before the climax of the story, Alicia inquires about the stars, which could be a slight indication of curiosity, but could just as easily be part of a program to show interest in her companion's interests. Another episode penned by Serling examined the more emotional characteristics of intelligence: "The Lateness of the Hour." In this episode, a young woman is unaware that she is a robot and acts and reacts as a human would. Perhaps Serling is suggesting that a true artificial intelligence would not know that it is artificial. When the woman-robot becomes aware that she is artificial, she breaks down and must be reprogramed. For consciousness to arise from intelligence he might be suggesting that there must be an emotional capacity to feel wonder, or joy or sadness. Of course, the inevitable trap of machines with emotions is paring the power of superior ability with emotional instability, as Serling warns in several episodes such as "From Agnes—With Love" (1964) or "In His Image" (1964).

Sentience is also a benchmark of consciousness or at least a way of measuring it, but what exactly is sentience? Is it being self-aware? If so, what could be an indication of sentience? A simple measure might be whether an organism, biological or mechanical, can recognize its own reflection in a mirror. Jerry Seinfeld once mused that growing up he had a room with a mirrored wall to give the illusion that the room was larger than it was, and his pet bird would try to escape from time to time only to collide with the mirrored wall, unaware that it was not a separate room. He understood why the bird was fooled by the illusion of the additional room, but why didn't it at least try to avoid the other bird coming straight at it? Birds not only lack self-awareness but apparently self-preservation as well. Alicia, a robot, does self-report feeling the pain of loneliness. If the report is a true account of an inner state of being, then this is some indication of self-awareness. Non-sentient beings can experience pain, and perhaps psychological pain, as in elephants grieving their dead, but understanding and articulating that inner state of pain must be the measure of self-awareness. For instance, a dog may whimper if its tail is stepped on, an instinctual reaction to pain, but it does not dwell on that pain after it has dissipated, nor does it relate that pain to other painful events or try to hierarchically categorize that pain against all possible painful events. Alicia understands the source of her pain (Corry's rejection) and what would alleviate that pain (Corry's acceptance of her).

Another crude indicator of self-awareness might be intentionality. Animals act with intentionality but only in the rudimentary moment. A lion, for instance, can create the intention to hunt and then strike out in search of prey, but humans can form complex intentions not only in response to the circumstances of the immediate future but rather across the potentialities of all conceivable futures. Alicia forms the intent to hide from the arriving spaceship and her crew the moment the ship is sighted in the night sky by Corry. The potential future of being discovered by the spaceship crew and perhaps separated from Corry initiates action in

Alicia. Again, Serling brings us back to ambiguity showing her inability to respond to an unpredicted situation when Corry leads the crew to her location and begs Alicia to prove to Allenby that she is a woman. His pleas go unheeded and she simply stares back at Corry in confusion. In the blissful scene prior to this, she was laying with Corry under the stars and asking curious questions in a humanlike manner, but now she is quite inhuman in her inability to adapt to an unpredicted situation: confrontation with Allenby. Alicia is at times very human, and at times very mechanical. She is also quite human in the eyes of Corry and quite machine in the eyes of Allenby.

Serling would most likely have been aware of the Turing test, but his stories of robotic intelligence predate and, in some ways, predict the thought experiments of Searle and other AI theorists. Serling leaves us a central question to ponder in "The Lonely": Was Alicia replicating consciousness or merely simulating consciousness. He introduces us to the problem with not atypical ambiguity when Corry first encounters Alicia. Corry's first reaction is hostility toward the robot because she is a reminder of the human interaction which he has been deprived. He feels "mocked" by her presence, questioning; "Why didn't they build you to look like a machine? Why didn't they build you out of metal, bolts, wires, and electrodes? Why did they turn you into a lie?"

Here is the introduction to the problem: Is something merely what it seems to be? Alicia looks like a human female and talks like a human female, but Corry questions whether this is a lie (simulation) or, as he comes to see, a truth (replication). In his rage, he throws Alicia to the ground. Her tearful reaction (whether replicated or simulated) is to say to Corry, "I can feel loneliness too." At this point, she passes the Turing test and Corry accepts her expressions of loneliness as something at least approximating genuine.

As the episode progresses through a montage of developing moments in Corry and Alicia's relationship there are subtle hints that direct the viewer to consider the artificial nature of Alicia's consciousness. During a chess game between them, Corry's inner monologue journals, "It's difficult to write down what has been the sum total of this very strange and bizarre relationship. Is it man and woman or man and machine?" His character is at a turning point as he reexamines his original assumption about the validity of Alicia's consciousness. But then his next line throws us back into the state of ambiguity so favored by Serling: "There are times that I do know that Alicia is simply an extension of me ... the things that she has learned to love are those things that I have loved." On its face, this sounds more likely the mimicry of simulation and not the strong position of replication of consciousness. But it could be an expression of a natural bonding between two consciousnesses not too unlike a child learning to love the things that a parent is interested in. The question in Corry's mind is whether she is a woman or a machine; put simply, is she what she seems to be? True consciousness on any objective level can only be inferred even in the case of human-to-human interaction. We can reliably relate our own state of being (I am sad or I am happy) but only subjectively report the state of another (she seems sad, or she seems happy); therefore, Corry's confusion about Alicia's state of being is not substantially different than might be experienced between two non-artificial intelligences.

Thomas Nagel explored this unbridgeable void of being in *What Is It Like to Be a Bat?*. In this philosophical thought experiment, Nagel imagines what it is like to be a bat, but concludes that only an approximation of what it is like to be a human imagining what it is like to be a bat is possible (436–439). The sensory apparatus of a bat, echolocation, is so foreign to human perception that we cannot know how the bat perceives the world using this unfamiliar form of radar. We can only imagine how a creature might see through sound, but invariably we are constrained by how we see the world and cannot accurately approximate the bat's experience.

Serling has elegantly portrayed the dilemma that perplexes current AI theorists. If we don't know the subjective inner experience of a person or, in this case, a thing, we must infer the inner experience from outward expressions of their inner state, never knowing if it is a lie or the truth or merely a projection of our own consciousness. Alicia may experience something like happiness (she does smile proudly when she makes a clever chess move), or it may simply be a programed response, which, in turn, elicits a desired response from Corry, a smile of affirmation.

One must hold a mechanistic point of view to believe that consciousness, or self-awareness, can be replicated in mechanical form. A mechanistic viewpoint of consciousness holds that, however it is expressed, consciousness is merely a biological algorithm playing across a neural network; information flowing from one part of the brain to another in response to mental or physical stimuli (Holt 18–22). If this is true, then strong AI, or replication, is only a matter of duplicating the physical/biological processes of the brain in a non-organic or mechanical fashion. Is this Serling's viewpoint? Through the eyes of the protagonist Corry, one could conclude that to be so. If we back up in the story, there is a telling moment just after Allenby delivers the crate containing Alicia, before Corry opens it to discover a robot inside. Allenby instructs Corry to simply open the crate, and the air will activate what is inside. From a metaphorical perspective this can be interpreted as a form of birth as Alicia's first contact with the air (or perhaps the breath of life if it is intended as a religious metaphor), brings her "to life."

Throughout the episode Serling is simultaneously stating that there both is and is not something qualitatively different between biological life and mechanical life. To understand the ambiguities of this point of view, imagine someone you knew suffered a terrible accident that resulted in irreparable brain damage. Now imagine that a mechanical brain with all the functionality and memory capacity of a biological brain could be imprinted with every memory that the biological brain contained. If this brain were transplanted into the brain-damaged accident victim, would that person still be the same as the one you knew? In the purely mechanistic point of view, there is no qualitative difference between the biological brain and the mechanical brain so long as the processes are duplicated sufficiently. Serling hints at how he might answer this question in the episode "Number 12 Looks Just Like You" (1964). This Charles Beaumont short story re-penned for *The Twilight Zone* tells not of a mechanical transformation but rather a complete physical alteration, resulting in a stark personality change. Consciousness is inalienably tied to the physical form. You might ask yourself this question from time to time: What if I was taller, or smarter, or better looking? For Serling the answer is simple and requires no introspection or imagination of other versions of yourself. A taller, smarter, or better-looking version of you would not be you. Any alterations in physical appearance or mental capacity would inevitably reshape the experiences that made you, you. Form and function are irrevocably linked.

In contrast to this mechanistic view is the Cartesian Dualist point of view, which defines consciousness not as an artifact of biological systems but rather as something more than the sum of its parts (Hoffman 310). Thinking is immaterial and the body is material. Consciousness exists above, or outside of its physical processes. For Corry, no such metaphysical distinction is necessary; Alicia is what she seems to be, a woman. For the viewer, however, Serling leaves some doubt. In the epilogue to the episode Serling states "All of Mr. Corry's machines—including the one made in his image, kept alive by love, but now obsolete." This is overlaid upon the panning image of Corry's shack, old car, and the lifeless body of Alicia. The religious tone of "in his image" and "kept alive by love" are cleverly juxtaposed with the previous scene of Alicia with her human face obliterated, showing a tangle of wires. The imagery and narration are at odds with one another. The words "kept alive by love" indicate that Alicia was not merely a mechanical brain, but that her very existence relied upon Corry; her mind was motivated by something unsubstantial and immaterial: love.

In season three, *The Twilight Zone* produced the episode "I Sing the Body Electric," based upon a short story by Ray Bradbury. This episode stands in sharp contrast with the nuanced ambiguity of Serling's writings. In that episode, a robot grandmother is hired to care for a widower's children and quickly becomes a dear member of the family. Her presence brings stability and joy to the family and, when they are grown, she explains she must return to a place without physical form to share all that she knows and prepare to be assigned to another family. The contrast here is not only that the episode lacks ambiguity or moral conflict, but that the phenomenological viewpoint is very clearly a stand with Cartesian Dualism. The electric grandmother is more than just the sum of her processing or mechanical computing; her consciousness will exist somewhere without physical form, something analogous to heaven. The electric grandmother is unquestionably sentient, self-aware, and has complex intentionality. She is also unbound from her physical form so that her brain, or CPU, are evidently not the source of her consciousness.

Is Alicia self-aware as she seems to be? Serling leaves this question in doubt. Alicia expresses both sadness and joy; she is curious and adaptive to Corry's emotional state. Still, her human portrayal is still slightly off, demonstrated in part by her monotone voice and use of clipped short sentences. This question of Alicia's consciousness is what Serling wants to linger in the minds of the viewers and clearly the point of the episode—there will be no big reveal at the end, only more ambiguity. This is evident in much of Serling's writing, and is certainly a mainstay of *The Twilight Zone*: leave the viewers wondering, "What exactly happened here?" In "The Lonely" we are confronted by the stark and desolate loneliness of a man in solitary confinement, but also a more existential loneliness illustrated by the inherent solitude of our unknowable fellow beings, each perhaps more or less than what they seem to be. Corry finds solace in the companionship of Alicia, but was she just an extension of his own consciousness or something unique, something alive? Given the rapid advancement in AI technology, it is quite likely that we will be asking the same things that Serling has asked in "The Lonely," in just a few short years. If our response is like that of Corry's, then the academic arguments of consciousness won't define our reaction to this advanced AI, but rather our relationship with that technology.

WORKS CITED

Bradbury, Ray. *I Sing the Body Electric*. Alfred A. Knopf, 1969.

"The Brain Center at Whipple's." *The Twilight Zone*, written by Rod Serling, directed by Richard Donner, CBS, 1964.

"From Agnes—With Love." *The Twilight Zone*, written by Bernard C. Shoenfeld, directed by Richard Donner, CBS, 1964.

Hoffman, Paul. "Cartesian Passions and Cartesian Dualism." *Pacific Philosophical Quarterly*, vol. 71, no. 4, 1990, pp. 310–310.

Holt, R.R. "Freud's Mechanistic and Humanistic Images of Man," *Psychoanalysis & Contemporary Science*, vol. 1, 1972, pp. 3–24.

"In His Image." *The Twilight Zone*, written by Charles Beaumont, directed by Perry Lafferty, CBS, 1963.

"The Lateness of the Hour." *The Twilight Zone*, written by Rod Serling, directed by Jack Smight, CBS, 1960.

"The Lonely." *The Twilight Zone*, written by Rod Serling, directed by Jack Smight, CBS, 1959.

"The Mighty Casey." *The Twilight Zone*, written by Rod Serling, directed by Robert Parish and Alvin Ganzer, CBS, 1960.

Nagel, Thomas. "What Is It Like to Be a Bat?" *The Philosophical Review*, vol. 83, no. 4, 1974, pp.435–450.

"Number 12 Looks Just Like You." *The Twilight Zone*, written by John Tomerlin, directed by Abner Biberman, CBS, 1964.

"The Obsolete Man." *The Twilight Zone*, written by Rod Serling, directed by Elliot Silverstein, CBS, 1961.

Searle, John R. "Minds, Brains and Programs," *Behavioral and Brain Sciences*, vol. 3, no. 3, 1980, pp. 417–450.

"The Shelter." *The Twilight Zone*, written by Rod Serling, directed by Lamont Johnson, CBS, 1961.

"A Stop at Willoughby." *The Twilight Zone*, written by Rod Serling, directed by Robert Parish, CBS, 1960.

Thompson, Dave. *The Twilight Zone FAQ: All That's Left to Know about the Fifth Dimension and Beyond.* Hal Leonard Corp, 2015.

Turing, Alan M. "Computing Machinery and Intelligence." *Mind: A Quarterly Review of Psychology and Philosophy*, vol. 49, 1950, pp. 433–460.

"Uncle Simon." *The Twilight Zone*, written by Rod Serling, directed by Don Siegel, CBS, 1963.

"Walking Distance." *The Twilight Zone*, written by Rod Serling, directed by Robert Stevens, CBS, 1959.

Zicree, Marc Scott. *The Twilight Zone Companion.* Sillman-James Press, 1992.

The Twilight of Humanism

ALEXANDER E. HOOKE

Another Dimension of Our Mind

Picture the bucolic suburban scene: Neighbors celebrate a venerable neighbor's sixtieth birthday with delicious food and heartfelt speeches. He's a doctor and has dutifully cared for many of the attendants and their children. It is an evening of conviviality and good cheer among kind and decent people. It looks to be the culmination of humankind guided by reason and compassion rather than zealotry, authority or superstition. Then something snaps. Humans are now faced with an impending invasion of aliens. The radio and television start blasting emergency notices that space ships or UFOs have been spotted in the distant sky and are heading for Earth. Worse, they are heading directly for these mini-utopias. Viewers soon witness an immediate transformation of the people. Street lights are flickering, nearby sounds and shadows arise from all corners. Suddenly, the neighbors suspect each other of being the real aliens. In "The Monsters Are Due on Maple Street" the threat of alien invasion turned out to be a false alarm. Recovering from the hysteria, the neighbors meet again but without conviviality, security or trust. They can no longer focus on the humanity in one another. For they have just perceived the potential monster in each other.

Suppose viewers continue their *The Twilight Zone* binge to watch "The Obsolete Man" and "The Trade-Ins." A naïve and harmless man is persecuted for reading the Bible and sundry books, thinking freely, and not being obsequious to the leader of a totalitarian state. He is condemned as obsolete in this future dystopia. The death sentence permits him to choose the means of execution. He invites the grand Chancellor to attend the moment of death, reading Biblical passages such as Psalm 23 ("The Lord is My Shepherd") while awaiting the bomb in his room to explode and obliterate him. "The Trade-Ins" plays on notions of transplanting souls and minds from our raggedy seventy-five-year-old bodies to those sculptured figures of twenty-five year olds. Rather than a vision of utopia, such an option would be a subversion of humanity's encounter with aging and mortality. In Rod Serling's humanist closing yet slightly facetious words, "For all you sentimentalists."

Serling presents an ambivalent perspective on the human species. Introducing "The Monsters are Due on Maple Street," he wryly notes, "There are weapons that are simply thoughts, attitudes, prejudices—to be found only in the minds of men." On the other hand, he can wax poetic about his fellow mortals, "Any state, any entity, any ideology that fails to recognize the worth, the dignity, the rights of man, that state is obsolete" ("The Obsolete Man").

Humanism—as an idea and value—has had an uneven reception that echoes Serling's ambivalence. There is an element of hubris in attaching an "ism" to one's own species. It implies an innate superiority to other species. It might place a blessing on a species that it is central to the design of Earth and its highest purposes. Perhaps it even connotes the human species is from nature but not of nature—namely, we ought to continually improve upon what has been granted us, whether by the gods or fates. Such notions of humanism have been undermined by facts, science and evolution. Humanism, its critics contend, has no rational foundation and is based on tenuous selection of criteria that often collapse once scrutinized. In terms of language, empathy, thought or sociability, evolutionists see humans as simply the latest extension of primates—not an exception.

French philosopher Michel Foucault, after his prolonged study of the birth of the human sciences, concludes his *The Order of Things* with a haunting forecast that our tools, languages and methods of gaining knowledge are unable to fully understand the creature who devises these tools and methods. He writes that "man is an invention of recent date" that has appeared and can easily disappear. Hence he concludes that under these conditions one can wager "that man would be erased, like a face drawn in sand at the edge of the sea" (328).

Twilight refers to that which is slowly receding while something else is arising. We often speak of the twilight years, the twilight of one's career, or the twilight that precedes the darkness of night. There is also the twilight that hovers, beacons and perplexes. The dimension between day and night, or lightness and darkness, is quite familiar at least since Plato's allegory of the cave where prisoners' only reality is the shadows of themselves cast upon darkened walls. Twilight invokes another dimension. It visits and tells of the mysteries underlying the presumed clarity of everyday lives, as if these shadows and faint images are themselves part of human reality. For Rod Serling, much of his magical work hovers in this twilight of humanism.

Shadows of the Absurd

A perennial favorite episode is "To Serve Man." Earthlings are suddenly alerted that aliens are about to invade. In the United States and particularly in New York City, where members of the United Nations are meeting, all sorts of questions and options are raised. Full military alerts and public announcements that citizens seek shelter quickly dominate the airwaves.

Soon the Kanamits land and one of them, approximately nine feet tall with a huge head, speaking by mental telepathy, approaches the United Nations. "We come in peace," he assures the members. "We only want to help you earthlings—please trust us that we only want to serve."

Only two persons are skeptical, expert linguists arduously trying to translate a book in the Kanamit language. Meanwhile, humans are so full of contentment that they readily accept the Kanamits invitation to visit their planet. The one linguist finally translates the book and learns its title: *To Serve Man*. Rushing to the spaceship to save her colleague about to ascend the steps, she shouts that infamous line: It is a cook book! Contrary to the lessons from Genesis and evolution, we see that humans are not at the top of the food chain. Indeed, their reason and belief in their own superiority is readily undermined by a more ingenious species.

Another case of human absurdity appears in the episode "People are Alike All Over." Serling's introduction sets the tone for another humbling moment, "You're looking at a species of flimsy little two-legged animal with extremely small heads whose name is Man." Two astronauts crash-land on Mars, though one is killed. The surviving earthling, who contends people are basically the same wherever they dwell, is welcomed by the human-like natives. Yet he quickly notices there is no exit. Instead he looks out to find the Martians all staring at him as if he is in a zoo. Mark Dawidziak emphasizes the ironic lesson of the ending. People are alike all over, but in terms of the willingness to place in cages those who are not quite like them (186). These two episodes represent a number of moments in which Serling engages thought experiments, humor and storytelling to illuminate his ambivalent perspectives on the twilight of humanism.

Interlude: Humanism and Its Malcontents

There is no single doctrine, manifesto or treatise that has successfully promoted and defended humanism as a political, ethical or sociological way of understanding and improving the world. It might be more accurate to use the plural. We can find humanistic principles in religion, secularism and atheism. There have been socialists, capitalists, naturalists claiming that their position offers the truest or best route to a more human world.

Corliss Lamont defines humanism as a "philosophy of joyous service for the greater good of all humanity in this natural world and according to the principles of reason and democracy" (9). He outlines a decalogue (principles, not commandments) of humanism, largely based on classical liberalism and the reliance on modern science. Erich Fromm contends that humanism is "the belief in the unity of the human race and man's potential to perfect himself" (vii), and this unity will be realized through a Marxian form of socialist democracy. Jean Paul Sartre defines existentialism as a humanism; after the horrors of World War II he is reluctant to emphasize the rule of rationality, unity and science. He instead underscores the individuality of passion and commitment that comes from having freedom and responsibility.

Amid such attractive versions of humanism, how could anyone object? Yet there is an array of critiques and objections to the various humanisms that have been promoted. The existential notion of a freedom (or free will) and even a fixed notion of personhood are dangerous illusions that Darwinists as well as neuropsychologists have ridiculed. Joshua Greene and Jonathan Cohen, in discussing the implications of a neuroscientific approach to law, have agreed that "our first-person sense of ourselves as having free will may be a systematic illusion" (236). For them, insisting on free will leads to a harsh view of criminal justice where retribution (punishing the offender as if he or she was free to do otherwise) prevails, in contrast to a Christian or Buddhist view that determinists embrace, namely, "to know all is to forgive all" (252).

There is also the problem that humanism invariably seems attached to or presumes some essential traits of human nature. Anti-humanists, trans-humanists or post-humanists contend that there is nothing special about the human species. We may be interesting, amusing, curious or pathetic, but not deserving of any special niche among all the other creatures on the planet. Moreover, the advances in robots, artificial intelligence, cyborgs and computers will soon convince us that human nature has been displaced by more rational, autonomous forms of existence. A recent book titled *Robot Sex* presents a variety of scholarly accounts often contending that the more humans rely on robots for companionship, servitude, even sexual pleasure, then robots might be given rights of autonomy and equality.

The Twilight Zone episodes were quite prophetic in this direction. Serling has a condemned murderer being punished with exile on another planet, only to fall in love with a female-like robot. A nerdy computer whiz has a crush on a colleague and tries to ask the computer for romantic advice. Turns out the machine gives him wrong counsel because the computer is jealous and seeks the nerd's complete devotion.

In this light Frank Scalambrino asks if *The Twilight Zone* has already moved its viewers to the possibility of "beyond being human." For him Serling evokes the earlier efforts of Surrealism in which artists and writers addressed that spontaneity of human action that eschews rational control and no fixed point to anchor the play of events, moments and fragmented thoughts. Rather than celebrating humanism and humanity's achievements, *The Twilight Zone*, like its predecessor Surrealism, offers "gripping images of human catastrophe" (18–19).

In the spirit of Surrealists such as André Breton and Salvador Dalí, Rod Serling revives themes about the shadows of ourselves—the dreams of returning to the past or skipping to the future, the desires to be in another body or another place all signal a wish to abandon mundane reality. Hence, Scalambrino emphasizes the centrality of Serling's introduction in which he always reminds that we are entering a zone whose boundaries are of the imagination. And that zone becomes more than an escape from mundane reality—for thirty minutes it becomes another reality, only more daring, intense, and singular. It also casts a different light on renewed sense of humanism, one that emphasizes commonalities found among humans everywhere.

Rod Serling might be amused by these speculations and theoretical postulates of a TV show that lasted only five years and over a half-century ago. Though *The Twilight Zone* was often categorized under the science fiction genre—given his penchant for time/space travel and humans encountering aliens of various sorts—Serling himself saw the episodes more as part of the human tradition of storytelling. In his words, "*The Twilight Zone* is about people—about human beings involved in extraordinary circumstances, in strange problems of their own or of fate's making" (Zicree, 96).

According to his brother Rob, seven years older than Rod, their childhood was largely shared when they enjoyed periodicals and publications such as *Amazing Stories, Astounding Stories, Weird Tales*. On the family's occasional New York trips from Binghamton to Syracuse, the car had no radio and needed a little family discussion. Their father insisted that no one talk "until Rod stopped talking." Older brother recalls how even at the age of seven Rod Serling could look out the car windows and sing, make up dialogues, provide tales about the scenery, ask oddball questions while leaving the family laughing hysterically during the two hour drive.

These anecdotes introduce an approach to Serling's humanism that eludes the conventional focus on human nature in terms of reason, tool users, intelligence and superiority over nonhumans. He finds the art of storytelling to be part of how humans relate to one another. This is not the same as exchanging information and establishing formal narratives.

Telling stories is embellishing, refining, modifying our anecdotes, experiences and thoughts to one another. Two frequent aspects of storytelling involve laughter and thought experiments, insofar as only humans seem to engage in humor and speculative questions about what could be. These aspects, however, do not always underscore the supremacy of humanity.

Laughter of various sorts became an essential aspect of *The Twilight Zone*. According to Stephen Scales, laughter is anchored to the twist that usually ends an episode. The laughter is not rooted in the characters who often looked perplexed, stunned, defeated, forlorn or lost. The laughter resides in the viewer who undergoes a cognitive dissonance. The story teller plants the seeds of emotional or psychological familiarity only to see the fruition arises when the story ends with a disruption or disturbance. In Scales' words, "The thin line between reality dreaming, and madness, aliens among us, paranormal events, time-travel, and inanimate objects coming to life are now part of our shared library of story-prototypes" (174). Herein lies the humor of Rod Serling's creation.

John Karavitis finds this humor in Serling's approach to second chances, those opportunities when after an initial failure we are offered another opportunity to succeed. And, as often in these episodes, a second chance results in additional failure. For example, in "A Nice Place to Visit" a thug shot dead by the police finds himself in a different realm. The thug wins at roulette, gets all the pretty girls, and soon becomes bored with this taste of heaven. He asks Pip if he can try the other place. Hah, reports Karavitis, we viewers can only laugh with Pip when he uproariously notes, "This *is* the Other Place" (160–161).

Over the last decade or more there has been a spate of books that attempt to reach general audiences who might have some interest in philosophical issues. These audiences are not academic professionals. They are thoughtful people who might have taken a philosophy course or come across movies, TV shows, literary fiction that anticipate quandaries such a truth, reality, meaning, beauty, goodness or justice. One of the more popular efforts is in the style of the thought experiment.

Julian Baginni's *The Pig That Wants to be Eaten* is one of the forerunners in this effort. In accessible language and frequent reference to problems raised by notable philosophers from Plato to John Rawls, Baginni asks readers to consider, for example, if their minds ("Brains in a Vat") were transported outside one's body. How might this change our notion of personal identity? Imagine a group of people are facing disaster ("The Lifeboat") and the only way for the group to survive is if several individuals leave (or die). Otherwise, the entire group faces extinction. Who decides and how?

The pig quandary is illuminating in terms of an ancient riddle. Baginni proposes the classic belief that everything has a purpose or telos. Birds are meant to fly, tigers hunt, bees make hives, mosquitoes make us miserable in summertime. To deny a creature's purpose could be a violation of its very being. Then Baginni notes, suppose a pig's destiny is to be eaten. If you are a vegetarian, are you violating the pig's telos? Many *The Twilight Zone* episodes pose thought experiments about the telos or purpose of human beings. If sociability, rationality or freedom is central to our destiny, then episodes such as "Obsolete Man" or "The Fever" highlight the limitations to realizing that destiny, for freedom can be easily denied for the good of the state and rationality can be cast aside in the delirium of grabbing easy money.

Without engaging the debate on the exact criteria of human nature, Serling presents accounts that underscore a sense of humanity that is not shared by non-human creatures. We recognize one another not by physiological, neurological or evolutionary traits that ostensibly define us. Instead, we recognize the humanity in one another by the telling of stories, sharing laughter over our foibles, and engaging in thought experiments that imply our world could be different, we can change how things are … for better or worse. This is the twilight of a humanism for tomorrow as presented in *The Twilight Zone*.

Everyone Has a Story

Serling's preambles often introduce characters and names. It is a sundry list of ordinary folks about to face extraordinary moments. There is Romney Wordsworth, bookish recluse facing execution for being a free thinker; Joey Crown, alcoholic trumpet player still waiting for one more chance to perform; Henry Bemis, bank teller seeking a time and place just to read; Janet Owens, born with a disfigured face with hopes to look normal; Henry Corwin, unemployed drunkard who suddenly becomes an avuncular Santa Claus; and even Talky Tina, a lifelike doll that can utter "I'm going to kill you" and so many others ("Living Doll").

Numerous thinkers, from Richard Rorty to Judith Butler, emphasize narratives as a mode of articulating the ideals or cohesiveness of society. American philosopher Alphonso Lingis is not convinced. For him stories cannot become official narratives because we rarely hear or tell the same story twice. Depending on the audience (grandparents, late night drinking buddies, friends, students, co-workers, strangers at a pub) we embellish some parts, emphasize or downplay the humorous or embarrassing elements, change personal commentaries, and then wait to hear the stories of others and amend ours accordingly. According to Lingis:

> Yet the story I tell myself about who I am and where is unlike any story ever told. I find that my situation, my vision, the accidents and windfalls on my

path do not fit into the available cultural patterns of epic, opera, tragedy, romance, ballet, comedy, vaudeville, sitcom, or farce. [...] Even if I am every-man and no one, I am so in a here and now that has never before occurred and will never be repeated [54].

This singularity of human stories is central to *The Twilight Zone* enterprise. Consider "A Passage for Trumpet" where Joey Crown is a talented trumpet player with a bad drinking problem. After apparent death from a traffic accident, viewers see Joey Crown in the company of the archangel Gabriel, savior of lost souls. He confronts Joey: What do you love more—the bottle or the music? This story could be told several ways. One version highlights personal struggles, another features the element of the spiritual dimensions of human life, and a third version emphasizes the role of chance and surprise in our lives.

One of the few hour-long episodes that impressed audiences, "Jess-Belle," features a love triangle in the Blue Ridge mountains. Serling's eloquent introduction underscores the universality of human storytelling:

The Twilight Zone has existed in many lands, in many times. It has its roots in history, in something that happened long, long ago and got told about and handed down from one generation of folk to the other. In the telling, the story gets added to and embroidered on, so that might have happened in the time of the Druids is told as if it took place yesterday in the Blue Ridge Mountains [470].

Here, the twilight of humanism emphasizes the tradition of story-telling as distinct to our species, but without the grandiose proposal that this tradition determines that we are the most rational or superior species. They illuminate humans as hovering between light and shadow, guided by archangels and beneficent spirits as well as clever witches and Satan's helpers. As retold through *The Twilight Zone*, we experience how this dimension thrives on laughter and thought experiments. The next sections attempt to elaborate on this dimension.

What If

Suppose humans could go back in time. What if they prevent Custer's last stand, the rise of Hitler, or the sinking of a battleship? The dilemma of "other minds" has sparked philosophical speculations about whether we can ever truly know someone's motivations, ambitions or hidden thoughts. We might offer a penny for your thoughts but soon regret having the capacity to read another's mind. What if we could transform a robot into an attractive human-like robot or a dutiful and caring grandmother? Humans have been defined as social creatures, but many are quite lonely or solitary types who are alienated from family or friends, wishing to be with someone, to love someone. What if a robot bearing eerily similar looks of a human offers such desperate souls some genuine accompaniment? We might have to revise what we count as friendship, universal rights, justice, or even love.

Thought experiments in *The Twilight Zone* present philosophical puzzles with compelling drama and suspense. Many were quite prophetic, particularly with the portrayal of human-like robots. Based on a short story by the famous science fiction author Ray Bradbury, the episode "I Sing the Body Electric" features a widower and his three children. To withstand threats from the mother-in-law, the widower takes his three children to see if the company can make them a caring grandmother. The children pick the hair color, voice, height, approximate age, and looks (similar to their mother), and then the company assembles the parts into a grandmother who days later approaches the home to introduce herself. Quickly, she becomes part of the family. As the children become adults and head off to college or another town, they ask Grandma of her plans. She is moved with gratitude but matter-of-fact. She will return to the company where her parts will be disassembled, placed in their proper categories, awaiting the next children seeking to put together their own grandmother. Here the thought experiment involves the tension between emotional attachment and objective perspective. Yes, on one level we assembled the object. Yet we also cared about him or her as much as any human being on the planet.

Equally startling is "The Lonely," written by Rod Serling. James Corry is serving a life sentence on another planet for murder. He is left with a package that contains a woman-robot, named Alicia. She is kind, courteous, respectful and attractive. At first Corry feels betrayed and fooled, wanting nothing to do with her and pushes her away. Upon falling Alicia sheds tears. Here the "what if" pushes us to decide whether Alicia should now be considered human.

One answer is offered in the concluding scene. The supply ship arrives with a cheerful announcement from the captain that Corry's verdict has been changed to not guilty. He's a free man and can return to Earth. Corry insists that he must bring Alicia. They are in love, she is part of his life, and he cannot return to Earth without her. Finally, Captain Allenby pulls out a gun and fires a shot into Alicia's head. This time the viewer does not see any tears dripping from Alicia's eyes—only wires and transformers inside her open skull.

The thought experiment of intelligent machines, computers and robots gradually taking on more human traits or displacing human beings might be Rod Serling's most prophetic speculation. Fifty-eight years since the broadcast of "The Lonely" a book titled *Robot Sex* was published. Featuring scholars from AI, law, religion, political science, philosophy, robot-humanities and economics, a number of thorny issues are raised that examine the very nature of the relation between machine and human. For example, suppose sexbots could look like children or defenseless women and thus suffice as a diversion for pedophiles or rapists while leaving unharmed innocent human beings. Surely this seems to be a worthy pursuit.

Not so fast, contend sexbot advocates. What if sexbots can look human, speak and interact like humans, offer and receive pleasure or emotion, then such creatures should be considered not just machines—but rather individuals with sexual agency and persons with basic rights, including the right not to be exploited. Thus the question is not the status of an object, but whether a machine can be endowed with qualities such as free will, responsibility and a sense of reciprocity. And yes, if the sexbot is pressed with an invitation for sex, it has the right to say no.

In "Deus Sex Machina," Julie Carpenter revives the possibility of choosing parts of the sexbot, from hair or skin color, bodily figure or gender, sexual preferences, even scent of the body. She wonders if the human-to-human model of companionship might become outdated. The sexbot introduces new models. At the same time she worries over the human interest in approaching such possibilities. "So is it narcissism or self-love or fantasy that gives someone a desire to not just seek, but *create*, an *other* for sexual intimacy? What is the power dynamic when a human is in a 'relationship' with a robot?" (279). Obviously, episodes from *The Twilight Zone* will not fully answer these questions. But many of the episodes introduce these questions that demand careful thought in order to appreciate the promises and pitfalls behind the "what if" encounter.

Thought experiments are not just philosophical puzzles for classroom discussion. Humans, unlike the rest of the planet's creature, continually alter the givens of their world. They are not content with the natural cycles and forces. Maybe our biped cave dwellers were much like us. That is, we all ponder to ourselves: What if humans could fly like the birds, swim like the fish, dig into the earth like rodents and ants, hunt like tigers and sharks. The Garden of Eden does not suffice. Humans want to see how life might be in the mountains and deserts, in the jungles and the frozen tundra. They risk the lives of innumerable creatures and members of their own species to create utopias or establish dystopias. The practical effects when humans act on the "what if" possibilities are central to humanism's twilight, artfully presented by Rod Serling.

The Laughable Animal

John Morreall, in his introduction to a collection of writings about the philosophy of humor, outlines three perennial theories for why we find things funny and amusing. Superiority refers to how we laugh over the misery or alleged inferiority of others, such as hillbilly or dumb blonde jokes, or the down fall of a powerful or self-righteous individual. Second, the relief theory emphasizes how humor generates one helpful way to address taboos and transgressions, such as laughter over tales of cannibalism, sexual deviances, family turmoil or heresy; this sort of humor can also appear in emergency rooms and concentration camps. Third, incongruity humor arises when things are at odds, our expectations and ideals are met with disappointment or sabotage, reason meets zealotry, dreams confront or escape reality, and human aspirations are countered by human foibles.

Much of the humor in *The Twilight Zone* embraces the third theory, though the first two theories are also in play. Consider "The Masks," an episode that takes place during Mardi Gras and will be the last evening of Jason Foster's life. He insists his four young visitors (daughter, son-in-law, and two grandchildren) stay until midnight and engage his game. If they decide to refuse and go partying, they will be cut out of the dying man's will.

The final hours embody a nervous and dark humor. Hours before midnight the guests don ugly and facially distorted masks the father designates for them while he chastises them for their arrogant and meaningless lives. They put up with the old man, keeping an eye on the clock so they can join the Mardi Gras festivities. As the clock strikes midnight they remove their masks, only with a horrifying look. Their faces now resemble the masks they just wore, but their new look is permanent rather than momentary. The last thing they want to do is show themselves among the Mardi Gras revelers. This trick would lose its twist if the masks reminded us of animals, such as Halloween costumes resembling a cat or dog. We might enjoy the playfulness of non-human creatures, but they inspire laughter only insofar as we project human qualities onto them. This anthropomorphism is absent in *The Twilight Zone*.

Nietzsche once observed in his *Twilight of the Idols,* "I sought great human beings, I never found anything but the apes of their ideal." This would be a worthy preface to innumerable *The Twilight Zone* episodes. For humans laugh because they are the only creatures who have senses of superiority, relief and incongruity in their dealings with other humans, as only they embody the humor when facing not only their reason but also their absurdity. We laugh because we are the laughable animal.

The Tip of Reality

In an opening that was never used, Serling notes, "This highway leads to the shadowy tip of reality; you're on a through route to the land of the different, the bizarre, the unexplainable." Serling's humanism does not promise enlightened views for the unity of *homo sapiens,* a solution to our problems by following reason and scientific principles, nor the realization of the essential traits that mark our supremacy over other species.

He instead finds commonalities among humans that we do not find among non-humans—be they animals or aliens. These commonalities are found when humans encounter among one another opportunities to tell and retell stories to one another, share a laugh or two over our foibles and tangled webs of hopes and experiences, and deliberating how the world might be different when deliberating the thought experiments we pose for one another. And in the end, borrowing from Mark Dawidziak about life's ironical lessons from *The Twilight Zone,* "beware what you wish for" could be added.

How many of us dream of reading another's mind—be it a friend's reflections, a boss's motive, a potential lover's desires, a neighbor's speculations? Games of chance and skill, such as poker, chess or bridge, rely on the ability to anticipate the thoughts of another. Much of nature's activities rely on deception; what if everything was transparent to us but we were not transparent to anyone else. The episode "A Penny for Your Thoughts" provides a lighthearted humor to the horrors that await us should we actually anticipate each other's hidden motives, attitudes and perspectives. As Mark Zicree puts it in terms of the show's enduring popularity, "The nightmare is a friend, the darkness a sanctuary."

In this light we can see how *The Twilight Zone* sheds light on the twilight of humanism. It appears not as a doctrine or ideology. Rather, it thrives on ambivalences, paradoxes and perplexities of what it can be like to be human. This twilight is best conveyed through storytelling, thought experiments, and moments of laughter. As long as these endeavors hover between light and darkness, clarity and shadows, viewers of *The Twilight Zone* will continue until their next stop—the tip of reality, or another dimension of the human mind.

WORKS CITED

Baginni, Julian. *The Pig That Wants to be Eaten.* Plume/Penguin. 2006.

Carpenter, Julie. "Deus Sex Machina: Loving Robot Sex Workers and the Allure of an Insincere Kiss." From *Robot Sex,* edited by John Danaher and Neil McArthur. MIT Press, 2017, pp. 261–288.

Dawidziak, Mark. *Everything I Need to Know I Learned in the Twilight Zone.* Thomas Dunne Books, 2017.

"The Fever," *The Twilight Zone,* written by Rod Serling, directed by Robert Florey, Image Entertainment, 2010.

Foucault, Michel. *The Order of Things: An Archaeology of the Human Sciences.* Pantheon/Random House, 1970.

Fromm, Erich, ed. *Socialist Humanism.* Doubleday, 1965.

"I Sing the Body Electric," *The Twilight Zone,* written by Ray Bradbury, directed by James Sheldon and William F. Claxton, Image Entertainment, 2010.

"Jess-Bell." *The Twilight Zone,* written by Earl Hamner, Jr., directed by Buzz Kulik, Image Entertainment, 2011.

Johnson, Marilyn. *The Dead Beat: Lost Soul, Lucky Stiffs, and the Perverse Pleasures of Obituaries.* Harpers/Collins, 2006.

Karavitis, John. "The Twists and Turns of Second Chances." From *The Twilight Zone and Philosophy: A Dangerous Dimension to Visit.* Ed. Alexander E Hooke and Heather Rivera, Open Court, 2019, pp. 155–164.

Lamont, Corliss, *The Philosophy of Humanism.* The Wisdom Library, 1949.

Lingis, Alphonso. *The First Person Singular.* Northwestern University Press, 2007.

"Living Doll," *The Twilight Zone,* written by Jerry Sohl (credited to Charles Beaumont), directed by Richard Safarian, Image Entertainment, 2011.

"The Lonely," *The Twilight Zone,* written by Rod Serling, directed by Jack Smight, Image Entertainment, 2011.

"The Masks," *The Twilight Zone,* written by Rod Serling, directed by Ida Lupino, Image Entertainment, 2010.

"The Monsters Are Due on Maple Street," *The Twilight Zone,* written by Rod Serling, directed by Ronald Winston, Image Entertainment, 2010.

Morreall, John, ed. *The Philosophy of Laughter and Humor.* SUNY Press, 1987.

"A Nice Place to Visit," *The Twilight Zone,* written by Charles Beaumont, directed by John Brahm, Image Entertainment, 2011.

Nietzsche, Friedrich. *Twilight of the Idols.* Trans. R.J. Hollingdale. Penguin, 1972.

"The Obsolete Man," *The Twilight Zone,* written by Rod Serling, directed by Elliot Silverstein, Image Entertainment, 2011.

"A Passage for Trumpet," *The Twilight Zone,* written by Rod Serling, directed by Don Medford, Image Entertainment, 2010.

"A Penny for Your Thoughts," *The Twilight Zone,* written by George Clayton Johnson, directed by James Sheldon, Image Entertainment, 2011.

"People Are Alike All Over," *The Twilight Zone,* written by Rod Serling, directed by Mitchell Leisen, Image Entertainment, 2010.

Sartre, Jean-Paul. *"Existentialism Is a Humanism."* From *Existentialism from Dostoyevsky to Sartre.* Ed. Walter Kaufmann, Meridan, 1975, pp. 345–369.

Scalambrino, Frank. *"Where Is the Twilight Zone?"* from *The Twilight Zone and Philosophy,* ed. Alexander E. Hooke and Heather Rivera, Open Court, 2019, pp. 13–20.

Scales, Stephen. "The Pleasure of the Twist." From *The Twilight Zone and Philosophy,* ed. Alexander E. Hooke and Heather Rivera, Open Court, 2019, 165–174.

"To Serve Man," *The Twilight Zone,* written by Rod Serling, directed by Richard L. Bare, Image Entertainment, 2010.

"The Trade-Ins," *The Twilight Zone,* written by Rod Serling, directed by Elliot Silverstein, Image Entertainment, 2010.

Zicree, Marc Scott. *The Twilight Zone Companion,* 2nd edition. Silman-James Press, 1989.

The Strange Zone
of Speculative Rhetoric

Jimmy Butts

Speculative work contains its own arguments. *The Twilight Zone*, in particular, reasons with and against the world as though something otherwise might be considered. In this sense, *The Twilight Zone* offers a kind of idealized rhetoric. The rhetoric involved in the television program has its own longstanding following. In other words, it works in the sense of persuasion for its audience. It is thoroughly attractive, but different than billboards or political speeches. While we know that *The Twilight Zone* was a uniquely rhetorical space because of product placements such as Ronson Lighters or Sanka coffee, the persuasive possibility built into the series went way beyond those limits. In its influential cultural position, *The Twilight Zone* has continued to persuade us to think otherwise about ourselves and our world. *The Twilight Zone* is uniquely rhetorical.

Science fiction, or speculative fiction more broadly, is a fundamentally and uniquely cross-disciplinary genre that can be used to think with. *The Twilight Zone* has helped us begin seeing differently by making claims that are notably both other-oriented and directed at our collective present situatedness. Some trouble arises in demarcating these two unique modes, mixing scifi and rhetoric. But speculative fictions work along the modes of social commentaries, thought experiments, philosophical exercises, prophecies, allegories, parables, hyperboles, and manifestos.

From *The Twilight Zone*'s first episode, penned by Rod Serling in 1959, "Where is Everybody?" to the last episode of the most recent reboot's first season in 2019, "Blurryman," written by Alex Rubens, the scenarios proposed are always about our own real world in some way. As such, the twisted versions of reality allow writers to moralize the norms of everyday life. The first episode considered what an astronaut might experience in isolation. The second episode proposed whether it is possible to cheat

Death. The third episode imagined the potentially positive influence of Fate. And so on. Across that sixty-year span, the show has tackled issues and concepts that were and were not "common to man." The show has changed sf along with changing and molding the medium of television itself, after the transition from radio. And Rod Serling's influential thumbprint has been present all along the way.

In this sense, these short episodes speculate. They ask, "What If...?" The blur that occurs between the real and unreal, the potential but not yet, is what is inherent to all rhetoric and good fiction. (In a moment of delirium, I am left wondering, however briefly, if all rhetoric is fictional in that it's constructed—certainly all fiction is rhetorical in some way.) So, thinking of speculative fiction and rhetoric together, gets us started thinking about that enmeshing as a kind of speculative rhetoric, a type of suasive work focused on exploring and positing strange, new possibilities. This designator, or identifier, or genre-term allows us to talk about this way that we can see rhetoric at work in speculative fiction broadly and in *The Twilight Zone* in particular. Speculative rhetoric connects these concepts.

Through all of this, the territorial work of language in general, and genre-terminology more particularly, offers generative space for thinking with. Science fiction and speculative fiction are targets of their own debated nomenclature. And rhetoric faces its own generic associations. Never mind what we call it, by getting on board with this sort of speculative rhetoric, crafting really imaginative arguments for the future comes to the fore. And this allows us to make claims to compose a better future, as well as able to wrangle our current reality with a buffer.

We are given to exploring the purpose of strangeness in the kinds of speculative narratives found in work like *The Twilight Zone*. Speculative work considers the world differently than our own; however, it always requires some relation to our own reality. As such, in principle, *The Twilight Zone* works along a liminality of strangeness, and a barrier of argument, proposing the world as otherwise, much in the same way the Ancient Greeks practiced the art of *dissoi logoi*, arguing different sides of the coin, something *in between* the truth of things, a zone of conjecture that allows both a and not-a to exist simultaneously.

When we face this inimitable series, we are faced with the basic questions about what science fiction or speculative fiction or fantasy are. From the first episode of the first season, in 1959, before we went to the moon, the series begins speculating. The first words of the narrative begin, "The place is here. The time is now. And the journey into the shadows that we're about to watch could be our journey." This could-be-ness of both science fiction and rhetoric allows a powerful partnership.

The introduction to *The Wesleyan Anthology of Science Fiction* explains: "Science fiction [...] writes about things that might be, although they are not yet and may never come to be" (Evans, et al. xv). In addition, *The Oxford Dictionary of Science Fiction* defines it like this: "a genre in which the setting differs from our own world, and in which the difference is based on extrapolations made from one or more changes or suppositions" (Prucher 171). Now, what I find so interesting about these definitions of scifi is that they make it sound like rhetoric. In other words, it imagines and suggests an alternative world using logical means.

So, it is worth taking the time to think about what science fiction really is, and then consider what scifi can do. Science fiction is a weird genre. Literally. That's one of the things that demarcates it. That it's weird. It's strange. This view also gains context when considered in relation to the theoretical work of Sigmund Freud's concept of the uncanny both in dream logic and creative writing. Of the psychological work of the uncanny, he writes, "This is that an uncanny effect is often and easily produced by effacing the distinction between imagination and reality, such as when something that we have hitherto regarded as imaginary appears before us in reality" (15). Freud also saw the zone in between fantasy and reality as a safe "Neutral Zone" where desires could be thought out and considered without danger (423). Fantasy works as a free space between desire and reality. The dreamwork of mediums like creative writing and rhetoric allow us to consider what could be without ill effect. This mirrors other conceptions, such as the strangeness suggested by Bertolt Brecht's concept of *Verfremdungseffekt* (or alienation effect) in theater (95). Strange figurations allow us to reorient the world into twisted versions of itself. Science fictional work like *The Twilight Zone* does this exceptionally well.

As the infamous intro to the first season goes, "This is the dimension of imagination. It is an area which we call The Twilight Zone." *The Twilight Zone* as a space of potential persuasion, of seeing the world otherwise, requires something of the viewer, as Samuel Taylor Coleridge put it, "a willful suspension of disbelief." Or, in the countersense put forth by J.R.R. Tolkien, the construction of belief. Tolkien writes in "On Fairy-stories":

> to make a Secondary World inside which the green sun will be credible, commanding Secondary Belief, will probably require labour and thought, and will certainly demand a special skill, a kind of elvish craft. Few attempt such difficult tasks. But when they are attempted and in any degree accomplished then we have a rare achievement of Art: indeed narrative art, story-making in its primary and most potent mode [61].

We see the success of this mode in the work of Serling's own twilight zone, a narrative working space that persuades and works over the viewers into a conception of an alternate reality.

Judith Merril in 1958 offers this for thinking about the genre:

> A few years back, the physical possibility of space flight was still enough in doubt to make space travel a favorite subject for science-fiction, which after all, is *speculative* fiction: meaning a story that answers the question, "What if ... ?" But in order to be *science*-fiction, the answer must not only be imaginative, but logically reasoned from the accepted knowledge of the day [171].

Speculative fiction was a broadening of the term science fiction in the late 50s, slightly contentious, favored by Robert Heinlein and others. It was literature that speculated on possibilities, using logical reasoning and creativity. This genre started to open things up for so many.

So, we are confronted with a kind of speculative rhetoric. What the science fiction field did was began to call their work merely "sf," which could stand for science fiction and/or speculative fiction, a further broadening. So, we may be quite near calling this perspective a kind of sf rhet, or something along those lines. Bruce Sterling gave us the name slipstream, which is quite nice for talking about alternative, otherworldly literatures. Slipstream rhetoric? There is suppositional, imaginative, inventive, fantastical, or just plain weird. There was a kind of term for marvelous literature, and marvelous rhetoric certainly has its own kind of charm.

Margaret Atwood wonderfully explains this genre delineation in a recent article:

> Bendiness of terminology, literary gene-swapping, and inter-genre visiting has been going on in the SF world—loosely defined—for some time. For instance, in a 1989 essay called "Slipstream," the veteran SF author Bruce Sterling deplored the then-current state of science fiction and ticked off its writers and publishers for having turned it into a mere "category"—a "self-perpetuating commercial power-structure, which happens to be in possession of a traditional national territory: a portion of bookstore rack space." A "category," says Sterling, is distinct from a "genre," which is "a spectrum of work united by an inner identity, a coherent aesthetic, a set of conceptual guidelines, an ideology if you will" [Atwood].

We see Atwood considering what exactly a kind of SF genre represents. Later, she continues, thinking about her own work:

> The writing of *The Handmaid's Tale* gave me a strange feeling, like sliding on river ice—exhilarating but unbalancing. How thin is this ice? How far can I go? How much trouble am I in? What's down there if I fall? These were writerly questions, having to do with structure and execution, and that biggest question of all, the one every writer asks him- or herself with every completed chapter: *Is anyone going to believe this?* (I don't mean literal belief: fictions admit that they are invented, right on the cover. I mean, "find the story compelling and plausible enough to go along for the ride") [Atwood].

The temporary ride that we're taken on in *The Twilight Zone* always invites us out into novel territory by working us over.

When we begin imagining what might be called speculative rhetorics—rhetorical approaches that are imaginatively future-oriented—we see strands or connections to the political branch of rhetoric by Aristotle's schema. Attraction or rhetoric exists as a primary means of reasoning out what could be. In the now *de facto* claim of Andrea Lunsford, everything is an argument. Everyday claims reflect this fundamental quality of communication including simple suggestions such as when your partner suggests, "We should have pizza for dinner tomorrow." But speculative claims about the future are in-built within rhetorical action because they presume a certain kind of reality, and is often future-oriented.

When Aristotle defines rhetoric as the "ability to discern the available means of persuasion in any given situation," we are left with two fronts of possibility. The first is how we persuade, and the second is the context of persuasion. Aristotle, too, was interested in the temporal nature of argument, explaining how within the three branches of rhetoric, his genres, deliberative, judicial, and epideictic rhetoric function in this way, related to time: "These three kinds of rhetoric refer to three different kinds of time. The political orator is concerned with the future. [...] The party in a case of law is concerned with the past. [...] The ceremonial orator is [...] concerned with the present, since all men praise or blame in view of the state of things existing at the time" (*Rhetoric* I. 1358b, qtd. in Lanham 165). So, Aristotle explicitly connects deliberative rhetoric, rhetoric connected to critical thinking, to future outcomes. This allows us to think that, yes, scifi *is* deliberative rhetoric, broadly speaking. Although, in my classes, we then blur Aristotle's designations and ask whether or not all rhetoric has to do with the future. After all, why make an argument, why speak at all, unless you want to affect the future somehow? We practice rhetoric when we want to change the future. That is how we change it—through conceptualizing something other than reality, a fiction.

Fictional texts have worked with philosophy and ethics and claims since before *Oedipus Rex* and *Antigone*. *Aesop's Fables* contain their own moralizing. It is not such a new thing to consider the rhetorical nature of fiction. Wayne C. Booth's *The Rhetoric of Fiction* explains the difference between didactic fiction as rhetorical and less explicitly didactic, which *merely* serves to communicate with readers (xiii). In separating out the two, he gives *Gulliver's Travels* and *1984* as examples of didactic literature as opposed to something "non-didactic" like *Middlemarch* or Faulkner's *Light in August* (xiii). The work of *The Twilight Zone* then certainly seems to align mostly for what Aldous Huxley was about in writing science fiction or even Jonathan Swift's work.

Johnathan Swift's "A Modest Proposal" is actually a good, classic example of the kind of speculative rhetoric that we see here. It isn't realistic. It's impossible. Eat children. It's ridiculous, like aliens are ridiculous. (Or are they?) But it is an argument made by thinking differently, but logically. This line of thought led me to find thinking about speculative rhetoric in this way as really, very useful.

In part, we began working with science fiction, because that is one of the few places where the future can be constructed, or at least imagined. This is not so much the future-oriented rhetoric one might find in The State of the Union address, but the kind of rhetoric that might be heard in a brainstorming meeting at Google.

This essential practice of making a claim through speculative work is summed up nicely in Spencer Holst's short piece "The Zebra Storyteller." It begins with a little Siamese cat who learns to speak Zebraic, the language of zebras. Anyway, zebras come along, and they are so surprised that the Siamese cat can speak their language that they're just fit to be tied, we learn. So, the cat takes advantage of their surprise, kills them, and eats them. He dines of filet mignon of zebra night after night. He even makes zebra neckties. Until one day, the storyteller of the zebras comes along, and imagines a story about a Siamese cat speaking his language. When he comes across the real Siamese cat who does, he's not surprised at all, doesn't like the look of him, and kills him. The storyteller lives happily ever after. The end. Then, the narrator wryly closes by telling us: "That is the function of a storyteller" (1).

Then, we furrow (or raise) our eyebrows as we often do at the end of a *Twilight Zone* episode and ask ourselves, "Wait. What is the function of a storyteller? To kill cats?" And then we get to thinking and working out the puzzle for ourselves, and we get it. That stories have purpose. They can be rhetorical. They can be warnings. They can help prepare us for different possible futures. And *The Twilight Zone* works in a packaged format that borrows from the science fiction short story, and later the scifi radio play. They are each short, manageable conceptual forays.

But scifi feels different than a Jane Austen novel. More useful perhaps.

Instead, when we read works found in collections like *The Wesleyan Anthology of Science Fiction* like Ray Bradbury's "There Will Come Soft Rains" (1985), Philip K. Dick's "We Can Remember It for You Wholesale" (1966), Samuel Delany's "Aye, and Gamorrah…" (1967), or "Out of All Them Bright Stars" (1985) by Nancy Kress, we find possibilities to consider—a science of persuading the audience to think otherwise. Kress notably explains that she pronounces her genre science *fiction* as opposed to her former husband who pronounced it *science* fiction (580). This fiction-work, this kind of inventive plausibility experimentation gives us weighty material with which to practice and develop critical thinking, which is defined by Diane Halpern as a process that must be thought of in terms of transfer across disciplines, and as "the kind of thinking involved in solving problems, formulating inferences, calculating likelihoods, and making decisions" (70). This work is precisely what scifi does so well. It is an entire genre founded upon thinking differently; the genre itself necessitates thinking outside the box, discovering strange ways of seeing the world around us and interpolating that in writing. It is a genre defined by how it makes us think and by unique approaches to writing itself. As rhetorician Carolyn Miller puts it, we are invited to try to see a genre not as what form it takes, but what through the lens of what it does—"the action that it is used to accomplish" (151). And science fiction in the vein of *The Twilight Zone* allows us to think and do quite a lot in terms of applying other conceptions of our universe.

What if aliens show up, we wonder. What if robots take over, we ask. We probe into the realm of climate change and media totalization, of technological breakthrough and inventions with planned obsolescence, for better or worse. It's better because it is, in essence, a series of ethical dilemmas, a series of thought experiments. This is valuable work. It is the work of scifi, and the work of exploring the tricks of composing good arguments and thinking differently. And lots of fiction poses ethical problems. Jane Austen does that. But I believe that scifi explicitly does it. For us. With us.

Let us consider a remarkable, fairly recent, real-world example of the usefulness of science fictional thinking. A few years ago now, Intel began to support the unique work of science fiction with *The Tomorrow Project*. And it's an interesting setup. *The Tomorrow Project* is a collection of science fiction storytellers, like Cory Doctorow, and personalities interested in technology—such as Will.i.am from The Black Eyed Peas—that have been brought together to imagine the future. Intel collects interviews, commentary, and most notably short stories in anthologies that help invent undiscovered technological prospects. This is the zebra storyteller, backed by corporate funding, but it is an interesting cultural artifact that allows for real speculation.

Due to recent interest in speculative realism and new materialism in philosophy, the field of rhetoric has taken up the speculative under a slightly different mantle. This other speculative rhetoric is being explored by folks like Alex Reid and others in the field of rhetoric, each seeing their versions of speculative rhetoric differently from one another, albeit along a more contiguous spectrum. As we career toward the future, this kind of work helps us prepare for novel situations. Alex Reid writes in a recent book chapter from *Rhetoric and the Digital Humanities*: "A speculative rhetoric begins with recognizing that language is nonhuman." Reid also nods toward Bruno Latour who suggests that this kind of speculative research is inherently interdisciplinary. Speculative literature simply works for a number of different fields.

Through this alternative speculative lens on composition, a different kairotic expediency presents itself—the need to prepare for what may come. Additionally, the genres connected with these approaches are exploratory, diverse, and interdisciplinary. By thinking about futures, and writing toward them, a number of different disciplines can be theoretically engaged.

What makes *The Twilight Zone*'s sort of persuasion unique then? Since the original broadcasts by CBS in 1959, the show has had its own kind of identity, its own ethos and style. *The Twilight Zone* is not the first speculative series, but it has become the touchstone in so many ways. Other series have followed the seminal series in suit, from *The Outer Limits* or *Amazing Stories*, to more contemporary series like *Black Mirror, Electric Dreams, Tales from the Loop*, or *Dimension 404* where Mark Hamill is the narrator. Different series have had different takes, some darker, some lighter, but always attempting similar approaches as *The Twilight Zone*—short, titillating, speculative takes on reality in episodic form.

The darkness of the claims embedded in most of these rhetorical takes is worth noting. The works are not just or not merely cynical, but certainly agonistic in that they run counter to normative thinking. Working along the tenuous line of comedy and tragedy, most episodes of *The Twilight Zone* end badly for the protagonist. These outcomes allow for rhetorical critique of a societal structure that is generally ordinary for our everyday lives. And yet, *The Twilight Zone* does not *merely* produce rhetorical criticism—it also builds and creates. As Bruno Latour writes in "Why Has Critique Run out of Steam?" the following inquiries: "What could critique do if it could be associated with *more*, not with *less*" (248) and also "The critic is not the one who debunks, but the one who assembles. The critic is not the one who lifts the rugs from under the feet of naïve believers, but the one who offers the participants arenas in which to gather." (246). This is precisely what Serling was able to construct through *The Twilight Zone*. The collective, anonymous authors of *Speculate This!* call for a productive speculation that does not merely deconstruct via cultural critique. They explain that "Projections of better tomorrows incorporate us in collective fictions" and that their "project articulates and practices what we call affirmative speculation" (5). No matter how bad the narrative gets, in the case of our beloved series, something is built along the way beyond isolation, darkness, and despair. We tend to naturally fill in the void with the negative.

And yet we wonder, "Why *can't* an episode end happily?" We have seen the success of such happy experiments, such as the award-winning episode of *Black Mirror* "San Junipero" that ends well. And yet, we know that some episodes do in fact end happily, or in a mixture of potential considerations. "Time Enough at Last" nearly ends happily enough for the protagonist, until he breaks his glasses. The mixture or tinge of darkness and light is exactly how narrative is laced with real possibility in *The Twilight Zone*.

The overarching argument of the series is that we should reconsider the real—our zone. Alternatively, the argument might simply be "what if." Longer cinematic sf—think space operas like *Star* Wars—loses the argument in the breadth of the characters and narrative. *Star Wars* certainly contains its own arguments about the world we live in, but they are complex and numerous. The brevity of a sf short story or single shot episode like *The Twilight Zone* allows the piece to exist as its own concise thought experiment. Each show presented a fairly simple premise that twisted or rethought reality in a different light.

While there was no physical narrator until the second season of the series, the narrator's closing remarks function as a second take. They slightly reread what we've just seen, and it is not typically the normal narrativization. Then there is the twisted possibility and sometimes rational explanation. The host of each episode keeps us hostage until we are let go of, returned to our own dimensions. Meanwhile, the didactic host attempts to persuade us concerning some ethical dilemma, a turning point that comes to its height right in the middle of the show—a true climax. As such, the show suggests that after all in the end each analog of reality is no analog at all, but a mirror representing us in terms of our most basic values and practices.

As one of the first television series to deal with racism and xenophobia, Rod Serling's political stakes were very real throughlines in the wild, fictional worlds spun by the series which came in during the swell of the Civil Rights era. Serling was impressively forward-thinking for his time and his values regarding social justice issues, which appeared within the series. They also appeared in the classes he taught and the public lectures he gave. He even wrote a eulogy for *The Los Angeles Times* for Dr. Martin Luther King, Jr., when he was assassinated with powerful language quoted in his daughter Anne's memoir "He asked only for equality, and it is that which we denied him" (180). In short, Serling was an activist. His wife Carol carried his message well beyond his death in 1975 until she herself passed at the beginning of 2020 (Sandomir). Rod Serling's speculative writing was not just fantasy; he wanted to enact real change. His teaching suggested the same immediacy with advice such as "MAKE PEOPLE THINK ... STUN THEM ... GRAB YOUR AUDIENCE IMMEDIATELY" (Marshall). This urgency of Serling's rings throughout the powerful messages still found in *The Twilight Zone* series today.

More recently, Jordan Peele has continued those social justice issues in his reboot of the series. In the last episode of the first rebooted season under the guidance of Jordan Peele, Serling returns, in a meta commentary upon *The Twilight Zone*'s own ongoing commentary—that it is a commenting specter upon everyday life. To be released from the zone at the end returns us to ourselves, but never without a lingering thought behind. This is precisely what language itself does so well. It allows us to think otherwise across the gaps of the real and imagine a world in recreating it in another sense—to theorize, to postulate. The gaps are the zone or distance between the real and the fictional, between the real and language itself. As linguist Ferdinand Saussure imagined it, communication leapt across a zone that exists between text and audience and also between language and reality (80).

There is a zone of speculative argument where science fiction and rhetoric overlap. *The Twilight Zone* as an anthology television show offers an anthology of different issues and possibilities. Rhetoric is a space-time portal, like fiction. SF or SR as speculative fiction/rhetoric work collaboratively to help us consider what we believe about our present moment and other alternative moments. As Lloyd Bitzer explained:

> a work of rhetoric is pragmatic; it comes into existence for the sake of something beyond itself; it functions ultimately to produce action or change in the world; it performs some task. In short, rhetoric is a mode of altering reality, not by the direct application of energy to objects, but by the creation of discourse which changes reality through the mediation of thought and action. The rhetor alters reality by bringing into existence a discourse of such a character that the audience, in thought and action, is so engaged that it becomes mediator of change. In this sense rhetoric is always persuasive [3–4].

The exact same things can be said of our current example. In this alternate speculative (fictive) rhetoric, there is quite a lot of power and influence—which is precisely what we saw play out across all the years of Serling's project in *The Twilight Zone*.

Works Cited

Atwood, Margaret. "On Science Fiction." *wbur* October 12, 2011. https://www.wbur.org/on point/2011/10/12/margaret-atwood. Accessed May 30, 2020.

Bitzer, Lloyd F. "The Rhetorical Situation." *Philosophy & Rhetoric* vol. 1, no. 1, 1968, pp. 1–14.

"Blurryman." *The Twilight Zone*, written by Alex Rubens, directed by Simon Kinberg, CBS All-Access, 2019.

Booth, Wayne C. *The Rhetoric of Fiction.* 2nd edition. University of Chicago Press, 1993.

Brecht, Bertolt, and Eric Bentley. "On Chinese Acting." *The Tulane Drama Review*, vol. 6, no. 1, 1961, pp. 130–36.

Doctorow, Cory, Douglas Rushkoff, and Brian David Johnson. *The Tomorrow Project Anthology.* Intel, 2011.

Evans, Arthur B., Istvan Csicsery-Ronay, Jr., Joan Gordon, Veronica Hollinger, Rob Latham, and Carol McGuirk, eds. *The Wesleyan Anthology of Science Fiction.* Wesleyan University Press, 2010.

Freud, Sigmund. "Creative Writers and Day-Dreaming." In *The Standard Edition of the Complete Psychological Works of Sigmund Freud, Volume IX (1906–1908): Jensen's 'Gradiva' and Other Works.* Hogarth Press, 1959, pp. 141–54.

_____, and Hugh Haughton. *The Uncanny.* Translated by David McLintock. Penguin Classics, 2003.

Halpern, Diane F. *Critical Thinking Across the Curriculum: A Brief Edition of Thought & Knowledge.* Routledge, 2014.

Holst, Spencer. *The Zebra Storyteller.* Station Hill Press, 1997.

Lanham, Richard A. *A Handlist of Rhetorical Terms.* 2nd edition. University of California Press, 2012.

Latour, Bruno. "Why Has Critique Run out of Steam? From Matters of Fact to Matters of Concern." *Critical Inquiry* vol 30, no. 2, 2004: pp. 225–48.

Marshall, Jeanne. "Rod Serling Teaches Writing." *Rod Serling Memorial Foundation.* August 22, 2005. https://rodserling.com/rod-serling-teaches-writing/. Accessed June 1, 2020.

Merril, Judith. "Wish Upon a Star." *Magazine of Fantasy & Science Fiction* vol. 15, 1958: pp. 6–87.

Miller, Carolyn R. "Genre as Social Action." *Quarterly Journal of Speech* vol. 70, no. 2, 1984: pp. 151–67.

Prucher, Jeff. *Brave New Words: The Oxford Dictionary of Science Fiction.* Reprint edition. Oxford University Press, 2009.

Reid, Alexander. "Digital Humanities Now and the Possibilities of a Speculative Digital Rhetoric." *Rhetoric and the Digital Humanities*, 2015: pp. 15–19.

"San Junipero." *Black Mirror*, written by Charlie Brooker, directed by Owen Harris, Netflix, 2016.

Sandomir, Richard. "Carol Serling, Rod's Wife and Tender of 'Twilight Zone' Flame, Dies at 90." *The New York Times.* January 23, 2020. https://www.nytimes.com/2020/01/23/arts/television/carol-serling-dead.html. Accessed June 1, 2020.

Saussure, Ferdinand de. *Course in General Linguistics.* Bloomsbury, 2013.

Serling, Anne. *As I Knew Him: My Dad, Rod Serling.* Citadel Press, 2013.

Sterling, Bruce. "Slipstream 2." *Science Fiction Studies* vol. 38, no. 1, 2011: pp. 6–10.

Swift, Jonathan. *A Modest Proposal and Other Writings.* Penguin Classics, 2009.

"Time Enough at Last." *The Twilight Zone*, written by Rod Serling, directed by John Brahm, Image Entertainment, 2013.

Tolkien, John Ronald Reuel. "Tolkien on Fairy-Stories: Expanded Edition, with Commentary and Notes." HarperCollins Publishers, 2008.

United Commons. *Speculate This!* Duke University Press, 2013.

"Where Is Everybody?" *The Twilight Zone*, written by Rod Serling, directed by Robert Stevens, Image Entertainment, 2011.

Serling and the Bomb

The Twilight Zone's *Nuclear Landscape*

MOLLY A. SCHNEIDER

Of all of the complex topics addressed in *The Twilight Zone* (CBS, 1959–1964), one that seemed especially well suited both to its genre and to its Cold War context was the threat of nuclear war. The series would imagine the hazards of nuclear destruction and "the bomb" multiple times throughout its five-season run, portraying apocalyptic fantasy not only in the classic episode "Time Enough at Last" (1959), but also in episodes such as "Third from the Sun" (1960), "The Shelter" (1961), "One More Pall-bearer" (1962), "No Time Like the Past" (1963), and "The Old Man in the Cave" (1963). Although creator Rod Serling would claim more than once that the bomb was an "untouchable" topic on commercial entertainment television because of network and sponsor reluctance, *The Twilight Zone* would nonetheless go on to address it with some frequency.

The Twilight Zone's discursive relationship to the frightening aspects of nuclear technology is not contained solely within the texts of the broadcasts themselves. Rather than approaching the episodes only at the level of narrative, then, I also look to the archive to investigate how the topic of nuclear war is addressed in some of Serling's viewer letters. Housed primarily in the Rod Serling Papers at the Wisconsin Center for Film and Theater Research, Serling's active correspondence with both his highly dedicated fans and his vigorous critics provides a wealth of context for *The Twilight Zone*'s nuclear imaginary, including some of the ways audiences may have thought about the show's role as a rare dramatic forum for grave societal concerns in the Cold War era. Moreover, this correspondence demonstrates the extent to which some audiences regarded Serling himself as a crucial voice in these contentious national discussions. As one television retrospective reminisced in 1989, "There was another reality on television, and it took place on 'The Twilight Zone,' in which the nightmare side of American life was opened up. The national soul was its subject, and its real villains were the selfish, the shallow, the rapacious" (Kaplan and Slansky 137). "The bomb" was not a cozy topic for network television, especially within the volatile political context of the greater Cold War, and a look at some of these letters can provide some pointed insight into the stakes of depicting nuclear apocalypse on commercial television at mid-century, as well as the extent to which some viewers regarded *The Twilight Zone* as a needed platform for such discussions.

Rod Serling, Television Sage

Before he created *The Twilight Zone*, Serling had already established himself as a prominent writer for dramatic anthology programs. The role of the television writer was a new fascination in American culture at mid-century, and many of the writers associated with anthology series in particular, including Serling, were household names. Because anthologies such as *Playhouse 90* (CBS, 1956–1960) and *Kraft Television Theatre* (NBC, 1947–1958) were often considered highly prestigious programs, the elite group of television playwrights associated with them sometimes enjoyed more freedom to address controversial topics, albeit still with powerful restrictions and sometimes strenuous battles with networks and sponsors. Serling was an especially vocal critic of television censorship, and he became well known for arguing that television had a duty to address important matters of public concern. This sentiment can be found not only in his countless media interviews and published editorial content, but also in his private letters with viewers, friends, and industry professionals.

It was Serling's already-established cache as a highly respected dramatist that brought legitimacy to his own anthology series, *The Twilight Zone*. It would also cause some confusion as to why such a prominent playwright would lend his name to a seemingly "strange" science-fiction and fantasy program. Although anthology series in general were well regarded as "quality" programming, shows that fell under the designation of science fiction and fantasy were rarely considered prestigious television. Indeed, Serling's move to write and produce *The Twilight Zone* was puzzling to many who felt that this type of program was beneath his talent and reputation (see Presnell and McGee 11). Serling, however, was able to leverage his influence as a celebrated writer to both retain some creative control as producer of *The Twilight Zone* and to bring higher regard to a program that used the trappings of allegory and alternate reality to make broader comment about society. As Jon Kraszewski notes, "*The Twilight Zone* was a series that highlighted authorship" (165), and "Serling won himself more creative freedom as a writer by making his own star persona a defining feature of *The Twilight Zone*" (140). Meanwhile, the allegorical register of many of the stories would give shelter to some of his social commentary and more controversial themes. As Serling established himself as both the literal and figurative moral voice of the show, he also cemented his reputation as one of the moral voices of American television more broadly. Not only was he "the guiding Aesop of *The Twilight Zone*" (Sander xix), he was also widely recognized as a sharp commentator on American society and a fierce proponent for the potential of television drama to address issues of world importance.

The horrors of war were an ever-present theme in Serling's work,[1] and his experiences as a paratrooper in the Pacific theater during World War II would significantly influence his writing. He would write a number of television scripts about the looming perils of the Cold War, both directly and indirectly, and these included several about the dangers of nuclear armament specifically. In nearly every case, these shows characterized the existence of nuclear weapons—in anyone's hands, including those of the United States—as a threat to all humankind. The bomb's destructiveness was not just in its literal explosive capabilities or radioactive fallout, but also in its ability to tear the world apart through panic and cruel inhumanity.

This theme fit rather squarely with the overall tenor of *The Twilight Zone*, which frequently used the context of extraordinary circumstances to provide a moral, ethical, or practical lesson about humankind. In nearly every portrayal of nuclear threat, the characters' downfall stems from a combination of hubris, selfishness, and lack of moral fortitude. For example, in season three's "One More Pallbearer" a malevolent egotist elaborately stages a false nuclear event in an attempt to exact retribution on people from his past who, he feels, have wronged him. When his plan backfires, he experiences a break from reality and hallucinates that there really has been a nuclear apocalypse, leaving him alone in a desolate wasteland of his own malice. The closing moral dubs the man "a dealer in fantasy who sits in the rubble of his own making" and "pallbearer at a funeral that he manufactured himself in the Twilight Zone." It was this episode that prompted one viewer to write to Serling and pointedly ask, "You have a thing about integrity, sincerity and the Bomb, don't you?" (Turner, letter, 12 January 1962).

Although Serling would perhaps dramatize the monstrousness of World War II and the Holocaust with greater frequency than the hazards of looming nuclear war with the Soviet Union, his reflections on the inhumanity of war would carry over. Serling also acknowledged that the nuclear era, ushered in by the bombings of Hiroshima and Nagasaki at the end of World War II, would bring new dangers. He maintained that all-consuming warfare in this new world would likely not involve prolonged invasion by boots on the ground, but a swift and terrible attack from afar via atomic or hydrogen bomb. As he wrote to a fellow "ex-Angel" (a former 11th Airborne Division paratrooper), "I think the whole idea of enemy occupation has become a dated and antique principle. Our next war will be nuclear and it strikes me that our major problem will be one of retaliation and simple survival" (letter to D. Giannetta, 16 June 1960). This position would be reflected in many of Serling's scripts, including several episodes of *The Twilight Zone*.

The "Untouchable" Bomb

Serling received a number of fan letters over the years proposing that he write a television play about the threat or the aftermath of nuclear war. Some of these letters express not only the need for television to discuss the pressing concerns of the nuclear age, but also the feeling that Serling might be just the writer to do it. One viewer wrote, "May I very humbly request and suggest that, as one of the rare playwrites [sic] competent to thus arouse our conscience, you endeavor through your talent to lead us toward recognition of our gravest problem—that of a shaky peace (or lack of a hot war,) and the perilous position in which all people find themselves in the shadow of the H-bomb." She felt it was especially important at that moment, "in the light of the belligerence of Mr. Khrushchev," to avoid "answering violence with more violence." To do so would be not only lazy, but disastrous, and the United States must take the lead in finding "new approaches to the solution of old problems." Echoing many of the concluding lessons that would come to define *The Twilight Zone*'s ethical framework, she implored, "It seems so easy to whip people into a frenzy of hate and despair, but far more difficult to arouse concern and awareness and bring about the resultant intelligent action. I feel sure that you could do this through the medium of your art—and there is so little effort toward this end and, many feel, so little time in which to achieve it" (Iltis, letter, 20 May 1960).

In some cases, viewers suggested specific stories that they would like to see Serling adapt for television. One young fan, an eighth-grade student from Sioux City, Iowa, sent a letter containing his history teacher's idea for a television story called "The Atomic War."

> It begins when after [sic] the 3rd World War begins. The Atomic bomb has been dropped and the radioactivity has started to kill the people on earth. After 4 months not a living thing is left on earth except one man witch [sic]

was sent into outer space. He is coming back from outer space, two weeks flying at the speed of light. When he gets back to earth two hundred had past [sic] and the radioactivity has sunk into the ground and he is all alone on earth and he was going crazy. The End [Miller, letter, 1 March 1960].

A few months later, another fan letter would suggest some existing material for a television program about nuclear destruction. This viewer wrote to suggest that Serling find a way to adapt Max Ehrlich's 1949 science fiction pulp novel *The Big Eye* for television, because she felt it "would be a great awakening for the American Public at this time" (Spiegel, letter, 18 May 1960). The jacket copy for the 1950 mass market paperback edition of *The Big Eye* reads in part: "The time was 1960 with Russia and America poised on the brink of atomic war. Then came the shattering news from Palomar Observatory that a new planet had been discovered—a planet that was rushing toward a collision with the Earth on Christmas Day, 1962." The viewer had found *The Big Eye* to be a "frightening" book, and she recounted, "I quickly put it aside and said to myself it couldn't happen here." Yet in the ensuing years, with "all of the terrible things that are happening," she sought to bring out the book again (Spiegel, letter, 18 May 1960). The viewer felt that this topic would be especially pertinent so soon after the failed 1960 Paris peace summit. The summit had fallen apart just two days before the date of her letter, after the shooting down of an American U-2 spy plane over Soviet territory had led to a breakdown in negotiations and Soviet Premier Nikita Khrushchev had walked out of the conference (see Williamson 60–65).

Perhaps most direct in his appeal was a viewer who wrote a four-page letter to Serling in 1959, praising his work and proposing the plot of a television play about the devastation of the United States in a nuclear attack. After a detailed pitch for an opening sequence, the viewer acknowledged with some dismay that perhaps this topic was too taboo for television. "Mr. Serling, this subject material is probably barred for some reason or other. Yet …, doesn't it seem logical that the 'watcher' who is constantly bombarded with 'messages' and 'educative slants' should be jolted into facing the present state of potential reality?" the viewer queried. "If this type of show is unrealistic, or apt to incite unnecessary anxieties, why then, do we produce bombs … and missles [sic] … and multi-million dollar subs?" Lamenting "the present barrage of silence toward this subject matter," the viewer argued,

Regardless of what our "thinkers" assume is right and wrong for the frail skins of Americans to watch…. I'd say they'd better get on the patriotic "ball" and start some constructive "slanting." […] A few shows on this theme would certainly make the "folks" build a fire under the Civil Defense deadheads. It might even cause enough interest to wake up the Secretary of Defense and point out his main job which is the immediate availability of Home Shelters for all home owners in the coastal cities.

This viewer plainly stated what he believed to be the grave implications of producing such a story on television, declaring, "Your producer has a wonderful power at his disposal. He can well save 20,000,000 lives if he so chooses." Such zeal was not uncommon in viewer letters to Serling, especially about topics such as war and worldwide conflict. Like so many others, this viewer expressed his profound desire, and perhaps desperation, for Serling to serve as a televisual savior for a terrified America. "I'm sincere and hope your tremendous artistry will be utilized for the salvation of our national future," the letter concluded. "Somebody's gotta get things going" (Rhea, letter, 29 May 1959 [erroneously dated 1958]).

Serling responded to the above letter with appreciation for the proposed story—"I was frankly enamored with it," he wrote—but regretfully noted that nuclear annihilation was not something dramatic broadcast television was prepared to earnestly address. "Unfortunately this involves another one of those 'untouchable subjects' that the mass media will not either try to attack or even make comment on. I wish to God something could be said since what's involved is simple survival. And by God, I think a discussion of this rates an airing!" (letter to F.K. Rhea, 4 June 1959). However, *The Twilight Zone* would premiere later that year, and, despite Serling's claims of untouchability, the show would indeed go on to dramatize the topic of nuclear attack multiple times.

Serling would also argue a few months later that a story about the past bombing of Hiroshima was not saleable to commercial television (letter to C. Vaughan, 27 November 1959), but he would go on to address it on *The Twilight Zone* in the fourth season episode "No Time Like the Past," wherein a physicist attempts to travel back in time to prevent historical tragedies. Having grown frustrated with humankind's self-defeating practice of walking "upright, and with eyes wide open, into an abyss of his own making" through "[h]is bombs, his fallout, his poisons, his radioactivity," the scientist decides he must endeavor to alter history. In one scene, he travels to 1945 in an unsuccessful attempt to warn Japanese authorities to evacuate Hiroshima before the bomb drops. Serling would again address the Hiroshima bombing, and the risks of future nuclear destruction, in his later 1964 television play *Carol for Another Christmas*, presented as part of a series of ABC specials promoting the United Nations. A variation on *A Christmas Carol* by Charles Dickens, the play follows an isolationist curmudgeon as he is visited by the ghosts of wars past, present, and future. According to Serling, the premise of *Carol for Another Christmas* was that "in a nuclear age ... a war has become obsolete; because it carries with it the absolute surety that we may win but we may also of necessity have to lose" (letter to Mrs. J. Lodgson, 15 January 1965).

Thus, even if Serling would highlight the difficulty of presenting a story of nuclear apocalypse on television, he ultimately was able to do so on multiple occasions, including on *The Twilight Zone*. His claims that television networks and sponsors would be hesitant to portray such a scenario were certainly true, although there had already been at least some notable examples of anthology dramas by other writers that had done this very thing. For example, *The Motorola Television Hour* (ABC, 1953–1954) had presented the television play *Atomic Attack* in 1954. Written by David Davidson, based on Judith Merril's 1950 novel *Shadow on the Hearth*, the play imagines a nuclear attack on New York City and the ensuing weeks of distress and uncertainty. In 1957, *Playhouse 90* had aired Dorothy and Howard Baker's *The Ninth Day*, a post-apocalyptic drama about a group of survivors attempting to repopulate after a bomb has wiped out most of humanity. These programs covered controversial nuclear ground more explicitly than was often permitted on network television, having benefited from the prestigious reputation of anthology dramas such as *Playhouse 90* and, in the case of *Atomic Attack*, cooperation from both state and federal civil defense authorities.

Serling himself had written more than one episode about the threat of the bomb before *The Twilight Zone*, including the celebrated *Playhouse 90* teleplay *Forbidden Area* (1956), although he had yet to fully dramatize the aftermath of nuclear fallout and the resulting suffering. Depicting such a disturbing and politically fraught story directly was indeed quite difficult in the face of "squeamish" networks and sponsors (Sarris 38), but he would eventually manage to do so in the fifth season *Twilight Zone* episode "The Old Man in the Cave," adapted from a short story by Henry Slesar. Set in 1974, ten years after a nuclear bomb has devastated the earth, "The Old Man in the Cave" portrays a small group of survivors who are running out of uncontaminated food and desperate for solutions. They look to prophecies from a mysterious "old man" in a cave, who turns out to be nothing more than a massive computer. The group disregards the computer's warnings, but its projections turn out to be correct, and all but one die from eating food contaminated by the radioactive isotope Strontium-90. Once again, Serling scolds humanity for its own self-destructive actions. His narration explains, "What you're looking at is a legacy that man left to himself. A decade previous, he pushed his buttons and, a nightmarish moment later, woke up to find that he had set the clock back a thousand years. His engines, his medicines, his science were buried in a mass tomb, covered over by the biggest gravedigger of them all: a bomb."

Before "The Old Man in the Cave" projected its more explicit nuclear wasteland, however, episodes like season three's "The Shelter" would warn of the broader cultural dangers that emerged from a climate of nuclear dread. An examination of "The Shelter" and the resulting viewer letters demonstrates both *The Twilight Zone*'s particular brand of social moralizing and the degree to which many viewers saw the show as an important platform to help mediate critical national discussions, ones that other programs might shy away from addressing.

"The Shelter"

"The Shelter" tells the story of a suburban neighborhood thrown into chaos and viciousness in the face of "the bomb."[2] A group of friends has gathered to celebrate Bill Stockton's birthday, and as they pay tribute to his high esteem in the community, they also tease him about the bomb shelter he has built in his basement. His is seemingly the only bomb shelter in the neighborhood, and it is regarded by his peers as an overcautious endeavor. The party is suddenly interrupted by a civil defense announcement warning of a possible impending nuclear attack. Citizens are advised to retreat to their prepared shelters or basements. As most of the neighbors have not prepared shelters, and some do not even have basements, they beg Bill to allow them inside his fortification. Bill only has space and supplies for his own family and must regretfully refuse entry. As the neighbors descend into panic, they furiously turn against Bill, and then against each other, as they attempt to knock down the shelter door with a makeshift battering ram. As soon as they have broken through, the radio announces that the warning had been a false alarm. As the adrenaline dissipates, the group of friends must confront their violent behavior toward each other.

"The Shelter" aired on the same night (although on a different network) as the premiere episode of the news magazine program *Here and Now* (NBC, 1961–1964), which coincidentally featured a discussion about the "the sudden boom in bomb shelter construction" ("Banjos, Baseball and Bomb Shelters"). To be sure, bomb shelters were a timely topic in 1961. However, as historian Elaine Tyler May notes, a relatively small proportion of Americans actually built shelters in their homes. Rather, their role as a potent symbolic touchstone of security far surpassed the number of physical shelters built. Although "[m]oments of increased tension in the cold war, such as the Cuban missile crisis, sparked flurries of shelter construction," much more widespread were the countless newspaper and magazine articles, television features, and civil defense messages that circulated in American culture. Promotions of nuclear preparedness, including the use of fallout shelters, "were attempts to reassure the public that they could protect themselves against nuclear annihilation." And yet, bomb shelters were not a purely comforting premise. Even as shelters became important objects of perceived safety and control in the face of terrifying possibilities, "at the same time, they intensified the nation's consciousness of the imminence of nuclear war, raising the specter of sudden carnage" (May 101–102).

In "The Shelter," the darker side of this dialectic forcefully emerges. As the neighbors' desperation increases, their selfishness and baser instincts take over. They band together not to help each other, but to claw at a piece of safety for themselves. The "moral" of "The Shelter" could have easily been a message about the importance of preparedness, as with government supported broadcasts like the abovementioned *Atomic Attack*. The story premise of "The Shelter" at first suggests this trajectory, and Bill does chide his neighbors for not heeding advice about how to protect their families. Ultimately, though, the program sidesteps a scolding message about self-reliance and instead indicts the ugliness that emerges from a climate of fear stoked by intercultural animosity and sectarian jingoism in the context of the Cold War. This point is made even clearer through the use of xenophobic and barely-veiled anti–Semitic vitriol about "your kind"—"pushy, grabby, semi-American" immigrant families—directed toward the Weiss family in a moment of nuclear panic.

In many ways, "The Shelter" could be considered a companion piece to the earlier and arguably more famous episode "The Monsters Are Due on Maple Street" (1960), whose premise of a suspected alien infiltration among neighbors is easily interpretable as an allegory of the divisiveness of Red Scare paranoia. In both episodes, the greatest danger comes not from without, but from within. Neither denies the existence of real peril— both acknowledge that there is indeed a threat from beyond our borders— but both also insist that the greatest destructive forces will be our own selfishness and fear. As the closing moral of "Monsters" argues, "The tools of conquest do not necessarily come with bombs and explosions and fallout. There are weapons that are simply thoughts, attitudes, prejudices—to be found only in the minds of men. For the record, prejudices can kill, and suspicion can destroy, and a thoughtless, frightened search for a scapegoat has a fallout all its own." The concluding sentence breaks any illusion that this episode is pure fantasy, declaring, "[T]he pity of it is that these things cannot be confined to the Twilight Zone."

As Rick Worland argues, "The twist ending of a *Twilight Zone* parable … was often a lesson in New Frontier–era Liberalism," or "Cold War liberalism," and the above lesson potentially "signals [Serling's] intent to link domestic politics to the larger dangers of the Cold War through the explicit mention of bombs and fallout" (106); thus, it forges a key connection between the threats of nuclear annihilation and the broader threats of Cold War cultural violence. Serling would use the conceit of nuclear destruction as a canvas upon which to paint some of his most common moral preoccupations as a writer: integrity, compassion, freedom of thought and expression, anti-discrimination, and the courage to rise above paranoia and mob violence.

Like in "Monsters," the cautionary message in "The Shelter" warns that Americans will destroy themselves all on their own, while the "enemy" sits back and watches. Yet, Serling's early narration announces that "The Shelter" is "not meant to be prophetic." Such violence "need not happen," and "It's the fervent and urgent prayer of all men of good will that it never shall happen." It is unclear, however, whether he refers to nuclear attack itself, or to the violent, fear-fueled self-destruction of American society.

Serling's closing narration insists that "The Shelter" has "[n]o moral, no message, no prophetic tract," but a simple "statement of fact" that "[f]or civilization to survive, the human race has to remain civilized." He would claim several times that *The Twilight Zone* had no political agenda or axe to grind, partly as a way of deflecting criticism and appeasing sponsors and networks who were nervous about controversial material. Nonetheless, it becomes clear in his scripts, some of his published material, and his private correspondence that he often very clearly had a moral or ethical message to express on television, and many viewer letters demonstrate that they did not believe the dubious claim that *The Twilight Zone* was devoid of social commentary (see Schneider 204–245).

Several favorable viewer letters explicitly expressed their appreciation for "The Shelter" because of the importance of its implications for American society. "A note to say thanks for last Friday's wonderful show, 'The Shelter,'" wrote one viewer. "Would that everyone in the country could have seen it" (Blyth, letter, n.d. 1961). Acknowledging the timeliness of the topic, another letter praised "The Shelter" for "posing some very pertinent and moral questions on all our minds" (Lash, letter, 9 January 1962). Yet another argued that "we surely need more of this type of writing on this type of subject to awaken our country" (Smith, letter, n.d. 1961).

A college student in California praised the episode and regretfully noted, "I feel it is a shame that everyone could not see the show.... [I]f I could, I would ask that the film be shown here and at all the other colleges in the nation." The notion that Serling's work served a pedagogical function, that it was important material worthy of being used in educational settings, appears repeatedly in viewer correspondence throughout Serling's career. Reflecting the sentiments of many other letters in Serling's collection, the student declared, "I feel that this film could be a great public service if it could be seen by more people. After all it could happen" (Puckett, letter, n.d. 1961). Serling responded via his secretary, who wrote that Serling "asked me to express his appreciation to you, and tell you that letters, such as yours, renews [sic] his faith in an audience he has always felt is not satisfied to just sit, watch, and be mesmerized. They are too bright.

Too aware. And they want to think a little—not just accept" (secretary to Rod Serling, letter, 25 October 1961). Serling would repeat this sentiment in many replies to viewers, suggesting perhaps his desire both to express his thanks and to flatter his adoring audience by commiserating about the often-unfulfilled cultural potential of television.

The notion that "it could happen here"—that Americans must not become complacent about their relative safety, and that they should not only prepare for, but try to prevent, tragic eventualities—is infused throughout many letters to Serling. Just as a great number of viewers had insisted that Serling's shows about Nazism and the Holocaust were important tools in helping Americans resist fascism and genocide, viewers like the college student above argued that programs like "The Shelter" might help Americans remain vigilant about the dangers of a nuclear world.

These letters are representative of a strong trend in Serling's fan mail overall—the idea that Serling was one of the only playwrights on television who had the courage to discuss important topics despite network and sponsor objection, and that his work was not just entertainment, but a vital public service in a turbulent time. A great many letters expressed both worry about current societal problems and exasperation at television's failure to address them. Serling was in an advantageous position that at times allowed him to leverage both his prominent reputation as a dramatist and the generic affordances of science fiction and fantasy to provide a platform for some of these discussions. Countless viewers thanked Serling for pushing to create television that asked audiences to think and consider important questions, in contrast to what they felt was network television's overall timidity and lack of substance. In many cases these viewers declared that *The Twilight Zone* was one of the rare shows to rise above what they perceived to be television's usual dreck, and in doing so they also revealed that it was important to them to think of themselves as more sophisticated and culturally engaged than the television industry often gave them credit for. Many criticized the networks and the sponsors for muzzling what they believed to be Serling's crucial national voice, and they clamored for more frank, mature dramas about matters of societal concern, including the alarming escalation of Cold War hostilities and nuclear saber-rattling. *The Twilight Zone*'s nuclear imaginary became an important facet of its role as a mediator of national anxieties and cultural values.

Conclusion

As this brief look at these episodes and viewer letters demonstrates, many audience members were deeply invested in the image of

Serling as a wise television sage for the Cold War era. Embedded in this near-devotional admiration is a strikingly earnest notion—perhaps not the confidence, but the hope, that television drama could save humanity if it were just allowed to do so. If we could not find salvation in nuclear technology, perhaps television technology could help bridge the gap, stem the tide, or cool the temperature of the "Cold" War. For many, *The Twilight Zone* is synonymous with Serling, and widely regarded as his magnum opus. Part of this may stem from a perception, accurate or not, that *The Twilight Zone* was the place where Serling could finally say what he wanted to say, what society needed him to say. In the face of something so inconceivable and incalculable in its scale as nuclear war, perhaps *The Twilight Zone* felt like one arena where those terrifying scenarios could be fantastically played out.

Certainly not all viewers appreciated Serling's messages. His archived papers contain plenty of letters from people who disagreed with his perceived politics or his artistic sensibility. Some accused him of being a bleeding-heart, unpatriotic pinko. Some, on the other hand, demanded to know why he was not forceful enough in his liberal politics. More than a few felt some of his scripts were too dark, too cynical, or too preachy. Some expressed impatience with *The Twilight Zone*'s penchant for heavy-handed moralizing, what one couple described as Serling's "eternal and wearying analysis at the end, middle, and beginning of your show" (Wilson, letter, 24 June 1961). Others complained that its "unexplainable" and "preposterous" stories were too disconcerting in a time already plagued by everyday fear and uncertainty. An elementary school teacher wrote, "In our own world of fanatic reality (H-bomb), there are too many true facts we can't explain. Is your added fiction a CONSTRUCTIVE contribution?" (McLean, letter, 5 March 1960).

What is clear, however, is that, for those who bothered to write a letter, the stakes of *The Twilight Zone* were high. Many viewers looked to the show, and to Serling in particular, to help them navigate a tumultuous cultural landscape. Some seemed to believe that fantasy and science fiction might be one of the only feasible avenues for addressing these often daunting and bewildering societal questions in dramatic television. One fan from Indiana pointedly wrote, "Twilight Zone is one of three programs that allows the public to use their minds, to 'think'.... Please keep thinking along the same lines" (Sweetow, letter, 18 May 1960). Even those who criticized *The Twilight Zone*—and in some ways *especially* those who criticized it—realized that it was potentially a very influential program on a medium that was proving itself to be more and more influential in American life. Ultimately, one can see in these discussions an expressed worry that *The Twilight Zone*'s depictions of nuclear destruction might not be science fiction or fantasy at all, that "the pity of it" was that these existential dangers could not be "confined to the Twilight Zone." Indeed, the Indiana viewer above quoted this very line from "The Monsters Are Due on Maple Street" in her letter to Serling, begging him to continue his work. "[M]aybe sometime, someday, people will listen, think, and stop destroying each other," she wrote. "P.S. I hope this letter reaches you before we all blow up."

Notes

1. See Carruthers and Popiel's essay on war in *The Twilight Zone*.
2. See Michael Meyerhofer's essay on "The Shelter" in the next section of this volume.

Works Cited

"Banjos, Baseball and Bomb Shelters" (advertisement for *Here and Now*), *The New York Times*, 29 Sep. 1961, p. 70.

Blyth, R. Letter to Rod Serling. N.d. [3 or 10 Oct. 1961]. Rod Serling Papers, Wisconsin Center for Film and Theater Research, Wisconsin Historical Society Library-Archives, U.S. Mss 43AN, Box 4, Folder 2.

Ehrlich, Max. *The Big Eye*. Popular Library, 1950.

Iltis, G. Letter to Rod Serling. 20 May 1960. Rod Serling Papers, Wisconsin Center for Film and Theater Research, Wisconsin Historical Society Library-Archives, U.S. Mss 43AN, Box 12, Folder 3.

Kaplan, Peter, and Paul Slansky. "Golden Moments." *Connoisseur*, Sep. 1989, pp. 135–149.

Kraszewski, Jon. *The New Entrepreneurs: An Institutional History of Television Anthology Writers*. Wesleyan University Press, 2010.

Lash, J.C. Letter to Rod Serling. 9 Jan. 1962. Rod Serling Papers, Wisconsin Center for Film and Theater Research, Wisconsin Historical Society Library-Archives, U.S. Mss 43AN, Box 4, Folder 3.

May, Elaine Tyler. *Homeward Bound: American Families in the Cold War Era*. Revised 4th ed., Basic Books, 2017.

McLean, M. Letter to Rod Serling. 5 Mar. 1960. Rod Serling Papers, Wisconsin Center for Film and Theater Research, Wisconsin Historical Society Library-Archives, U.S. Mss 43AN, Box 11, Folder 5.

Merril, Judith. *Shadow on the Hearth*. Doubleday, 1950.

Miller, T. Letter to Rod Serling. 1 Mar. 1960. Rod Serling Papers, Wisconsin Center for Film and Theater Research, Wisconsin Historical Society Library-Archives, U.S. Mss 43AN, Box 11, Folder 3.

"The Monsters Are Due on Maple Street," *The Twilight Zone*, written by Rod Serling, directed by Ronald Winston, Image Entertainment, 2011.

"No Time Like the Past," *The Twilight Zone*, written by Rod Serling, directed by Justus Addiss, Image Entertainment, 2011.

"The Old Man in the Cave," *The Twilight Zone*, written by Rod Serling, directed by Alan Crosland, Jr., Image Entertainment, 2013.

"One More Pallbearer," *The Twilight Zone*," written by Rod Serling, directed by Lamont Johnson, Image Entertainment, 2011.

Presnell, Don, and Marty McGee. *A Critical History of Television's* The Twilight Zone, *1959–1964*. McFarland, 1998.

Puckett, T.C., Jr. Letter to Rod Serling. N.d. [Sept. or Oct. 1961]. Rod Serling Papers,

Wisconsin Center for Film and Theater Research, Wisconsin Historical Society Library-Archives, U.S. Mss 43AN, Box 4, Folder 2.

Rhea, F.K. Letter to Rod Serling. 29 May 1959 [erroneously dated 1958]. Rod Serling Papers, Wisconsin Center for Film and Theater Research, Wisconsin Historical Society Library-Archives, U.S. Mss 43AN, Box 9, Folder 3.

Sander, Gordon F. *Serling: The Rise and Twilight of Television's Last Angry Man.* Plume, 1994.

Sarris, Andrew. "Rod Serling Viewed from Beyond the Twilight Zone." *Television Quarterly,* vol. 21, no. 2 (1984), pp. 37–41.

Schneider, Molly. *Americanness and the Midcentury Television Anthology Drama.* 2016. Northwestern U, PhD Dissertation.

Secretary to Rod Serling. Letter to T.C. Puckett, Jr. 25 Oct. 1961. Rod Serling Papers, Wisconsin Center for Film and Theater Research, Wisconsin Historical Society Library-Archives, U.S. Mss 43AN, Box 4, Folder 2.

Serling, Rod. Letter to C. Vaughan. 27 Nov. 1959. Rod Serling Papers, Wisconsin Center for Film and Theater Research, Wisconsin Historical Society Library-Archives, U.S. Mss 43AN, Box 10, Folder 1.

_____. Letter to D. Giannetta. 16 June 1960. Rod Serling Papers, Wisconsin Center for Film and Theater Research, Wisconsin Historical Society Library-Archives, U.S. Mss 43AN, Box 12, Folder 7.

_____. Letter to F.K. Rhea. 4 June 1959. Rod Serling Papers, Wisconsin Center for Film and Theater Research, Wisconsin Historical Society Library-Archives, U.S. Mss 43AN, Box 9, Folder 3.

_____. Letter to Mrs. J. Lodgson. 15 Jan. 1965. Rod Serling Papers, Wisconsin Center for Film and Theater Research, Wisconsin Historical Society Library-Archives, U.S. Mss 43AN, Box 4, Folder 5.

"The Shelter," *The Twilight Zone,* written by Rod Serling, directed by Lamont Johnson, Image Entertainment, 2011.

Smith, S. Letter to Rod Serling. N.d. [Sept. or Oct. 1961]. Rod Serling Papers, Wisconsin Center for Film and Theater Research, Wisconsin Historical Society Library-Archives, U.S. Mss 43AN, Box 4, Folder 2.

Spiegel, Mrs. H. Letter to Rod Serling. 18 May 1960. Rod Serling Papers, Wisconsin Center for Film and Theater Research, Wisconsin Historical Society Library-Archives, U.S. Mss 43AN, Box 12, Folder 3.

Sweetow, I.J. Letter to Rod Serling. 18 May 1960. Rod Serling Papers, Wisconsin Center for Film and Theater Research, Wisconsin Historical Society Library-Archives, U.S. Mss 43AN, Box 12, Folder 3.

"Third from the Sun," *The Twilight Zone,* written by Rod Serling, directed by Richard L. Bare, Image Entertainment, 2010.

"Time Enough at Last," *The Twilight Zone,* written by Rod Serling, directed by John Brahm, Image Entertainment, 2010.

Turner, N. Letter to Rod Serling. 12 Jan. 1962. Rod Serling Papers, Wisconsin Center for Film and Theater Research, Wisconsin Historical Society Library-Archives, U.S. Mss 43AN, Box 4, Folder 3.

Williamson, Richard D. *First Steps Toward Détente: American Diplomacy in the Berlin Crisis, 1958–1963.* Lexington, 2012.

Wilson, Mr. and Mrs. M. Letter to Rod Serling. 24 June 1961. Rod Serling Papers, Wisconsin Center for Film and Theater Research, Wisconsin Historical Society Library-Archives, U.S. Mss 43AN, Box 4, Folder 2.

Worland, Rick. "Sign-Posts Up Ahead: *The Twilight Zone, The Outer Limits,* and TV Political Fantasy 1959–1965," *Science Fiction Studies,* vol. 23, no. 1 (1996), pp. 103.

The *Twilight Zone* Goes to War!

Elsa M. Carruthers *and* Paul Popiel

Often called "The Angry Young Man of Hollywood" because of his outrage and arguments with studio executives over censorship, racism, bigotry, and blind patriotism, Rod Serling struggled to write teleplays and screenplays with the kind of social commentary he felt was important ("Rod Serling: Submitted for Your Approval"). He was fiercely antiracist and deeply concerned about the world. As a young man wanting to serve his country during World War II, he enlisted in the Army, and we can only assume that he took those youthful ideals along with some hard-won life lessons, distilling them into great writing.

Serling used the fantastic as a means to discuss the unpopular. During an interview, his wife, Carol Serling, said of his frustrations, "He had said, 'You know, you can put these words into the mouth of a Martian and get away with it.'" "If it was a Republican or Democrat they couldn't say it. I mean, he wanted to deal with the issues of the day. We're looking at bigotry, racism, prejudice, nuclear war, ethics, witch-hunts, loneliness. All of these things were verboten" (2002 NPR Morning Edition retrospective and interview with Serling's widow Carol Serling). Furthermore, Serling's own experiences in war fed into his writing the fantastic to engage with difficult topics, including topics that were difficult for him. Interviewed for the *American Masters* profile "Rod Serling: Submitted for Your Approval," a former soldier from Serling's unit shared: "He didn't just have war experiences; they were branded into his hide soul and mind and I think he produced some of the finest writing he ever did," said his Army buddy ("Rod Serling: Submitted for Your Approval"). The experiences of enlisting, training, reporting for duty, combat/deployment, and then attempting to readjust to civilian life are so life changing and common, that veterans often feel a sort of kinship even across service branches and conflicts.

Battle takes a physical and psychic toll on soldiers, often to devastating degrees. Serling himself was profoundly impacted by his time as a paratrooper during World War II, and as the writer of the majority of tele-plays for *The Twilight Zone*, the evidence of his service time and the linger-ing effects it had on him are clear. In his own words, "I was traumatized into writing by war. By going into a war in a foreign country in a com-bat situation and feeling a desperate need for some sort of therapy to get it right out of my gut write it down. This is the way it began for me" ("Rod Serling: Submitted for Your Approval").

In a sense, we can say that he took to writing as activism. "He car-ried his *Playhouse 90* sensibility right into The Twilight Zone," finding that stories of social commentary that could not sell anywhere under other circumstances, if put in a fantasy story could say all sorts of things, said Richard Matheson. Most of his philosophy can be seen in his war episodes. "The war was always with him. I think up until the time he died he was still having nightmares at times" Carol Serling ("Rod Serling: Submitted for Your Approval").

Battle Fatigue/Shell Shock

"I don't want to be here. I don't want to be here!" says Lieutenant Carter in "Death Ship" (1963) and at some point, or another, every sol-dier has said that to themselves. People enlist when they are barely into adulthood and for most soldiers, they find themselves away from home for the first time. Training, no matter how realistic, is little comparison to the unrelenting realities and hardships of deployment. Astronauts, while not engaged in war, sometimes have a military background and also experience some of the same feelings as soldiers because of the difference between their lives on Earth and their experiences in space exploration.

One of the unique experiences of soldiers/astronauts is a sort of time compression while off on deployment. The soldier is working nonstop for months or years and the relative sameness of it gives one the impression that time isn't really passing. Meanwhile, at home, loved ones and friends are experiencing time at a seemingly different rate, with birthdays, anni-versaries, etc., winding away while the soldier is deployed. There is a sense of loss and being out of place for a freshly returned soldier that can only be described as time-lag. Even regular letters, phone calls, and pictures aren't a substitute for seeing loved ones in person. Soldiers often need a chance to "catch up" on it all.

Though Zicree dismissed this episode as "suffering from flat acting that results in an interesting concept that never generates much energy" (Zicree, 350). "The Parallel" (1963) was, in fact, quite an insightful piece. Take away the space-mission conceit, it is a story of a man returning home from deployment. There is a period of adjustment that occurs, the person left behind has taken on more tasks and "held down the fort" while the soldier was away. They have both changed somewhat, though the soldier likely has changed more. Indeed, there is a moment when Major Gaines is speaking to his wife and they are both uneasy. She tries her best to put him at ease, assuming he is readjusting to home as any other time he returned from a mission, but there is just something *off*.

When they kiss, both are momentarily repulsed. They simply don't know each other. This is a common occurrence for couples when one person is back after a long absence; the estrangement between a couple during the period after a return home is difficult to talk about and even more difficult to deal with in a healthy way. Nervous, the wife tries, as so many military spouses do, to "make things normal" for Gaines. So much so that he makes several comments about it, asking her not to "tip-toe around me." She promises not to, but calls Gaines' buddy anyway, for reassurance that her husband is all right and that he will soon be back to his "normal" self.

His daughter isn't as diplomatic. "Daddy, you're different. I don't know, but you're different. There's something wrong!" ("The Parallel"). She is obviously frightened and uncomfortable around him. This too is common for military children but excruciating for the returned parent. The child is wary of the returned parent and can seem cold or distant.

Touched on in this episode is also that sense of time-lag mentioned above. Gaines is troubled by the little things that seemed to have changed or that he didn't notice before he went on the mission. This is of course explained away in the episode as it being the home of his parallel counterpart, Colonel Gaines. For returning soldiers, this feeling is unsettling and disruptive, and often listed as a symptom of PTSD (Battle Fatigue or, earlier called Shell Shock) and/or reentry anxiety ("The Parallel").

Survivor's guilt frequently accompanies the anxiety of coming home. In "King Nine Will Not Return" (1960), Captain James Embry, a former Army pilot, is shocked to see a headline in the local paper detailing the discovery of his downed B-25 Mitchell bomber from seventeen years earlier. He wakes in a hospital room and his doctors believe he is suffering from battle fatigue and survivor's guilt. He is. He was ill the day before the mission, seventeen years before and another pilot along with his whole crew perished in Tasmania. Ever since, Embry was haunted by the loss of his crew and the guilt of not making the mission.

In true *The Twilight Zone* style, Embry also somehow went back there, and took in the wreckage and saw his crew one last time. The psychiatrist examining Embry tells him emphatically that it was not way his fault. Later, the psychiatrist tells the admitting doctor, "he will be all right now, now that he can get all of the guilt and grief out of his gut." This bit of dialogue is an eerie bit of self-echoing of Serling's remarks about writing after the war ("Rod Serling: Submitted for your Approval").

"The Thirty-Fathom Grave" is another exploration of survivor's guilt. Unlike Captain Embry, Naval Chief Bell is literally haunted by the men he accidentally killed by dropping the signal lamp, knocking the red filter off and alerting the Japanese to their location. They were immediately attacked. He was the sole survivor. Twenty years later, during a small engagement, Chief Bell is horrified by the specters of the men who died that night. He keeps telling the Captain that the men were "calling muster on him." No amount of reassurance from his captain helps Chief Bell.

He is unable to let go of his grief and guilt. Sure enough, he dives to the wrecked submarine and joins the others. After a ten-hour search and rescue mission to recover Bell, the Captain laments, "Funny thing how long it takes some men to die. Or to find any peace at all. Sometimes I think that's the worst thing about war. Not just what it does to the bodies, what it does to the minds" ("Thirty-Fathom Grave").

Anxieties of coming home and the survivor's guilt can be symptoms of Post-Traumatic Stress Disorder (also known as battle fatigue or, even earlier, shell shock) and/or reentry anxiety ("Returning Home from Deployment"). Survivor's guilt is multifaceted. Perhaps it is because soldiers are constantly reminded that they are part of team and that their lives depend on members of their units and beyond that, their branch of service, and so on, to members of other branches. "Leave no man behind" and "don't forget your buddies" are common refrains that remind us to look out for each other. Each soldier is trained and repeatedly drilled in tasks that would be lifesaving to their fellows. Soldiers not only learn basic combat lifesaving techniques, first aid, and first responder skills, but also safety practices, such as clearing hallways and tight quarters of debris and trip hazards, and other tasks specific to their MOS (Military Occupation Specialty) or NEC for the Navy. All of this training lends to a culture of looking out for others and taking responsibility for the lives and welfare of fellows.

While Captain Embry, and many of his real-life counterparts agonize over whether or not the circumstances would have been different, there is a realization that events are completely out of one's control. It is both frightening and seems like a cheat; like survival is merely luck of the draw. Surely the others that perished deserved to live just as much and that is where guilt lies. Serling, through this brilliant bit of writing, addresses the profundity of this feeling.

Though similar, Chief Bell in "Thirty Fathom Grave" is actually a closer study of the complexity of survivor's guilt and one's responsibility to the welfare of others. He feels haunted over a mistake he made. Whether or not he should feel the guilt is difficult to say with any certainty. On the one hand, he no doubt had hours of drills to prevent such a tragic outcome, on the other, accidents happen all of the time. The brilliance of Serling's writing is that he took this culture of caring for our neighbors and through a lens of military story, allowed civilians, even young children, to understand what it means to carry the weight of responsibility for others.

Loved Ones Left Behind

"Oh Bob, darling. Welcome Back!" says his wife as Major Gaines greets her at the door after a short mission. Her relief and happiness are palpable. It isn't difficult to relate to a sense of profound joy, no matter how fleeting, she must have felt as she learns that her loved one is safe and unharmed. It is the same for every military family. There is hope that all will be well while the soldier is away, while there is also an awareness that they may at some point or another, get a call, visit, or telegram informing them that their loved one is injured or deceased.

One of the few episodes to address the grief of loved ones left behind is "In Praise of Pip," which explores the worry of parents whose children have "shipped off." As with military spouses, it is an awkward and tense "wait and see" situation, only the child is an adult, and the information isn't as forthcoming to parents as it is to a spouse. A nightmare about a battlefield wrenches Max Phillips awake. It is unclear if the nightmare is conjured from his own wartime experiences, or his connection with his son, or from the fear he carries for Pip's safety, who is stationed in Vietnam. Regardless, Max is clearly worried about his son.

When the landlady, Mrs. Feeney, comes to straighten up the room, he asks about the mail. "Nothing from the kid?" "No, not this time, but don't worry about him. He's all right," she tells him because she wants to allay Max's unease over Pip. Later, when Mrs. Feeney reads a telegram from the Army to Max over the phone, Max is overcome with grief to learn that Pip is injured and not likely to survive, "Pip is dying. My kid is dying. In a place called South Vietnam. There isn't even supposed to be a war going on over there, but my son is dying. It's to laugh. I swear it's to laugh." When Max tells his boss, "I gave away the best part of me," it is a heartbreaking revelation. Here we see every parent's anguish at such news. Their child is far away from home, distance and location making it impossible to visit or call and they likely missed or will miss the moment of their child's passing. They will outlive their child without having been able to say a proper goodbye. The show ends on a bittersweet note; Max sacrifices himself for Pip. Such a sacrifice could only happen in *The Twilight Zone*, but how many parents would gladly offer up themselves in place of their children if such as thing was possible? ("In Praise of Pip").

Another episode, "The Passersby," deals with grief, but also touches on the patriotic and moral furor that draws so many young people to enlist. A woman watches as hundreds of men march past her ruined home until Sergeant Ebbie stops for some water. He, along with the others are heading down a long road that both Union and Confederate soldiers are marching. He stops overnight, exhausted and finding it rough to travel since one of his feet is blown away. The woman is happy enough to have him as he reminds her of her late husband, killed in the line of duty.

Repeatedly during the episode she wistfully tells Ebbie about her husband and reminisces about their time together, wishing that he hadn't go off to war in the first place. In a telling exchange, they discuss the patriotic fervor that swept the men up to enlist. "There were smiles and not many tears," she says of the parades of celebrating the men as they reported for duty. She tells him that they were so sure that the men would all be coming back home, an unspoken understanding that they were on the "right" side of the conflict suggested in her tone and certainty. Ebbie then recounts that his father was finally proud of him when he enlisted. "He was a proud one when I marched off to war to become a man." Sadly, he did become a man and had his life cut short in battle.

Though we come to understand that the men marching by are dead, having succumbed to the ravages of the battlefield, it is difficult not to see the endless marching and not connect them to the living veterans of every war that have been all but forgotten about as soon as the wartime was over. The stress and trauma of combat have changed them forever, so that even if they are back in body, not many veterans are completely back in spirit. It is as if those veterans died as well, leaving friends and family to mourn for the people they once were.

Not only does Serling's image of the long parade of wounded men trotting off into the unknown evoke the vanity of sending young people off to fight in battles they don't have any stakes in, but it is almost a condemnation. It is as if he is saying we will continue to conduct large scale war until there aren't any more people to fight them because no one questions the necessity, or worse, the morality of war. As Richard Matheson once said of Serling, "There is a sense of outrage in Serling's writing about our own stupidity" (Rod Serling: Submitted for Your Approval).

Relieving (Reliving?) "The Glory Days"

One of the unfortunate side effects of soldiering is a certain level of desensitization that is necessary to do one's job in combat. Being in combat situations and having to fight and potentially kill enemy soldiers is profoundly life-changing and soul wrenching for most people. "We've done enough killing to last us a lifetime. More than a lifetime. You got a yen to do some killing. Okay. We'll kill for you but don't expect us to stand up and cheer about it," Sergeant Causarano tells his unit's new Lieutenant when he demands that they kill a small band of Japanese soldiers trapped in a cave. The lieutenant was very eager to prove himself and thought the best way to do so was to order his men kill as many Japanese soldiers as possible. Causarano tries at first to reason with him, explaining that the men were no threat and that it was wrong to harm them. To no avail.

When that same lieutenant is somehow transformed into a Japanese soldier whose commander had told him to attack the Americans, he is horrified to hear his own words barked back at him. The full moral weight of what he had ordered is now resting on his shoulders. If not directly renouncing the ruthlessness of some soldiers and military commanders, this episode certainly does lend itself to that interpretation. In writing it, Serling seemed to have been condemning power-hungry, cruel leaders that use the soldiers under their charge for their own purposes.

The kind of training that goes into desensitizing combat soldiers also corrupts. Obliquely referencing it, Fenton, in "The Encounter," decries:

> You by any chance afraid of me? Well, I can think of a couple of reasons. One, being my background. I was in a fighting outfit. Do you know what that means? Well it's not like the recruitment posters, I can tell you that! A nice clean-cut lad who helps old ladies cross the street. He has to be a highly trained combat machine with split second reactions in place of emotions. He's on wire, he's on his toes. His nerve endings are dead! And he's as cold and as hard as this helmet! In fact, there's nothing more terrible to meet on a dark night than a fighting man with an M1, a Thompson, a grenade, or even his bare hands.

There is a sense of pride in his proclamation that he was in a "fighting outfit"; Fenton survived arduous training and grueling combat. But there is also an unspoken sadness. Fenton lost a some of his humanity in the process.

What happens when there is a total loss of humanity? For the few soldiers who revel in violence and live for the glory days of the war, their days are spent in recalling and recounting those times to anyone who will listen. In "Deaths-Head Revisited" former SS Captain Lutze returns to Dachau to relive his "glory days." He is enjoying himself until the "caretaker" appears before him. Lutze is shocked but quickly recovers, laughing at the man he tortured for sport.

Such men and women are truly dangerous and there really isn't a place for them in the world. Lutze uses the very same words we hear today from racists and bigots when he tries to convince Becker that his crimes weren't serious. He tells Becker it is time to "move on" that "it was a long time ago" and that "it means nothing now" ("Deaths-Head Revisited").

Othering of the Enemy and Loss of Innocence

The obsession with sameness and otherness is what makes it possible to kill. By necessity there must be an "us" and "them." "The Encounter" is a tense, unnerving story of a World War II veteran venting on a young Japanese American twenty years after the war. Mr. Arthur Takamori is going door to door to offer landscaping services. Fenton, bitter and already a bit drunk, invites the young man up for a beer. When refused, Fenton then invites him up, ostensibly to earn some extra money "to help me clear out all this junk" but it is plain he has harmful intentions.

Takamori is immediately on alert. He is extremely reluctant to go upstairs or to even enter the building. He tries to say he doesn't have the time, but Fenton won't have it. "All right, but just for ten minutes," Takamori relents after Fenton badgers him into accepting. Almost immediately, Fenton escalates his belligerent tone. He asks Takamori his name, and scoffs. "Arthur, why Arthur?" Takamori responds, "Why not? I was born in this country. I am just as American as anybody."

Fenton grouses over the reply. "Well who says you're not? You're too darn sensitive." But he is still behaving like a bully and he repeatedly bars Takamori from leaving. He also makes several racist remarks including, "In the Pacific we were told you guys weren't even human. You were some kind of species of ape. And not to worry about burning you out of caves, Now all of a sudden, you're fine people. Highly cultured."

Between his offensive outbursts, Fenton continually tries to engage Takamori. "I've been pushed and pulled this way and that until now I hate everybody!" Fenton screams at Arthur. He tells the young man that he is all alone. He has lost everything, and he can't quite make out why. When he sees that the young man is coming under the sword's power, he gestures toward his old service medals and says, "All right, I'm scared. But not of dying. Of living! I've got a box of decorations over there. Decorations!" as if to say it was all for nothing. And this is the most tragic moment for Fenton. He is confronted with the fact that he murdered a man who had already surrendered, and he lost the most important part of himself as a result.

It is excruciating to watch Fenton try and fail to articulate his feelings of remorse, guilt, loss of innocence and sense of self and self-respect. He said earlier that he's "not a bad guy," but he clearly doesn't believe it himself. He had no idea how to return to the young man he was before the war and he pushed everyone away since. Fenton's experience is not an unusual one for combat soldiers ("The Encounter").

As an aside, Takamori's "confession" in this episode is extremely problematic and it was pulled from syndication until 2016 (Wiki Fandom). "In reality, there was no Japanese-American traitor at Pearl Harbor guiding enemy planes. In fact, there is no case of sabotage by a Japanese-American during all of WWII. The suggestion of such an action—even in a fictional context—could easily have brought protests" (Zicree, 423). Though this episode was not written by Serling, it is clear that he worried that some veterans held racist and bigoted beliefs long after their tours of duty. Episodes like "The Shelter" and "The Monsters are Due on Maple Street," which he did write, are evidence of that concern.

Fascism/Totalitarianism/Tyranny/Racism as Trigger for War and Result of War

It is no coincidence that just a decade after World War II, in The McCarthy Era, with the lingering racism, fascism, and anti-Semitism so many Americans harbored in their hearts, that Serling would have a preoccupation with totalitarianism and dictators. So many of the episodes in the original run centered around the evils of fascism and totalitarianism. Many of these episodes can be viewed as both precursors to war and the aftermath. "Number 12 Looks Just Like You," "Eye of the Beholder," and "Obsolete Man" are set in worlds where we can assume a previous war has resulted in a totalitarian State. These episodes are not only warnings about the oppressiveness of everyday life under such regimes that would demand complete conformity of appearance, thought, and action, but that to break free would require rebellion and likely another war.

One of the terrible things about fascism is how insidious it is. It can start so slowly that by the time it is noticed, it is too late. In "On Thursday We Leave for Home," Captain Benteen slowly becomes a bully, and then a tyrant. Like any great leader, he took command of "his people," as he called them, giving much needed structure, morale, and support while they live out there days on a remote desert planet. When one of the colonists, Baines, complains about Benteen's orders, Benteen rightfully reminds him that without laws, "the young take the food from the old, the strong would take from the weak." It would be the worst kind of anarchy.

But Baines' insubordination has successfully put a chink in Benteen's command. Shortly after, when a rescue ship finally arrives to take them all home, Benteen is immediately put off of Colonel Sloane who calls Benteen "Mr. Benteen" because the Captain rank was honorary. Rankled, he

corrects the Colonel. "It's Captain." He is further put off when Sloane and
the crew come into the cave as he is delivering his orders to the people,
and they disregard him for the moment in favor of asking questions about
Earth. They are excited and eager to learn more.

Benteen tells Sloane in no uncertain terms that the people are under
his command and the major gives him a pitying look. Increasingly upset,
Benteen is still in favor of returning home until the colonists insist on set-
tling with long-lost family in various parts of the country, not all together
as Benteen wishes. Baines is the first to speak up, rebelling against Benteen's mandate that they stay together. He has infantilized the other colonists to the point that he feels that he is the only person in the world who
would be able to keep them safe back on Earth.

Benteen makes a last-ditch effort to get the people back in line. Infu-
riated that it didn't work, he refused to go aboard the ship as it prepares
to take off. Even when Colonel Sloane and Baines try their best to cajole
him into coming along, Benteen stays hidden away until he could hear the
engine start. He comes out of hiding to "talk" to his people, only realizing his horrible mistake as the ship takes off ("On Thursday We Leave for
Home").

Examine the phenomenon of foreign control. You examine it and
there is a conspiracy. You will note with absolute clarity that the lines lead
directly to Palestine! They lead directly to Africa! They lead directly to the
Vatican. There is a conspiracy! There is an insidious developing conspiracy. A conspiracy personified by the Yellow man, by the Black man, and
by the foreigners who come in and infiltrate into our economic structure.

Peter Vollmer says in "He's Alive," and by the end of the episode,
when Vollmer is killed, but the shadowy figure of Hitler is already finding another acolyte, we plainly see how difficult it is to kill these ideas once
they are allowed to be expressed.

Aftermath

Overall, war in *The Twilight Zone* is as much an internal battle as an
external one. So many of the episodes have a feeling of futile inevitabil-
ity. There really is a universality to war and a futileness to questioning its
necessity while in the moment. The choice to reembrace a kinder, just, and
peaceful world without any cynicism prove to be the biggest battle of all.

In one of the most refreshing episodes to deal with the aftermath of
war, "Two," is set on the first day of the sixth year after a presumed nuclear
holocaust.[1] Two lone survivors, one male and one female, from opposing
armies find themselves in a ravaged town. While the male is no longer

interested in continuing the fight, pointing out that they are probably the only two people left and that it didn't matter that they were once on opposite sides, the female isn't so sure. She keeps on until she takes some shots at him, finally driving him away from her.

By the time she has had a change of heart, he is visibly moving on. He has ditched his uniform for a suit jacket and in an endearing fashion, tries to tie a colorful scarf into a cravat. He smooths it down against his bare chest before putting a handkerchief into the jacket in place of a proper pocket square. When she appears across the street, he yells at her to go away. It isn't until she appears from behind a car in a dress she had admired earlier, that he is relaxed enough to come down from the second story balcony he was preening on. When she walks behind him and gently steps up to him in acceptance, the audience sees that they have completely abandoned their roles as soldiers and are walking together to a better future with one another ("Two").

The Twilight Zone *into the Future*

Perhaps if Serling could have predicted the rise of late stage capitalism and its devastating effects on democracy, he might have given later episodes of *The Twilight Zone* a darker tone. In the end we see that *The Twilight Zone* went to war against racism, totalitarianism, authoritarianism, wholesale war for private industry profits, anti-Semitism, large-scale greed, runaway capitalism, and callous selfishness. In short, *The Twilight Zone* went to war for us.

But it was a war it couldn't win. Though *The Twilight Zone* warned us about the evils facing modern society and taught us that kindness, acceptance of all people, and bridging the gaps between societies could bring about a better world, people really only half-listened. The problems it talked about persist today despite the efforts of good people to banish them from society. Maybe that's one of the reasons people still watch the original episodes and continue to re-imagine the series for modern times. Because as long as those evils exist, the war isn't really won and new generations of people need to watch *The Twilight Zone* to learn the lessons from the past that it tries to teach and maybe be the generation that finally takes them to heart and wins the war.

NOTE

1. See Molly A. Schneider's essay in this collection for an extensive reading of Serling and nuclear war.

WORKS CITED

"The 'angry young man' of Hollywood, Rod Serling became something of a personal hero to us." Cinephilia and Beyond, 2017. https://cinephiliabeyond.org.

Black Mirror. Created by Charlie Brooker. Channel 4 and Netflix, 2011–present.

Carroll, Noël, and Lester H. Hunt, editors. *Philosophy in The Twilight Zone*. Hoboken, NJ: Blackwell, 2009.

Causewell, Melody. *Our Everyday Life*. https://oureverydaylife.com. Accessed 3 May 2020

"Death Ship," *The Twilight Zone*, written by Richard Matheson, directed by Don Medford, Image Entertainment, 2010.

"Deaths-Head Revisited," *The Twilight Zone*, written by Rod Serling, directed by Don Medford, Image Entertainment, 2010.

Department of Veterans Affairs, Veterans Programs, PTSD, www.ptsd.va.gov/. Accessed 3 May 2020.

"The Encounter," *The Twilight Zone*, written by Martin M. Goldsmith, directed by Robert Butler, Image Entertainment, 2010.

"Eye of the Beholder," *The Twilight Zone*, written by Rod Serling, directed by Douglas Heyes, Image Entertainment, 2010.

"He's Alive," *The Twilight Zone*, written by Rod Serling, directed by Stuart Rosenberg, Image Entertainment, 2010.

"In Praise of Pip," *The Twilight Zone*, written by Rod Serling, directed by Joseph M. Newman, Image Entertainment, 2010.

LiCapria, Kim. "Did Rod Serling's *Twilight Zone* Use Sci-Fi to Push Politics Past Network Censors?" Truth or Fiction. 3 April 2019. www.truthorfiction.com. Accessed 13 June 2020.

"The Little People," *The Twilight Zone*, written by Rod Serling, directed by William F. Claxton, Image Entertainment, 2010.

"The Monsters Are Due on Maple Street," *The Twilight Zone*, written by Rod Serling, directed by Ron Winston, Image Entertainment, 2010.

"Number 12 Looks Just Like You," *The Twilight Zone*, written by John Tomerlin, directed by Abner Biberman, Image Entertainment, 2010.

"The Obsolete Man," *The Twilight Zone*, written by Rod Serling, directed by Elliot Silverstein, Image Entertainment, 2010.

"The Old Man in the Cave," *The Twilight Zone*, written by Rod Serling, directed by Alan Crosland, Jr., Image Entertainment, 2010.

"On Thursday We Leave for Home," *The Twilight Zone*, written by Rod Serling, directed by Buzz Kulik, Image Entertainment, 2010.

"The Parallel," *The Twilight Zone*, written by Rod Serling, directed by Alan Crosland, Jr., Image Entertainment, 2010.

"The Passersby," *The Twilight Zone*, written by Rod Serling, directed by Elliot Silverstein, Image Entertainment, 2010.

"The Purple Testament," *The Twilight Zone*, written by Rod Serling, directed by Richard L. Bare, Image Entertainment, 2010.

"A Quality of Mercy," *The Twilight Zone*, written by Rod Serling, directed by Buzz Kulik, Image Entertainment, 2010.

"Returning Home From Deployment," *Military One Source* 3 Jan. 2020, www.militaryone source.mil. Accessed 3 May 2020.

Rivera, Heather L., and Alexander E. Hooker, eds. *The Twilight Zone and Philosophy*. Chicago: Open Court, 2019.

"Rod Serling: Submitted For Your Approval." *American Masters Presents*. CBS, Image Entertainment, Chatsworth 29, Nov. 1995.

"The Thirty Fathom Grave," *The Twilight Zone*, written by Rod Serling, directed by Perry Lafferty, Image Entertainment, 2010.

Twilight Zone: The Movie. Directed by Steven Spielberg, John Landis, Joe Dante, and George Miller. Burbank: Warner Brothers, 1983.

"Two," *The Twilight Zone*, written by Montgomery Pittman, directed by Montgomery Pittman, Image Entertainment, 2010.

Zircree, Marc Scott. *The Twilight Zone Companion*, 2nd ed. Silman-James Press, 1992.

PART II

"Remember that one episode?"

From Demonic "Opie" to Latchkey Kid

The Narrative/Character Shifts in "It's a Good Life" from Television to Film

Erin Giannini

Based on Jerome Bixby's 1953 short story "It's a *Good* Life," *The Twilight Zone* episode of the same name (1961) left a significant mark on subsequent popular culture. The tale of a young boy, Anthony Fremont, with the god-like power to read minds and emotions, as well as kill or resurrect animals and humans, both the story and the episode "It's a *Good* Life" focus on a single day in a long nightmare for the residents of Anthony's hometown of Peaksville. Anthony has cut off the town from the rest of the world. As a child, he does not seem to comprehend the consequences of his actions (e.g., a diminishing food supply) or the complexity of adult emotions; he lashes out at any perceived unhappiness or anger, forcing the townspeople to pretend everything is "good" regardless of what he does. The story's influence is clear. Animated series *The Simpsons* and *Johnny Bravo* offered outright parodies, in the "Treehouse of Horror II" (3.7) segment "It's a Bart Life," and the episode "Johnny Real Good" (1.12b), respectively, and numerous series across genres have made references to being "wished into the cornfield" (the fate of objects and people who bother the god-like Anthony Fremont in his various iterations), including *Bunheads* ("It's Not a Mint" 1.17) and *Buffy the Vampire Slayer* ("Older and Far Away" 6.14). "It's a *Good* Life" thus belongs in the company of certain episodes of the original series whose source has not necessarily been supplanted, but have a pop culture afterlife beyond the series, such as "To Serve Man" (3.24), "The Monsters Are Due on Maple Street" (1.22), and "Time Enough at Last" (1.8).

While the parodies and references have their own connections and interpretations of the original episode,[1] my interest throughout this essay is the connective and interpretative differences between the original epi-sode and the Joe Dante–directed segment of *Twilight Zone: The Movie*, which remains one of only a handful of films that use an anthology format. While films such as *Four Rooms* (1995) and *New York Stories* (1989) offer examples in the comedic and dramatic genres, it gained significant trac-tion in the horror genre during the 70s and 80s, of which *Twilight Zone: The Movie* was only one.[2] Aside from anthology films' most common genre (horror), the concept of the all-powerful child has become a similar trope, appearing in multiple formats, including *Dragon Ball* (anime), *The Incred-ibles* (animated film), and television (*The 4400*, *Charmed* [1998]). One of the most recent examples is in the 2019 Amazon/BBC adaptation of Terry Pratchett and Neil Gaiman's 1990 novel *Good Omens*, which features an eleven-year-old antichrist with ultimate power, Adam Young.[3] Both the format (anthology) and the trope (powerful child) are consistent across all the interpretations of Bixby's original story. It is the differences in how both the text and the character of Anthony Fremont are interpreted in the different social and generation contexts of the original series and the film that form the bulk of my analysis.

"You'd better start thinking happy thoughts": The Entitled, Monstrous Child

The post–World War II era, which saw the rise of bedroom commu-nities and suburbs, increased prosperity for a significant percentage of the U.S. population (relative, at least, to the proceeding decades) and the rise of television, was the first in the century to put the child—especially boys—at the center of parental and social attention. Absent an economic depression or large-scale war for the first time in 30 years, *Life* magazine could unironically publish a double issue on "The Good Life," whose cover offered a collage of athletes, artists, and hobbyists, presumably with the free time to pursue their passions. With this free time, however, came the specter of what children would do with it, inciting what would be one of the first "moral panics" over youth culture. As Stanley Cohen defined it, in his seminal work on the subject, moral panics were "[a] condition, epi-sode, person or group of persons … defined as a threat to societal values and interests" with "its nature … presented in a stylized and stereotypi-cal fashion by the mass media; the moral barricades … manned by editors, bishops, politicians and other right-thinking people" (Cohen 9). The rela-tive freedom from privation and war—as well as, it's suggested, the earlier freedoms younger people experienced during World War II, with absent fathers and working mothers, and were loathe to give up—could easily turn to delinquent behavior (Smith 18). The concern was enough to merit the creation of a senate subcommittee to study the causes and potentially curb the perceived rising tide of juvenile offenses. They eventually landed on comic books as the main offenders.

During his testimony in defense of the comics industry, Bill Gaines (who went on to publish *Mad Magazine*), asked the committee: "Are we afraid of our own children?" (Gomez 2014). Gaines' question lacks a certain amount of nuance; as Louis Menand argues in his analysis of the 1954 hearing, the expert witness arguing against the comics, psychologist Fredric Wertham, was not a reactionary but made quite cogent points regarding how these comics portrayed violence against women and trafficked in harmful stereotypes of people of other races and ethnicities (Menand 2008). Yet the rhetoric he employed at the Senate hearing, including suggesting that the constant exposure of youth to these images was propagandizing violence to such a degree that "Hitler was a beginner compared to the comic book industry" (Coville), seems vastly overstated. Further, his book, unsubtly titled *Seduction of the Innocent* and illustrated with examples from crime and horror comics (complete with Wertham's commentary on each) drew a scientifically unrigorous connection between the reading of these comics and delinquent behavior—particularly that the comic books offered a roadmap to successfully getting away with criminal behavior—by relying primarily on anecdotal evidence from the already at-risk teens he worked with to make his case for the comics' danger to children and teens, that later critiques found less than credible (Tilley 383–413). That being said, while not explicitly stated by either the committee or their witnesses, the subtext and tenor of the questioning during the hearing suggest that there is something to be feared from the young; in particular, that they are malleable, corruptible, and possibly dangerous.

The Anthony Fremont that appears in "It's a *Good* Life" (3.8), aged up from 3 years old in Bixby's short story to 6 in the episode, is not subtextually dangerous; he is malevolent. Like the fabled child discussed within the Senate committee, mind warped by violent comics, Anthony's presence holds the entire town of Peaksville in fear of his moods and ravages. Indeed, Anthony's god-like powers have isolated the town from the rest of the world, meaning that no outside help is available to the townspeople. They must constantly profess to be happy and shield any negative thoughts, lest Anthony turn his mind to them. He hates singing, creates violent images on the television for entertainment, and if crossed, can transfigure or kill someone with a thought. At the end of the episode, when one of townspeople, Dan Hollis (Don Keefer), confronts Anthony and begs the other adults to use the moment to kill him and free them, he is turned into a jack-in-the-box and is banished "to the cornfield" (i.e., killed). The adults cower in fear, and the episode ends with Anthony still in charge and the town and its residents' fates uncertain.

While the setting of the short story and the episode are the same—a small, rural town in Ohio—both the small town setting and the casting of the freckled, red-headed Bill Mumy as Anthony seems a direct reference to a series that debuted the year before this episode aired: *The Andy Griffith Show*. In the story, Anthony is described in terms that suggest he is not quite human, with a "bright, wet, purple gaze." This Anthony, introduced swinging on a fence with a bright smile, could easily pass for Ron Howard's Opie, and Peaksville a slightly more rural version of Mayberry. Yet it simultaneously offers the counterargument to the previous decade's focus on the child as giving them too much power. That is, the entire community of Peaksville is forced to think of nothing but what would and wouldn't please the monstrous child in their midst: the food he desires, the sounds he does (or doesn't) want to hear, even what everyone watches on television. As Susan Faludi writes in her analysis of twentieth-century masculinity: "It was evident in the periodic rampages of suburban boys that always seemed to go unchecked … that this was their birthright—to be imperial bullies over their miniature domains" and to be "automatically entitled and powerful" (Faludi 25). Visually suggesting both Howard's Opie and Mayberry itself thus serves as a critique of the primacy of the child. By putting him front and center and catering to his needs, the episode suggests, we've created this monster.

"You want to send me away, just like my real mother and father": Anthony as Latchkey Child

A 2004 marketing study of the five living generations (from what they term the "G.I. Generation" to millennials) concluded that Generation X (1965–1980) "went through its all-important, formative years as one of the least parented, least nurtured generations in U.S. History" (Clack 2004). While these children of the Baby Boomers were not the first to be dubbed "latchkey kids" (the term originated during World War II), the concept came into general use to describe children in families in which either full-time work or divorce made one or both parents regularly unavailable. As the decade progressed, there was increasing concern that these children, left on their own too much, were overstressed, lonely, and possibly prone to developing personality disorders related to perceived abandonment (Granberry 1987).[4]

While the figure of the latchkey child lead to its own moral panics (most notably, Satanic panic, particularly filtered through heavy metal and role-playing game such as *Dungeons and Dragons* [Janisse and Corupe 2016]), it is the lack of supervision and sense of loneliness that screenwriter Richard Matheson and director Joe Dante foreground in their interpretation of "It's a *Good* Life," in 1983's *Twilight Zone: The Movie*, one of the four short films based—faithfully or loosely—on classic episodes of the original series and helmed by well-known genre and mainstream directors: Steven Spielberg, George Miller, John Landis, and Dante. The film's interpretation of "It's a *Good* Life" shares a similarly small town setting as the short story and the episode; however, it is not cut off from the rest of the world, and the few townspeople seen do not seem to live in outright fear of Anthony. Indeed, one even pushes him to the ground, tired of Anthony's video game interfering with television reception; only to be warned by fellow patron Tim (Bill Mumy) that attacking Anthony is a bad idea.

Yet Tim's warning seems unnecessary; this Anthony takes no revenge. It is Helen Foley (Kathleen Quinlain)—the character's name one of the numerous metatextual references in the segment[5]—who helps Anthony and stands up to the man bullying him. When she accidentally wrecks his bicycle, she offers him a ride home. Rather than the town, it is the house that is isolated, serving as a metonym for Anthony himself. Even most of his violent acts—sending his parents away, psychically kidnapping two women and a man to serve as his "new" family   seem driven by loneliness rather than malevolence. The house itself suggests one seen in the cartoons constantly playing on Anthony's television, and the upstairs appears in black and white, with the dutch angles and decorations associated with early animation, as well as suggesting color and settings of the original series. If comic books were the "seducers" of 1950s children, the danger posed by Anthony's ability to change his environment to one that mirrors what he's seen on television reflects the prevailing idea that televised violence was the new "seducer" (National Institutes of Mental Health 1982), even though what Dante is able to show in the film would not have met broadcast standards, despite the film's PG rating. Even his rages are connected to what he's seen on television; transporting his "sister" Ethel (Nancy Cartwright) into a cartoon and transporting a Tasmanian devil character out of one, transforming a rabbit Uncle Walt pulls out of his hat into a gremlin, and removing his sister Sarah's mouth so she can't yell at him. Rather than the danger of the unchecked child of the original, the film seems to be warning against the dangers of children left to parent themselves, with snack foods for sustenance and the television as babysitter.

Indeed, when Helen, who is a teacher in search of a new life, indicates that the candy apple and pudding dinner Anthony's "family" is served isn't healthy, Anthony's anger is directed not at Helen for pointing it out, but

the others for not doing so. The segment concludes with Anthony sending the rest of the "family" back where they belong, and Helen agreeing to
mentor and teach Anthony to control and use his powers for good. As they
drive away, Anthony uses his abilities to make the desert-like surround-
ings bloom with multicolored flowers. With the exception of Spielberg's
interpretation of the episode "Kick the Can" (3.21), the ending of this "It's a
Good Life" is one of the more upbeat and hopeful of the film.[6] He is happy
because someone is willing to nurture him, using his powers not to force a
connection but to forge a new one based on care and respect.

Conclusion

The fact that not only has the original series spawned three revivals
(1987, 2002, 2019), but a film and a score of imitators (*Black Mirror* creator Charles Brooker credited the series as inspiration [Brooker 2011]),
implies that many of its stories continue to resonate with not only writers and creators, but the viewing audience as well. Consequently, many
lend themselves to reinterpretation in multiple eras; e.g., "The Monsters
Are Due on Maple Street" (1.22) was re-conceived as "The Monsters Are
on Maple Street" for the 2002 revival. The threat of aliens is replaced by
that of terrorists (1.32), but the theme—that fear makes humans act monstrous—remains intact across both episodes. This is less the case with "It's
a *Good* Life" and its transition from television to film, and from the 1960s
to the 1980s. Instead of presenting Anthony as a pint-sized totalitarian, as
both Bixby and Serling did, Matheson's Anthony is no less powerful, but
infinitely lonelier, making him more pathetic than omnipotent. Both types
of Anthonys still carry currency within popular culture: *Family Guy*'s
baby genius Stewie Griffin (voiced by Seth MacFarlane) suggests both
the literary and Mumy's Anthony; *Supernatural*'s young antichrist Jesse
Turner (Gattlin Griggith) not only warps the reality around him based
on urban myths and television series, as Anthony does in the film, but is
also frequently left to fend for himself ("I Believe the Children Are Our
Future" 5.6). As Dominic Lennard lays out in *Bad Seeds and Holy Terrors*,
the idealization and romanticization of childhood as a time of innocence
and children themselves as vulnerable and in need of protection, is largely
a product of a fusing of Romantic (and Rousseau-ian) views of the child as
"natural" and "innocent" and socioeconomic shifts in views of child labor
(Lennard 7–8). Throughout his study, Lennard asserts that the concept of
childhood as "innocent" and the constant shock of child villains (particularly in the horror genre), says less about the reality of childhood than
the adult conception of it. It is adult fears about children (unknowable,

inscrutable, and possibly amoral) that are addressed in these texts. The figure of the powerful (frequently evil) child thus "possesses a degree of shocking autonomy that fantastically illustrates the agency and power children are denied in our society" (11), and questions adult assumptions of childhood as "an apolitical site of nostalgia" rather than its reality (13).

This nostalgic view is not limited to children and childhood. In his analysis of 1950s nostalgia across multiple facets of popular culture, Michael Dwyer posits that, rather than confined to the 1980s and the Reagan presidency, it is better considered as at least a 15-year span: 1973–1988 (Dwyer 3). While films such as *American Graffiti* (1973) and series like *Happy Days* (1974–1984) featured the still-young Ron Howard as a symbol of (relatively) wholesome 1950s America, it's interesting to note that some of the more mainstream 1980s films that used the 1950s as their setting involved the now-adult Baby Boomers (or their children) traveling through time via magic (or science) to correct the mistakes of their pasts (e.g., *Back to the Future* [1985] or *Peggy Sue Got Married* [1986] [Dwyer 18–44]), while others, such as Barry Levinson's *Diner* (1982) and David Lynch's *Blue Velvet* (1986), contend with encroaching adulthood and responsibility and darker, noir elements beneath sunny, small-town exteriors, respectively.

There is no nostalgia on display for the idyllic small town life and innocent child of the era in either Bixby's 1953 short story or Serling's interpretation in 1961. Peaksville may be magically cut off from the rest of the world through Anthony's power, but in some respects it only exacerbates the divide between rural and urban environments that is not unique to either the era or to the U.S. itself, in which smaller or more rural communities frequently lag behind their urban counterparts in terms of both cultural acceleration and technology. It is possible that Anthony is able to exert his power so effectively because of he has managed to cut off the town from the wider world. This is underscored in the 2002 revival series of the *Twilight Zone,* with the episode "It's Still a Good Life" (1.31), featuring an adult Anthony Fremont and his equally powerful daughter, which also offers the metafictional touches (e.g., Bill Mumy reprises his role as Anthony; his daughter Liliana plays Anthony's daughter Audrey) and focus on generational differences (Audrey brings back the world and people Anthony sent away) of Dante's interpretation, as well as ending with Audrey convincing her father to engage with the world beyond his hometown (1.33). Dante's Anthony also has little desire to be cut off from the world; he takes himself to the local diner—a fair distance from his house—to play video games and conjures a new family for himself when his original family wanted to "send me someplace bad," instead of being alone. It is the film's Anthony, both in his choice to create a stereotypical family: father, mother, uncle, sister and the classic—occasionally black and white—cartoons that are his primary entertainment, who seems to exhibit nostalgia for an era gone long before he was born. What both the original episode and the film imply is that such nostalgia is toxic, while taking wildly divergent paths to reach that conclusion.

NOTES

1. While the *Buffy* episode "Older and Far Away" makes an overt dialogic reference to "It's a *Good Life*"—the character of Xander (Nicholas Brendan) suggests that "the only thing missing is a cornfield"—the overall plot of the episode, in which the main characters trapped in a house by the accidental wish of Buffy's (Sarah Michelle Gellar) troubled younger sister Dawn (Michelle Trachtenberg), suggests the similarly trapped nature of the town of Peaksville in the original.

2. Others include *From Beyond the Grave* (1974), *Trilogy of Terror* (1975), *Heavy Metal* (1981), *Creepshow* (1982), *The Company of Wolves* (1984), and *Cat's Eye* (1985).

3. Genre series *Supernatural* actually offered its own homage to *Good Omens'* all-powerful child previous to the adaptation in the 2009 episode "I Believe the Children Are Our Future" (5.6).

4. Ironically, these same issues that made Generation X latchkey kids a cause for concern in the 1980s have resulted in a recent spate of articles suggesting Gen X is uniquely qualified to enact social distancing and navigate stay-at-home orders because of their upbringing (Dabney 2020; Beals 2020; Baker 2020).

5. Mumy isn't the only *Twilight Zone* veteran in the segment; while the film as a whole features more than one (e.g., Burgess Meredith provides the narration), four appear in "It's A *Good Life*": Kevin McCarthy, who plays "Uncle" Walt, appeared as Professor Walter Jameson in "Long Live Walter Jameson" (1.24); Patricia Barry ("Mother"), was cast twice ("I Dream of Genie" [4.12] and "The Chaser" [1.31]), and William Schallet ("Father") had a small role in the episode "Mr. Bevis" (1.33). The segment also features references to "A Stop at Willoughby" (1.30), "Walking Distance" (1.5), and "Of Late I Think of Cliffordville" (4.14), as well as a tribute to *Twilight Zone* writer Charles Beaumont.

6. In the case of the *Twilight Zone* film, this is more than usually true. Not only does George Miller's take on "Nightmare at 20,000 Feet" conclude with airline passenger John Valentine (John Lithgow) dismissed as insane and en route to a mental hospital, driven by the monster who appears in the opening and closing segments, but John Landis' "Time Out" has its antagonist driven off in a cattle car, unseen by his friends, to a concentration camp. This, of course, is the same segment of the film in which actors Vic Morrow, Myca Dinh Le, and Renee Shin-Yi Chen were killed due to a helicopter accident during filming. "Time Out" was originally supposed to end with Morrow's bigoted character saving the children and thereby redeeming himself. See Weintraub (2012) for an analysis of how the accident shifted safety protocols in Hollywood. See Kevin J. Wetmore, Jr.'s, chapter in this volume for more details.

WORKS CITED

Baker, Falma. "Who Is Generation X and Why Does Self-Isolating Come So Easily to Them?" *Metro News.* 16 March 2020. metro.co.uk.

Beals, Rachel Koning. "A Rare Win for Gen X? Boomers Gave Us Latchkey Childhoods That Prepared Us for Coronavirus Quarantine." *Market Watch.* 22 March 2020. www.marketwatch.com.

Bixby, Jerome. "It's a *Good Life*." In: Silverberg, Robert, ed. *The Science Fiction Hall of Fame, Vol. 1: 1922–1964.* New York: Orb Books, 2005, pgs. 433–448.

Brooker, Charlie. "Charlie Brooker: The Dark Side of Our Gadget Addiction." *The Guardian*. 1 December 2011. https://www.theguardian.com.

"The Chaser," *The Twilight Zone*, written by John Collier and Rod Serling, directed by Douglas Heyes, Image Entertainment, 2003.

Clack, Erin E. "Study Probes Generation Gap: An Industry Update." *Children's Business.* May 1. 2004.

Cohen, Stanley. *Folk Devils and Moral Panics: The Creation of Mods and Rockers.* London, MacGibbon and Kee, 1972.

Coville, Jamie. "1954 Senate Subcommittee Transcripts." TheComicBooks.com. http://www.thecomicbooks.com.

Dabney, Courtney. "It Took a Global Pandemic, but Generation X Is Finally Getting Some Love." *Paper City Magazine*. 26 March 2020. www.papercitymag.com.

Dwyer, Michael D. *Back to the Fifties: Nostalgia, Hollywood Film, and Popular Music of the Seventies and Eighties.* London: Oxford University Press, 2015.

Faludi, Susan. *Stiffed: The Betrayal of the American Man.* New York: Perennial, 1999.

Gaiman, Neil, creator. *Good Omens.* The Blank Corporation, Amazon Studios, and BBC Studios, 2019.

Gomez, Betsy. "60 Years Ago Today: The US Senate Puts Comics on Trial!" CBLDF blog. 22 April 2014. http://cbldf.org.

Granberry, Mike. "Latchkey Kids: A Study in Frustration: After-School Alternatives Called Costly, Inadequate, or Rare." *Los Angeles Times*. 11 October 1987. www.latimes.com.

"I Believe the Children Are Our Future," *Supernatural: The Complete Fifth Season*, written by Andrew Dabb and Daniel Loflin, directed by Charles Beeson. Warner Home Video, 2010.

"I Dream of Genie," *The Twilight Zone*, written by John Furia, Jr., directed by Robert Gist, Image Entertainment, 2005.

"It's a Good Life," *The Twilight Zone*, written by Jerome Bixby and Rod Serling, directed by James Sheldon, Image Entertainment, 2005.

"It's Not a Mint," *Bunheads: The Complete Series*, written by Daniel Palladino, directed by Daniel Palladino, Disney—ABC Domestic Television, 2013.

"It's Still a Good Life," *The Twilight Zone: The Complete Series*, written by Ira Steven Behr, directed by Allen Kroeker, New Line Home Entertainment, 2004.

Janisse, Kier-La, and Paul Coroupe, eds. *Satanic Panic: Pop-Cultural Paranoia in the 1980s.* Surrey: Fab Press, 2016.

"Johnny Real Good," *Johnny Bravo: Season One*, written by Seth MacFarlane, directed by John McIntyre, Warner Home Video, 2010.

"Kick the Can," *The Twilight Zone*, written by George Clayton Johnson, directed by Lamont Johnson, Image Entertainment, 2005.

Lennard, Dominic. *Bad Seeds and Holy Terrors: The Child Villains of Horror Film.* Albany: SUNY Press, 2014.

"Long Live Walter Jameson," *The Twilight Zone: Season 1—The Definitive Edition*, written by Charles Beaumont, directed by Tony Leader, Image Entertainment, 2004.

Menand, Louis. "The Horror: Congress Investigates the Comics," *The New Yorker*. 24 March 2008. https://www.newyorker.com.

"Mr. Bevis," *The Twilight Zone*, written by Rod Serling, directed by William Asher, Image Entertainment, 2003.

"The Monsters Are Due on Maple Street," *The Twilight Zone*, written by Rod Serling, directed by Ronald Winston, Image Entertainment, 2003.

"The Monsters Are on Maple Street," *The Twilight Zone*, written by Rod Serling, directed by Debbie Allen, New Line Home Entertainment, 2004.

National Institutes of Mental Health. "Television and Behavior: Ten Years of Scientific Progress and Implications for the Eighties, Vol. 1: Summary Report." ERIC: Institute of Education Sciences, 1982. https://files.eric.ed.gov.

"Of Late I Think of Cliffordville," *The Twilight Zone*, written by Malcolm Jameson and Rod Serling, directed by David Lowell Rich, Image Entertainment, 2005.

"Older and Far Away," *Buffy the Vampire Slayer: The Complete Sixth Season*, written by Drew Z. Greenberg, directed by Michael Gershman, Twentieth Century Fox Home Entertainment, 2004.

Smith, Ken. *Mental Hygiene: Classroom Films, 1945–1970*. New York: Blast Books, 1999.

"A Stop at Willoughby," *The Twilight Zone*, written by Rod Serling, directed by Robert Parrish, Image Entertainment, 2003.

Tilley, Carol L. "Seducing the Innocent: Frederic Wertham and the Falsifications That Helped Condemn Comics," *Information and Culture: A Journal of History*, vol 47, no. 4, 2012, pp. 383–413

"Time Enough at Last," *The Twilight Zone*, written by Lynn Venable and Rod Serling, directed by John Brahm, Image Entertainment, 2003.

"To Serve Man," *The Twilight Zone*, written by Damon Knight and Rod Serling, directed by Richard L. Bare, Image Entertainment, 2005.

"Treehouse of Horror II," *The Simpsons: The Complete Third Season*, written by Al Jean, Jeff Martin, George Meyer, Sam Simon, and John Swartzwelder, directed by Jim Reardon, Twentieth Century Fox Home Entertainment, 2003.

Twilight Zone: The Movie. Directed by George Miller, Joe Dante, John Landis, and Steven Spielberg, performances by Dan Ackroyd, Vic Morrow, Scatman Crothers, Kathleen Quinlan, and John Lithgow, Warner Brothers, 1983.

"Walking Distance," *The Twilight Zone*, written by Rod Serling, directed by Robert Stevens, Image Entertainment, 2003.

Weintraub, Robert. "A New Dimension of Filmmaking: How Tragedy on the Set of the Feature-Length Adaptation of *The Twilight Zone* Changed the Way Movies Are Made." *Slate*. 26 July 2012. https://slate.com.

"Stopover in a Quiet Town," the Horror Film, and Dread of the Child

Dawn Keetley

Many horror creators (among them such notables as George A. Romero, Stephen King, and Jordan Peele) have been influenced by *The Twilight Zone*, but there has yet to be a study of how particular episodes have woven themselves into actual horror films. Numerous clear lines of influence can be mapped—from "Mirror Image" to *Psycho* (Alfred Hitchcock, 1960), from "The Monsters Are Due on Maple Street" and "I Am the Night—Color Me Black" to *Night of the Living Dead* (George A. Romero, 1968), from "Number 12 Looks Just Like You" to *The Stepford Wives* (Bryan Forbes, 1975), from "You Drive" and "A Thing about Machines" to *Duel* (Steven Spielberg, 1971) and *Christine* (John Carpenter, 1983), from "Twenty Two" (1961) to *Final Destination* (James Wong, 2000), and, more recently, from "The Trade-Ins" to *Get Out* (Jordan Peele, 2017) and "In His Image" to *Us* (Jordan Peele, 2019).

One of the more influential installments of *The Twilight Zone* is the under-appreciated season five episode, "Stopover in a Quiet Town," which reverberates, I argue, through three modern horror films: *Children of the Corn* (Fritz Kiersch, 1984), *The Cabin in the Woods* (Drew Goddard, 2011) and *Vivarium* (Lorcan Finnegan, 2019). The episode dramatizes two themes in particular, one that has clearly been central to the horror film and one less obviously so. First, "Stopover" anticipates a central characteristic of modern horror: humans have little to no control over their lives. Indeed, lack of freedom is as good as synonymous with the horror genre. Second, the episode evinces a profound dread of children—targeting, specifically, the ways young people control the lives of adults. In its exploration of both of these themes, "Stopover" can be linked with the

113

better-known season three episode, "It's a Good Life," which portrays even more starkly the tyrannical power of a child over the adults around him.[1] In these two *Twilight Zone* episodes, then, children attenuate characters' free will: control is a zero-sum game that, at least from the baby-boom era onward, adults lose to young people. This dread of all-powerful children, and a consequent animus against that power, is also evident in modern horror films, although it has not been explored as much as other ways in which children enter the horror film—as the "bad seed" or the possessed child. The texts I am considering here, moreover, show how children exert a power over adults that isn't only personal but that ripples out to include the environment, even the planet.

"Stopover in a Quiet Town": Three Points of Influence

"Stopover in a Quiet Town" was written by Earl Hamner, Jr., and directed by Ron Winston. It features a New York couple—Bob (Barry Nelson) and Millie (Nancy Malone) Frazier—who wake up after a particularly festive party in a strange bed in a strange house in what they soon discover is a very strange town. They have little memory of getting there—just a drive, a shadow passing over them—and they have no idea where they are. As the couple investigates, they discover that the town is completely deserted and that the food, appliances, animals, trees, and grass are all fake. They think they discover a solitary man in a car, but it's a mannequin. They think they manage to get on a train out of town, but it just chugs round in a circle until they are back where they started. At the end, we discover, in a classic *Twilight Zone* twist, that Bob and Millie are merely the playthings of a gigantic alien child. The child picks Bob and Millie up, laughing, as her mother admonishes: "Be careful with your pets, dear. Daddy brought them all the way from Earth." Specific parts of this plot get repeated in three subsequent horror films, anchoring the way in which all four texts share important thematic preoccupations.

Children of the Corn

The extended middle of "Stopover," in which Millie and Bob search the town for people, for some clue as to where they are, and, finally, for a way out, is echoed in 1984's *Children of the Corn*. In Fritz Kiersch's adaptation of Stephen King's 1977 story, married couple Burt (Peter Horton) and Vicky (Linda Hamilton) end up in the deserted town of Gatlin, Nebraska, after they hit a boy who comes running out of a cornfield. Millie and Bob's attempt in "Stopover" to escape the small town by train, only to end up right where they started—"We've gone in a circle," Bob says bitterly— is reprised in Burt and Vicky's futile efforts to avoid Gatlin (after being warned by a gas station owner) and drive instead to the larger town of Hemingford. At every intersection, they turn away from Gatlin and yet always end up closer to the town. They finally end up driving in circles on dirt tracks lined by tall rows of corn: "We're never going to get out of here," Vicky proclaims. And they do indeed end up back at the gas station: "We're right back where we started from," Burt says.

When Burt and Vicky get to Gatlin, they wander the empty town just as Bob and Millie did. In "Stopover," Bob launches into a tirade about how he hates small towns where people "peak from behind curtains"; in *Children*, people actually do peak from behind curtains. The protagonists' isolation is emphasized, moreover, in mirrored scenes involving telephones. In "Stopover," Bob grabs at the phone on the wall of the house they wake up in as if it's a lifeline, and it comes away in his hand, not even wired in. The scene is reprised when Burt and Vicky explore a house in Gatlin and Burt goes immediately to pick up the phone, only to have the receiver come away in his hand; the cord has been cut. Finally, in both "Stopover" and *Children*, the main characters end up in churches—places where they hope they'll find community, normality. The narratives diverge at this point since Bob and Millie find only an empty church while Burt finds the children of Gatlin engaging in a bloody ritual. In both scenes, though, the camera lingers on portraits of Christ, corn husks added as hair in the church in Gatlin. These mirrored portraits of Christ foreshadow how, in both "Stopover" and *Children of the Corn*, the protagonists are earmarked for sacrifice; indeed, in "Stopover," Millie and Bob have *already* been sacrificed, colonized as pets for an alien child.

The Cabin in the Woods

The Cabin in the Woods was written by Drew Goddard and Joss Whedon, directed by Goddard, and produced by Whedon. It follows five college students as they head for a break in a secluded cabin; unbeknownst to them, at least initially, they are actually being set up as sacrifices to the "Ancient Ones," and all they have the power to do is choose the means of their own destruction. As in "Stopover" and *Children of the Corn*, the protagonists are unable to leave the site of their confinement; their world has limits they can't see, as one of them discovers when he tries to jump a ravine on his motorcycle and hits an invisible wall. As in "Stopover," especially, the characters in *Cabin* are unwitting players in a drama determined by larger forces, both human and nonhuman. The strikingly similar endings of both makes this very clear. In both "Stopover" and *Cabin*, a giant hand emerges from above and destroys existence as the human characters know it.

The hand, a kind of *deus ex machina* in both texts, also epitomizes the characters' lack of choice. In "Stopover," the absence of choice is clear: Millie and Bob were at some point literally taken, without their knowledge, by an alien, and confined to her playset. The question of choice is more complicated in *Cabin* as the young protagonists are lured but not abducted to their particular sacrificial ground. The characters have some level of power and self-awareness. As Marty (Fran Kranz) says at one point, when he hears subtle whispers urging him to leave the cabin (and head straight to the zombie rednecks conjured up to kill him), "You think I'm a puppet? … Gonna do a little puppet dance? … I'm the boss of my own brain." Of course, Marty isn't "the boss of his own brain," as he tries to assert, and he does go for a walk anyway. Like Bob and Millie, Marty and his friends are playing on someone else's stage, moving to someone else's directions. Late in the film, however, Marty and Dana (Kristen Connolly) do make a choice, specifically the choice that provokes the divine hand that destroys the Earth. And this choice and its consequences actually parallels the ending of "Stopover": it keeps power in the hands of the young, and in both cases that power is apocalyptic, world-destroying.

Vivarium

Shown at festivals in 2019 and released widely in March 2020, *Vivarium* is directed by Irish director Lorcan Finnegan and written by Garret Shanley. It centers on Gemma (Imogen Poots) and Tom (Jesse Eisenberg), a couple who wander one day into a store where houses in a development called "Yonder" are up for sale. The scaled model homes are identical, and, as it turns out when the salesman takes them to see the development itself, so are the homes. After the salesman shows Gemma and Tom Number 9, he inexplicably leaves them. They try with increasing desperation to get out of Yonder, driving around and around the unnervingly indistinguishable houses and streets until they run out of gas. Their stuckness in an eerily empty place echoes "Stopover," *Children of the Corn*, and *Cabin in the Woods*—and indicates that Gemma and Tom may be much less in control than they think. The title, "vivarium"—"a place, such as a laboratory, where live animals or plants are kept under conditions simulating their natural environment, as for research,"[2] or, as pets—certainly echoes the explicit revelation of "Stopover" that Millie and Bob are themselves merely "pets."

There are direct references in *Vivarium*, large and small, to *Twilight Zone's* "Stopover"[3]: in both, the couple travels in circles, thinking they're getting away but finding themselves back where they started; both couples are trapped in empty places; in both, the food they find is artificial; in both, the characters at some point wonder whether they are actually dead and in hell; and, in both, characters realize—making some larger symbolic point—that nothing around them is "real." Indeed, a strikingly similar moment in both *Vivarium* and "Stopover" is when both sets of characters make discoveries involving fire and fake grass. In "Stopover," after Millie laments that nothing in the town is real, Bob points to the "nature" that surrounds them—to trees and grass—to prove her wrong. When he flicks a match onto the grass, however, he discovers that, in fact, nothing is real. "Why, this isn't grass. It's papier-mâché," he says. Tom and Gemma make the same discovery when a cigarette similarly gets thrown onto grass that burns unnaturally to reveal a circle of some yellow plastic substance. In both of these scenes, characters learn that they are, indeed, in some sort of "vivarium," in a world that is most definitely not "real." For both sets of characters, these moments crystallize the need to escape, however futile that attempt turns out to be.

Unfreedom and the Power of a Child

The specter of unfreedom, that any sense of control is completely illusory, infuses "Stopover in a Quiet Town," *Children of the Corn, Cabin in the Woods*, and *Vivarium* with a profound sense of dread—one of the fundamental emotions associated with the horror film (along with, for instance, fear, shock, and revulsion). Cynthia Freeland claims that dread is "a fundamental response to aspects of our human condition." She goes on to argue that dread may "stem from a sense of threat posed by an evil agent" but that it also might be "existential, registering fear not of some malign agents but of precisely the reverse—that the world has no ruling agents and that we humans are alone in a world that fails to satisfy our expectations for purpose, meaning, and justice" (192).[4] There is a third option, though, that to some degree dissolves the divide between Freeland's two sources of dread (malignant agent or no agent): humans could be "ruled" by indifferent agents, entities that are profoundly unaware or uncaring of human subjectivity. This world would be bereft of meaning, at least within a human frame of reference, and yet it would also be subject to rule by an agent. "Stopover in a Quiet Town," *Children of the Corn, Cabin in the Woods*, and *Vivarium* all posit the child as that agent, in control not of humanity *in toto* but of adults specifically.

The particular narrative structure of the typical *Twilight Zone* episode enables it to tap into multiple forms of dread. The series does so by shifting the frame of the narrative, specifically through the infamous con-cluding twists for which *The Twilight Zone* is perhaps best known. Carl Plantinga has argued that some of *The Twilight Zone*'s surprise endings serve as what he calls "frame shifters," which abruptly wrench the viewer (and/or the characters) out of their habitual patterns of thinking and push them into new "frames," alternative ways of viewing the world (39–40). *The Twilight Zone*'s surprise endings, in other words, involve a "frame shifting" that is both narrative and epistemological. This "frame shifting" can serve to redouble the dread provoked by an episode. In "Stopover," the characters at first appear to be "struggling, alone, in a world bereft of meaning," but the abrupt shift in frame at the end discloses an omnip-otent agent, not malignant but simply unconcerned with the characters' "humanity."[5] *Children of the Corn*, *Cabin in the Woods* and *Vivarium* fol-low the narrative pattern set by "Stopover," and what distinguishes all four of these texts, in the end, is their assertion of the ruling agent as child. The dread-inducing agent is the child.

In both "Stopover" and *Children of the Corn*, control over the protag-onists' lives is clearly vested in children: Bob and Millie live in an artificial world of a child's design; they just don't know it. The same is true for Burt and Vicky. Once they enter Gatlin, they are watched, their fates charted, by a cult of children—and the force of the sacrificial drive of this cult is directed against adults; the children voluntarily sacrifice themselves when they turn nineteen, when they themselves become adults, and any outsider adults are also sacrificed. *Children* also echoes the companion episode to "Stopover"—"It's a Good Life"—which is set in a Midwestern farm com-munity and involves a tyrannical child sending adults who displease him to the nearby cornfield, never to be seen again: in both "It's a Good Life" and *Children*, then, the cornfield is the site of sacrifice.

The extent to which *Children* encodes the power of children was on display in September 2019 when Fox News commentator Laura Ingraham compared sixteen-year-old climate activist Greta Thunberg—and, pre-sumably, the other young activists Thunberg has inspired—to the cult in Kiersch's 1984 film. She quoted Thunberg's rebuke of (older) world leaders for their concern about the economy when, "We are in the beginning of a mass extinction." Ingraham then asked "Does anyone else find that chill-ing?"—answering her question by playing a clip from *Children of the Corn* (Amatulli). Thirty-five years after its release, *Children of the Corn* lingers in the popular memory as an apocryphal warning about the "unnatural" power of children over adults.

Vivarium draws directly on "Stopover" in its central plot that tracks how a couple's freedom is taken away by a child. While viewers only realize in the final scene of "Stopover" that Bob and Millie are a child's playthings, in *Vivarium*, this realization emerges earlier and more gradually. Gemma and Tom find a baby in a box outside their house one day, and they feel compelled to raise it. The baby grows unnaturally fast (echoing the giant alien child of "Stopover") and soon dominates every aspect of their lives. From the beginning, the baby signals entrapment. Indeed, it comes with a note: "Raise the child and be released." The boy, as it grows (and it is soon very clear it's not human), screams at Gemma and Tom if they do not do exactly as it wants. Tom eventually tries to kill it, but Gemma cannot go that far and rescues it. After Tom dies, at the bottom of a hole he has been compulsively digging that signals nothing if not his own imprisonment, Gemma herself eventually tries, and fails, to kill the child. In despair, late in the film, she screams, "What am I? What is this? What am I in this?" A disembodied voice replies, "You are a mother. You prepare your child for the world." "What happens then?" Gemma asks. "You die," is the reply. It's at this point that the allegory of *Vivarium* becomes clear, and it's one also made more obliquely in "Stopover" and "It's a Good Life." *Vivarium* is about the trap of parenting, something adults "choose" but often without knowing or foreseeing all the implications of that choice, including the ways in which it is life-consuming, life-destroying. The only "release," *Vivarium* implies, is death.

Indeed, it is possible to read "Stopover" as being about the trap of parenting all along. Bob and Millie wake up in bed together with no memory of what happened the night before except that both of them were very drunk. Millie dimly remembers a "shadow" looming over them, which we're supposed to presume (after we've seen the ending) is the alien child. Could the episode actually serve, though, as a covert commentary on how people stumble blindly, unintentionally (and sometimes while drunk) into pregnancy and parenthood? This reading would certainly explain the frantic way in which Millie and Bob struggle to flee the stifling small town, a town that would undoubtedly (like Yonder in *Vivarium*) be considered a perfect place to raise a child, but that is definitely not perfect for Millie and Bob given their urban existence and predilection for wild parties. As the couple desperately tries to escape the town, moreover, the only thing they hear, occasionally, is the elusive laugh of a child, a sound that seems to emanate from everywhere and nowhere, a sound that threatens to engulf them in ways they grasp, if at all, only unconsciously. But it fills them with dread, highlighting their fear of having that child who already, unbeknownst to them, controls their every move.

In *Cabin in the Woods*, the power of the young effects nothing less than the end of the world. The hand that destroys Earth at the end of the film is not literally that of a child, as in "Stopover," but the ancient gods are prompted to their act of destruction because of the choice of two young people. Marty and Dana are told that Dana must kill Marty or else the Ancient Ones will rise up and destroy the Earth. Marty says that, if that's how things are, if all his friends (and himself) have to die to save the planet, maybe "it's time for a change." Dana agrees: "Time to give someone else a chance." Dana refuses to offer up her friend as a sacrifice, and Marty refuses to be sacrificed, and so the world is ended. Two young people decide it's "time for a change" so millions of people are destroyed. While viewers have most likely identified with Marty and Dana until this point, their decision could be interpreted as rather spectacularly narcissistic. What Marty and Dana do is assert the supreme importance of youth; they assert that young people—their interests, their moral choices, their being—are sacrosanct. In this, *Cabin* is very much perpetuating the same dynamic as "Stopover," *Children of the Corn*, and *Vivarium*: they all dramatizes the power of children to control adults' lives, including the power to end their lives.

If these texts evince an animus against the power of children, this animus can, I think, be extrapolated to figure a commentary on overpopulation, which is, after all, about the fear of too many children.[6] What also signals that overpopulation may be at issue here—and that at all of these texts may be open to an ecological reading—is that they all intriguingly combine a sense of the omnipresent power of children with a demonstrable loss of "nature," an attenuation of wilderness.[7] The key moment that ties "Stopover" and *Vivarium* together, for instance, is the adults' discovery that "nature" has been erased from their environment. "Nothing is real in this town," Millie declares, after they discover that a squirrel perched on a tree is fake. "Show me one thing that's real." Bob points out that the tree is real, but it topples over to disclose that it too is artificial—and then the dropped cigarette reveals the unnaturalness of the grass. In *Vivarium*, the similarly unnatural grass covers an artificial yellow dirt, and in both texts, nature of any kind, including animals, are demonstrably absent. The same is true of the literal "vivarium" the college students stumble into in *Cabin in the Woods*, consisting of "woods" completely engineered by technicians and sealed off from actual nature, as we see when a large bird flies into its invisible wall. Kiersch's *Children of the Corn* seems like an outlier, replete as it is with scenes of lush corn, but Kathleen Hunt has insightfully argued that the "eerily menacing" and wildly proliferating corn in Kiersch's adaptation of King's story allegorizes the global overproduction of "monocropped" corn, which now appears in vast swathes of products from processed snacks to beverages and from shampoo to gasoline. "*Children of the Corn*," she continues, "registers the consequences of capital-driven surplus production through the corn's ominous excess." The nature in *Children* is unnatural after all; biodiversity has been replaced by only one crop that stretches out as far as the eye can see.

Linking the looming power of the child and a vanished natural wilderness, an omnipresent artificiality, these narratives suggest the cost of designing a world for exploding numbers of children, including the suburbs that sprang-up in the post–World War II baby-boom era (the historical context for *The Twilight Zone* and starkly depicted in *Vivarium*) as well as the rise of industrial agricultural practices (such as monocropping). Marty and Dana's decision to end the world in *Cabin in the Woods* could be seen as a rather obvious warning of the global dangers caused by young people, by the fact of their omnipresence. And *Cabin* can indeed be read as a story about the dangers of too many children. Significantly, it begins with one of the technicians of the facility, Hadley (Bradley Whitford), telling another that his wife is going overboard on child-proofing their home: he can't even open his own cupboards. He laments that her actions seem a bit premature, since "We don't even know if the whole fertility thing is going to work." This otherwise rather random opening signals that *Cabin* is indeed about reproduction—about the drive to reproduce, even when artificial means must be undertaken—and about how, even before birth, children control the lives of the planet's adults.

Against the multiple forms of power young people exert in *Cabin*, from Hadley's unconceived child to Marty and Dana's final world-ending choice, the film asserts a counter narrative, one that sacrifices children: the slasher plot, the five-young-people-go-to-a-cabin-in-the-woods plot. This plot defends against the threat of overpopulation in directing its violence at young people. Adam Lowenstein has insightfully elucidated the pleasures of a "subtractive spectatorship" in *Friday the 13th* (Sean S. Cunningham, 1980)—a pleasure derived from the ecological drive to clear the landscape of characters: "Those humans whose lives disturb the landscape are methodically removed, until only the landscape itself and a token living (or perhaps undead) presence remains" (138). It is crucial, although Lowenstein does not address this fact, that the characters who are removed from the landscape are young. The director of the facility in *Cabin* (Sigourney Weaver) does make this fact clear when she tells Marty and Dana that it is always young people who must be sacrificed, in rituals that mimic the slasher plot. She says that the ritual Marty and Dana are subject to is designed to punish them "for being young." The ritual "has always required youth." Albeit very covertly, the "ritual" that is central to the sacrificial logic of *Cabin* and the slasher plot more broadly, then, is one that clears away the young and thus takes up the global problem of overpopulation, of too many children.

The line that can be traced from "Stopover" through *Children of the Corn*, *Cabin in the Woods*, and *Vivarium*, is one that represents above all the threat of the child, sign not only of individual unfreedom but also, through the lurking threat of overpopulation, of present and future eco-logical devastation. "Stopover in a Quiet Town" (as well as "It's a Good Life") begin a particular formation of horror that challenges what Lee Edelman has called "reproductive futurism"—the ways in which "the fan-tasy subtending the image of the Child" is integral to political discourse; everything must be for "the Child" (2).[8] Both "Stopover in a Quiet Town" and "It's a Good Life" portray this fantasy of the omnipotence of "the Child" as a nightmare. The horror films that are influenced by these *Twi-light Zone* episodes elaborate on the nightmare that is a life in service to the "Child." It is the individual nightmare of adults (parents in particu-lar) and it is the collective nightmare of the ecological damage done to an overpopulated world.

NOTES

1. "Five Characters in Search of an Exit" is also tangentially related as it, like "Stopover," ends with the revelation that a child is in charge and that the characters whom viewers have come to identify with are toys.

2. https://www.dictionary.com/browse/vivarium.

3. I wrote to Lorcan Finnegan to ask if he had seen "Stopover," and he told me that writer Garret Shanley was indeed inspired by it. Personal correspondence with Lorcan Finnegan, March 10, 2020.

4. The variant of dread articulated by Freeland, is distinct from, even opposed to, the dread Carroll has identified as a staple of *The Twilight Zone*. In Carroll's reading, the series features abundant "Tales of Dread," which present the viewer with a universe controlled by supernatural forces that consistently enact justice. As he puts it, the Tale of Dread "aspires to elicit the uncanny feeling or apprehension that the world represented in the fiction is itself authored—that is, governed ontologically by a presiding intelligence" (31); that "intelligence" or "agency," moreover, is "dedicated to righting wrongs" (32). Carroll's notion of dread, then, is one predicated on "justice," specifically on the certainty that a character's bad actions will be punished (29). Carroll's argument is persuasive, and there are indeed many *Twilight Zone* episodes in which characters are given their due. "Stop-over," however, represents a very different kind of universe, one that refutes the notion of justice, and elicits a very different kind of dread.

5. Some of the best episodes that fall into this category, and that demonstrate the frame shifting Plantinga describes are "People Are Alike All Over," "The Little People," "To Serve Man," "Five Characters in Search of an Exit," and "The Monsters Are Due on Maple Street."

6. For a discussion of the politics of overpopulation, see Garrard 55–59.

7. For a discussion of catastrophic declines in wilderness areas, see Watson et al.

8. Garrard has argued that Edelman has launched the sole critical challenge to "modern reproductive assumptions" (56).

WORKS CITED

Amatulli, Jenna. "Laura Ingraham Compared Teenage Activist Greta Thunberg to 'Chil-dren of the Corn.'" *HuffPost*, 24 September 2019, https://www.huffpost.com/entry/laura-ingraham-greta-thunberg-children-of-the-corn-fox-news_n_5d8a28e9e4b0c2a8 5cb1a9d9?ncid=engmodushpmg00000006

Carroll, Noël. "Tales of Dread in *The Twilight Zone*: A Contribution to Narratology." *Philosophy in* The Twilight Zone, edited by Noël Carroll and Lester H. Hunt, Wiley-Blackwell, 2009, pp. 26–38.

Edelman, Lee. *No Future: Queer Theory and the Death Drive*. Duke University Press, 2004.

"Five Characters in Search of an Exit," *The Twilight Zone*, written by Rod Serling, directed by Lamont Johnson, Image Entertainment, 2013.

Freeland, Cynthia. "Horror and Art-Dread." *The Horror Film*, edited by Stephen Prince. Rutgers University Press, 2004, pp. 189–205.

Garrard, Greg. "World Without Us: Some Types of Disanthropy." *SubStance*, vol. 4, no. 1, issue 127, 2012, pp. 40–60.

Hunt, Kathleen. "'Bring Him the blood of the outlanders!': *Children of the Corn* as Farm Crisis Horror." *The Politics of Horror*, edited by Damien Picariello, Palgrave-Macmillan, 2020, pp. 173–85.

"I Am the Night—Color Me Black," *The Twilight Zone*, written by Rod Serling, directed by Abner Biberman, Image Entertainment, 2013.

"In His Image," *The Twilight Zone*, written by Charles Beaumont, directed by Perry Lafferty, Image Entertainment, 2013.

"It's a Good Life," *The Twilight Zone*, written by Rod Serling, directed by James Sheldon, Image Entertainment, 2013.

Lowenstein, Adam. "The Giallo/Slasher Landscape: *Ecologia del Delitto*, *Friday the 13th* and Subtractive Spectatorship." *Italian Horror Cinema*, edited by Stefano Bachiera and Ross Hunter. Edinburgh University Press, 2016, pp. 127–44.

"Mirror Image," *The Twilight Zone*, written by Rod Serling, directed by John Brahm, Image Entertainment, 2013.

"The Monsters Are Due on Maple Street," *The Twilight Zone*, written by Rod Serling, directed by Ronald Winston, Image Entertainment, 2013.

"Number 12 Looks Just Like You," *The Twilight Zone*, written by Charles Beaumont and John Tomerlin, directed by Abner Biberman, Image Entertainment, 2013.

Plantinga, Carl. "Frame Shifters: Surprise Endings and Spectator Imagination in *The Twilight Zone*." *Philosophy in* The Twilight Zone, edited by Noël Carroll and Lester H. Hunt. Wiley-Blackwell, 2009, pp. 39–57.

"Stopover in a Quiet Town," *The Twilight Zone*, written by Earl Hamner, Jr., directed by Ronald Winston, Image Entertainment, 2013.

"A Thing about Machines," *The Twilight Zone*, written by Rod Serling, directed by David Orrick McDearmon, Image Entertainment, 2013.

"The Trade-Ins," *The Twilight Zone*, written by Rod Serling, directed by Elliot Silverstein, Image Entertainment, 2013.

"Twenty-Two," *The Twilight Zone*, written by Rod Serling, directed by Jack Smight, Image Entertainment, 2013.

Watson, James E.M., et al. "Catastrophic Declines in Wilderness Areas Undermine Global Environmental Targets," *Current Biology*, vol. 26, no. 21, November 2016, pp. 29–34.

"You Drive," *The Twilight Zone*, written by Earl Hamner, Jr., directed by John Brahm, Image Entertainment, 2013.

Grief, Loss, and the Unknown

The Hauntological Phantasm of Richard Matheson's The Twilight Zone

Melissa A. Kaufler

> To die—to sleep.
> To sleep—perchance to dream: ay, there's the rub!
> For in that sleep of death what dreams may come
> When we have shuffled off this mortal coil,
> Must give us pause.
> —Shakespeare, Hamlet (III, I, 65–69)

To omit Richard Matheson from a discussion of *The Twilight Zone* would be an egregious mistake as his philosophies have left an indelible mark on the series. At the outset of the series, Matheson was one-third of the original *Twilight Zone* writing team with Rod Serling at the helm and friend Charles Beaumont as number two. This worked extremely well, for Matheson's approach to loss is not dissimilar to both Serling's and Beaumont's.[1]

Throughout his writing career, Matheson called upon the works of Shakespeare to inform his storytelling. Matheson (like Beaumont) could extract singular lines of dialogue written hundreds of years prior and with them spawn entire novels, television shows, and even films that expound on loss and the unknown. His body of work—vast and in many genres—weaves a consistent thread of loss and hauntings based upon the absence of what has been lost. Matheson himself has even admitted that tragedy and loss have been sources of inspiration (Hawtree).

It is a legitimate question: what is left where something is lost? A ghost:

The ghost is primarily a symptom of what is missing. It gives notice not only to itself but also to what it represents. What it represents is usually a loss, sometimes of life, sometimes of a path not taken. From a certain vantage point the ghost also simultaneously represents a future possibility, a hope [Gordon 63–4].

The Twilight Zones of Richard Matheson, much like his larger body of work, are haunted—a term usually reserved for evil spirits in old Gothic houses. However, ghosts are so much more—whether it be a lost love, person, or a lost future. A ghost is the absence of something one possessed in the past but no longer does, and the grief that is felt with that loss is the ghost that haunts that person.

Matheson was a storyteller, and to tell a story is "always to invoke ghosts, to open a space through which something other returns" making "all stories, more or less, ghost stories" (Wolfreys, xii–xiv). This is especially true of fiction which is, "more or less," hauntological.

Hauntology

Today, in America—and most of the world—we are living in an era best characterized by the elusive concept of "hauntology." A term coined by Jacques Derrida in his work *Spectres of Marx*, "hauntology" is meant to describe the study of how our collective ideations of the past and future inescapably invade or "haunt" our present (Derrida 10). According to Italian Marxist Franco Berardi, the idea of a brighter and better future is not one that is "natural," but rather, it is something that has been culturally mythologized since the conclusion of the modern atrocities that are the Holocaust and Second World War. He goes on to say that the ascendance of such a silently pervasive concept and expectation of a limitless future of possibilities in the post-war world has been "rooted in modern capitalism" and the robust expansion of a capitalist economy which "resides exactly in the accumulation of the surplus value that results in the constant enhancement of the spheres of material goods and knowledge" (Berardi 18–19). Berardi claims that the future that was collectively "expected" in a post-war world was based on an "unspoken confidence that human beings [would] never again be treated as Jews were treated in their German nightmare" (Berardi 19). This collective notion of looking "forward" and "ahead" in life was, for a time, an effective way of escaping the inevitable socio-economic decline by way of unrestricted capitalism and rampant consumerism beginning in the fifties and sixties. It wasn't until the seventies when this promise of a better tomorrow began to appear less likely. As the seventies trudged on towards the eighties, people started to lose faith for a host of reasons including the end of the post-war economic boom and introduction of the neo-liberal policies that have brought us to our present.

No one knew this was happening at the time, and Matheson certainly did not. This was a "slow cancellation" that began in the seventies as the late Mark Fisher puts it (Fisher 2). Having experienced loss at an early age before bearing witness to the atrocities of war, Matheson realized the value of escapism—something of which we have become increasingly familiar in the last two decades of economic struggles, decline in production of new art and creativity, and how it has become increasingly more expensive to simply be alive and exist.

To bring us up to speed on our current moment which began taking root in post-war America, it is important to understand where we are now, especially amid a global pandemic. So, what *does* happen when the big, bright future we were waiting for is "lost" and we are met with an underwhelming present? The preface to Berardi's book helps answer such a question:

> What happens to political thought, practice, and imagination when it loses hold on "the future?" It goes into crisis. The analytic, psychological, and libidinal structures of twentieth-century revolutionary politics were beholden to the temporal form of the future—it even gave the first movement of the avant-garde its name: Futurism. The future was on the side of the revolution. It was a great and empowering myth, but few believe it any longer: the future is over. Its last vestiges were squandered in the schemes of a heavily futurized financial capitalism [Genosko and Thoburn 3].

As a result, our current culture is unavoidably "haunted"—recycled so heavy-handedly as we create monstrous mashups of what has already been done, yet we attempt to pass it off as fresh and new. In reality, we are saturated with reminders that "time is out of joint." Even *The Twilight Zone* as a series is on its third reboot, courtesy of Jordan Peele. Though Matheson began writing before the collective "cancellation" of the future really took hold, Matheson knew the value of the future as a necessary concept—an idea—and what it could offer people in terms of solace and hope or in some cases, a warning. He wrote some of his most poignant and beautifully haunting pieces in the seventies (*Bid Time Return, What Dreams May Come*), and it isn't hard to understand why. In order to be haunted, one will have had to have lost someone or some*thing*. For Matheson, his childhood offers an explanation of his own hauntings and personal "lost future."

Matheson: The Man and the Writer

Among his contemporaries and science fiction readers, Matheson's personal contribution to the horror and science fiction genres is often described as something that helped personalize and "bring hauntings home"—sometimes too close to home. Matheson's style took a departure of older tropes involving malicious ghosts, foreboding abandoned castles, murder, betrayal, and the whole gamut of other elements of more traditional and "gothic" horror.

> Richard Matheson's influence in the genre of dark fantasy has been enormous. Major horror critic Douglas E. Winter credits him with having "created the modern landscape of fear, taking it from the Gothic arena of misty moors into our shopping malls and quiet suburban neighborhoods—right into the house next door" [Nolan 9–10].

Even before this general feeling and subsequent grief of the "slow cancellation of the future" began to pervade collective society in the mid-seventies, Richard Matheson's experience of grief of his own "lost future" with a nuclear family began to inescapably inform his writings. That said, one cannot begin to look at the works of someone Stephen King once likened to the Elvis of his craft without first knowing some background on the man who dreamt the unreal into reality (King 11).

Born in New Jersey to Norwegian immigrants in 1926, Richard Burton Matheson was the eldest of three children. Matheson's father abandoned his family, forcing a young Matheson, his mother, and siblings to carry on and adapt despite the absence of a father figure. In conversations with fellow writer and friend William F. Nolan (*Logan's Run*), Matheson is said to have described his father as someone who was "uncertain and insecure and took refuge in alcohol." Nolan goes on to quote Matheson's own theory that alcohol "served to numb his [father's] fears and anxieties" and served as an escape from the pressures and expectations of life. As it would for any young child, Matheson was deeply affected by this loss and the subsequent grief. He and his family turned inward to rely heavily on one another as a united front against a cruel world (Nolan 10–11). This cloistered, inward-turned family dynamic between Matheson, his mother, and his siblings had both a positive and negative impact on his development—something that explains a great deal about his writings. On one hand, Matheson was taught early on how important love is in its different forms: husband and wife, child and parents, separated lovers (for whatever reason: death, time, different dimension). On the other hand, Matheson credits these circumstances for making him "extremely introspective at a very early age" where he "withdrew and lived inside [himself]" (Nolan 11–12). While he said his mother found an escape by joining the Christian Science Church, he himself escaped into reading fantasy, leading to an eventual interest in science fiction after college.

Considering that Matheson had to cope with and grieve his own personal "lost future" of an intact family unit at a very early age, it is of little surprise that such a large portion of his work was written with the intent of "helping others." Perhaps this why his work is still relevant and even so much more important now, even talking about a largely twenty-first-century concept such as hauntology. For some, confronting trauma from the past is itself a traumatic experience. Perhaps Matheson observed his mother's turn to religion as an attempt to circumvent the haunting grief of her husband leaving and having to raise three children alone. Matheson took refuge in writing as a way to confront his lost future in a way that offered a safe escape. One could even go as far as to say that *The Twilight Zone* is a metaphor for the place where we can go to process the unimaginable. Nevertheless, Matheson's inane talent for capturing the human condition in writing went far beyond just science fiction and dark fantasy.

Poignantly named *The Beardless Warriors*, Matheson's 1960 war novel drew inspiration from his own military service during the Second World War. The novel's title features the adjective "beardless" as an emphasis on just how young these men were as they were being sent off to end a war—not yet old enough to really have facial hair. Even the premise alone that Matheson lays out for his readers is already one of inevitable loss: young men yanked away from the promise of a future and thrust into a situation that often exposes both the ugliest parts of humankind with a high risk of death (Gorman 155–56).

Yet another example of Matheson's apt understanding of the human condition is his 1975 time-traveling romance novel that tackles love and loss with a loving dedication to his mother of whom he writes, "Recollection of our past together is the happiest of time travel." Published nearly 20 decades after *The Bearded Warriors,* Matheson gave us *Bid Time Return* which tells the story of Richard Collier—a playwright so weary of his time that his creative writing suffers and he withdraws from social relationships as he becomes increasingly obsessed with a vintage portrait of a beautiful woman that leads him to dabble in time travel. The description alone of the novel-turned-film is evidence of that.

Richard Collier is exhausted and bore of everyday life and how that, in addition his success as a playwright, has left him devoid of inspiration. The very notion that Richard feels he must "return" to a previous time to unearth real inspiration in the form of his inexplicable devotion to a woman whose photograph has mesmerized him is hauntological. Richard's present is not what he had hoped it to be: he's put under pressure to produce his plays for profit ("profit" being capitalism's bottom line) and while he is celebrated for his work at the outset of the film, it is clear he is also viewed less in his humanity and more in terms of his work product.

The only way Richard could escape this *was* to go backwards or at least "somewhere" in time—just not the present. The present is the time from which he needed escaping, and the future is only the *promise* of an ideal, better tomorrow.

For *Bid Time Return*, as he had with much of his work, Matheson said that he had fully immersed himself in his writing process:

> My main character walked around the hotel with a cassette recorder, describing what he saw and speaking his thoughts aloud. I did the same. His observations and feelings were mine, as I imagined myself to be Richard Collier. I found the experience intriguing and exhilarating. It engrossed me completely [Matheson 116].

It is hardly a coincidence that the narrator and main character, Richard Collier, shared a first name with the man who dreamt him into reality.

Matheson's entire body of work is saturated with similarly excellent examples of how hauntological themes of loss and grief are universal. His celebrated novel *The Shrinking Man* (1956) deals with the increasing vulnerability and grief of a man who literally shrinks as the world remains the same around him, while *A Stir of Echoes* (1958) explored hypnosis and a man unwillingly gaining the ability to hear other's thoughts and receives messages from the past against his will. *Hell House* (1971) tells the tale of man presumed to be dead for over thirty years and the small gaggle that seeks to investigate his abandoned home after previous deadly attempts features an expert in parapsychology.[2]

Lastly, it would be an ironic and colossal failure to omit at least the mention of one the most critically-acclaimed science fictions works of the twentieth century at the moment in which this is being written—*I Am Legend* (1954): a post-apocalyptic novel where the last man on earth is the sole survivor of a global pandemic that was adapted not twice, but thrice for the big screen.

Matheson's Twilight Zone

As previously mentioned, Matheson thoughtfully sought to offer an explanation to the inexplicable by attempting to provide reason and meaning in response to a loss that has occurred. Many of the 25-minute teleplays that he wrote for his friend Rod's science fiction television program on CBS functioned similarly to his longer, more in-depth works.

Season 1: *The Last Flight*

Flight Lieutenant William Decker is a British World War I pilot who discovers rather quickly that he is lost—lost in time. Claiming his engine went silent while in descent through the clouds in 1917, he lands in 1959 at an American airbase in France after having abandoned in fear his flying partner, Mackaye, without assistance mid-battle. While the theme of lost futures is a prevalent one throughout the series—especially Matheson's teleplays—this is a little different: instead of a lost future, he's lost his present, his flying partner, and nearly forty decades of his life. William is immediately incarcerated and thought to be crazy to the Americans in present day 1959. Through them, William learns that the day he has arrived just happens to be the day his old flying partner, now a decorated war hero, is making a visit to this base. Before long, William realizes it would have been impossible for Mackaye to have survived the battle in which he abandoned his partner and that he would not be arriving on base that day if William did not return to save him. In a moment of heroism, William manages to escape from captivity with the intent to save Mackaye.

Soon after, Mackaye, now as an Air Vice Marshal, arrives and the Americans on base begin inquiring about Flight Lieutenant William Decker where we quickly learn that he successfully returned to 1917—giving his life and saving Mackaye.

Again, Matheson invokes Shakespeare in Serling's closing narration:

> Dialogue from a play, Hamlet to Horatio, "There are more things in heaven and earth than are dreamt of in your philosophy." Dialogue from a play written long before men took to the sky. There are more things in heaven and earth, and in the sky, that perhaps can be dreamt of. And somewhere in between heaven, the sky, the earth, lies the Twilight Zone [*The Last Flight*].

Sometimes, we discover that there are things we cannot explain. Other times, we discover that there are things that shouldn't be known in the first place. In most cases, being unable to see into one's future is a blessing, but not always.

Season 2: *Nick of Time*

This is one of Matheson's most famous teleplays and it features a young William Shatner. A man named Don, played by Shatner, is on his honeymoon with his bride, Pat, when their car breaks down. As they begin to search for a place to grab lunch while they wait hours for repairs, we learn that Don is up for a competitive promotion at work that he doesn't want to lose—it's a minimal loss in comparison to what the newlyweds are about to discover at the local diner. (Spoiler alert: Don gets the promotion!)

When they sit down inside the small-town diner, they notice a little machine that says for only a penny, the little mystic seer atop that machine would tell your future to a "yes" or "no" question. All in good fun at first, Don soon becomes enraptured with the one-cent machine and its mystic seer. At first, this irritates Pat, but she grows increasingly worried as her husband continues to ask his questions to the seer.

Don asks the machine if the car is ready and when the mystic seer says it's "already done," Pat is relieved. A moment later, the repairman comes into the diner and tells them that they got "lucky" and found the spare car part they needed. Before they leave the diner, Don ramps up his obsession with the machine almost in desperation. Fearing for her husband's well-being, Pat cries, "We can have a wonderful life together, if we make it wonderful ourselves. I don't want to know what's going to happen. I want us to make it happen together" (*Nick of Time*). These words bring Don out of his increasingly-obsessive behavior just in the "nick of time" as he and Pat reaffirm their love and their shared belief in their future together.

Happy with their decision, Don and Pat exit the diner to retrieve their car and leave the small town that almost trapped them with a false promise of prophecy. Just as they exit, we see a distressed-looking couple enter the same diner. There is a look of trauma—by failing to tame their obsession with the future and the unknown in relation to the mystic seer, they have forever enslaved themselves in this town—a larger metaphor for fear and the unknown. One must appreciate the irony that this nameless couple was so fixated on knowing their future, they ended up losing their present as a result. Don and Pat really did get "lucky" as Serling begins to impart to us with Matheson's warning:

> Counterbalance in the little town of Ridgeview, Ohio. Two people permanently enslaved by the tyranny of fear and superstition, facing the future with a kind of helpless dread. Two others facing the future with confidence—having escaped one of the darker places of the Twilight Zone [*Nick of Time*].

While the idea of knowing what has not yet occurred is a seductive one, it is also a disastrous one. Equally seductive is a quick trip back in time when one is feeling tired of their own time period.

Season 3: *Once Upon a Time*

It is a treat that the star of this particular episode is acclaimed silent film star Buster Keaton. While his presence in the episode is an obvious example of something hauntological, the opening and closing of the episode features title cards and saloon-style piano score in the style of films in the 1920s. While these Old West tropes overtly pay homage to Keaton's early career in silent films, they are inherently anachronistic not just in the 1950s, but also in the 1890s (nearly two decades before silent films became mainstream) and therefore "haunt" the episode. Other than Serling's traditional opening and closing narrations, there is no verbal dialogue. Like the title implies with its fairytale reference, this episode is one of the few episodes in the series with a lighthearted tone and embodies Keaton's signature slap-stick humor style. In line with its levity is an interesting observation: unlike other *Twilight Zone* time travel episodes, Woodrow does not have to convince anyone around him that he's from another time.

In the true spirit of a silent film, this episode overdramatizes the "struggles" of a curmudgeon named Woodrow Mulligan who, in 1890, works for a scientist who invents what he calls a "time helmet." Effectively a time machine, the time helmet transports whoever wears it to a time of their choosing. Woodrow, weary of the time in which he lives and openly showing his disdain for it, he wonders if he could go back to his glorified version of the past. His curiosity gets the best of him and he places the time helmet on his head to take him to a place where it there is "peace and quiet" and things aren't so expensive. Accidentally, Woodrow sets the year to 1962 where he is thrust into what is (was) present day. There, he is quick to discover how much he regrets his decision as he stumbles through something dangerous of which is wholly unfamiliar—automobile traffic. He manages to lose the time helmet and in his pursuit of it, takes note of how prices have skyrocketed and the world has become loud and hectic.

With less than thirty minutes to retrieve the time helmet and return to his own time, Woodrow finally begins to realize what he has lost: everything he wanted—which he already possessed—but never could appreciate. Woodrow makes it safely back but not without a few hiccups and making a friend along the way. Upon his return, he is in awe but appreciative of his world and his place in time.

> "To each his own"—so goes another old phrase to which Mr. Woodrow Mulligan would heartily subscribe, for he has learned—definitely the hard way—that there's much wisdom in a third old phrase, which goes as follows: "Stay in your own backyard." To which it might be added, "and, if possible, assist others to stay in theirs"—via, of course, The Twilight Zone [*Once Upon a Time*].

Yes, the notion of "the grass is greener" comes to mind, but there's something larger than that. Perhaps we are all meant to be exactly where we are, as we are, and in the time we're meant to be. Matheson shows us through the humorously endearing Woodrow Mulligan that perhaps we cannot—or do not—always appreciate what is our status quo until we have lost it. Case in point, another of Matheson's teleplays in Season 3 imparts a similar message, but with a much darker tone.

Season 3: *Little Girl Lost*

This is the story of Chris and Ruth who are awakened abruptly in the middle of the night by disembodied cries of their younger daughter, Tina.[3] After discovering that Tina is physically nowhere to be found, Chris calls his from Bill to come over to their house. Bill, a physicist, figures out rather quickly that Tina has disappeared under her bed and into another dimension. The family dog, Mac, soon disappears through the same opening under the bed as Tina.

Rather than tell the story of two parents whose daughter suddenly disappears and the anger and desperation that they go through, Matheson takes an emotionally paralyzing experience and makes it more palatable. He even helps gives meaning and hope by exploring the possibility of another dimension and a potential way for Tina to return home safe. In this way, it forces us—if we are actively watching and listening—to even subconsciously insert ourselves in his characters' shoes and we begin to wonder how we would handle such a loss. Matheson then uses Serling's closing narration to deliver his message, which is something Matheson did exponentially well and undoubtedly contributed to his universal success. As Chris grabs hold of Tina and Mac the dog, his physicist friend Bill pulls the three of them by Chris' leg back into their own dimension. As Ruth whisks Tina out of the bedroom, Chris, in utter disbelief, asks Bill what had just happened. Bill pauses and says, "It was closing up all the time you were in there. Another few seconds and half of you would have been here and the other half…" as voice trails off as the camera pans out to a shot of a Chris with his hand over his mouth as the beginning of Serling's narration finishes Bill's sentence:

> The other half [of him], where? The fourth dimension, the fifth? Perhaps. They never found the answer. Despite a battery of research physicists equipped with every device known to man, electronic and otherwise, no result was ever achieved. Except perhaps a little more respect for an uncertainty about the mechanisms of the Twilight Zone [Matheson, *Little Girl Lost*].

The idea of Serling as omnipresent narrator who suddenly crosses over unnoticed into the scene where this is taking place is itself alone hauntological. The larger point here being that no matter how advanced our research and technology had come—even in the early sixties—there are things that we were never meant to know.

Season 4: *Mute*

Season Four of the *Twilight Zone* brought audiences the infamous hour-long programs instead of the usual, tight twenty-five minute episodes. Matheson authored only one teleplay this season and surprise—it centers around a young girl in Germany who, as a child, loses her parents tragically in a house fire. However, the twist is revealed at the episode's outset: Ilse Neilsen was part of an experiment as a toddler where she and several other children were to be raised only communicating through telepathy. Living a sheltered life with her parents who also communicate telepathically offered a safe haven and sense of belonging—a home. Upon losing her home, her parents, and the future she thought she would have, a young Ilse struggles desperately to adjust to a world where everyone is talking verbally.

After being traumatized by the loss of her parents, Ilse is thrust into a new life and new school that is so far from what she's known. She continues to struggle to feel a sense of love and belonging with her new, adoptive parents. Her new mother, Cora, is particularly sympathetic to Ilse's situation, usually acting as her best and really only advocate. She exhibits a level of patience and care for Ilse from the moment she meets the orphaned girl, and Ilse's ability to read her Cora's mind allows her to learn that her adoptive mother also lost someone once—her own daughter. In this, they both find some comfort in each other. Serling's closing narration, as usual, drives home Matheson's message:

> It has been noted in a book of proven wisdom that perfect love casteth out fear. While it's unlikely that this observation was meant to include that specific fear which follows the loss of extrasensory perception, the principle remains, as always, beautifully intact. Case in point, that of Ilse Nielsen, former resident of the Twilight Zone [*Mute*].

The loving and healing nature of Ilse's adoptive mother mirrors Matheson's feelings towards his own mother. Perhaps Matheson was inspired by his own mother's love and semblance of a home after his father had walked out and Matheson's "future" was "lost." However, there is another side of losing a loved one and it isn't quite as uplifting.

Season 5: *Spur of the Moment*

Dressed in all white and seated upon a white horse, we are introduced to Anne Marie Henderson—our young protagonist—who is described as "the face of terror" as she gallops home in a panic after a black figure on a black horse begins chasing after her. As she arrives home, she is instantly received by her worried father, mother, and her fiancé, David, who attempt to comfort her so that she may enjoy her engagement party later that evening. Moments later, Anne's ex-fiancé, Robert, shows up at her front door begging her to leave her current fiancé and return to Robert.

We are transported twenty-five years later to Anne's present day and we discover that the black figure on the black horse was, indeed, an older Anne trying to warn her younger self. Devastated and defeated that she failed to properly warn her younger self, she pours herself a drink and talks back to her mother. In a belligerent and bitter tone, present day Anne asks her mother a rhetorical question before launching into the anger of her grief:

> You know what I saw today? [...] I saw a ghost, mother. My own. [...] Intriguing, isn't it? To be haunted by one's own self. Positively intriguing. [...] I'm talking about ghosts, mother. Phantoms, visitations, reminders from the past and the future. I went out riding today out where I usually go, beyond the meadow. I was on a ridge and I saw this young girl ride toward me…. ME. Me, mother! As I looked at 18! Do you remember the day of my engagement party? Do you? June 13, 1939. I even remember the date. Do you remember how I came in terrified because some woman had attacked me and daddy, dear daddy, had them search for her in vain. Well, I was that woman, mother. I am that woman! And you want to know something funny, something marvelously funny? That's not the only time I've seen her. Bizarre, isn't it? I keep seeing her again and again. Keep seeing myself again and again on that day, that one particular day. You know the expression "go chase yourself?" Well, that's what I've been doing. Chasing myself. Do you remember what Robert said to me that day? "Maybe it's a warning," he said. I thought he was joking. Well, it was a warning. I was warning myself not to marry the wrong man. But I married him anyway, didn't I? And now I have paid the price. I have become that grotesque phantom that frightened that poor childlike girl half to death 25 years ago. A sterile, alcoholic phantom married to a man who's run this estate into ruin. If only I had known I was being warned [*Spur of the Moment*].

Anne's detailed level of self-actualization and "bitter" wisdom in her tirade is uncharacteristic of Matheson's usual protagonists. Matheson operates on the assumption that the audience would see Anne's interactions with Robert and assume she made the wrong choice by marrying a boring David, but that is intended.

Her angry soliloquy flashes back to the moment at her engagement party where she is about to make her biggest mistake. David shows up and Anne sees him, runs to him, and embraces him. He says, "I love you, come away with me." She says, "Oh, David, David, I want to…." He pushes her and says "Now Anne. Now, decide! There's no more time." Anne responds, "Oh, David, you are my true love. My adored one, make me happy. Please, make me happy." He responds over and over that he will make her happy and we begin to fade back to present day as we still hear a voice pleading "I love you, come away with me" (*Spur of the Moment*).

Matheson operates on the assumption that the audience would see Anne's interactions with Robert and assume she made the wrong choice by marrying a boring David, but that is intended. The big reveal happens when David—not Robert—enters the room. He's still saying he loves her, but it is clear by his malicious tone that he is taunting her. Anne has chosen incorrectly.

She flees the house leaving David crying, running off on her horse as she did at the start of the episode and shrieks "Anne! Wait! Come back!" to her younger self, thus commencing the pursuit we first witnessed at the opening of the episode as Serling's closing narration begins to play but now focusing on present day Anne's face, not young Anne's.

> This is the face of terror. Anne Marie Mitchell, 43 years of age, her desolate existence once more afflicted by the hope of altering her past mistake. A hope which is unfortunately doomed to disappointment. For warnings from the future to the past must be taken in the past. Today may change tomorrow, but once today is gone, tomorrow can only look back in sorrow that the warning was ignored. Said warning as of now stamped "not accepted" and stored away in the dead file in the recording office of the Twilight Zone [*Spur of the Moment*].

Now, Anne is once again "the face of terror," but not because she is terrified like young Anne was at the outset of the episode. At 43 years of age, the lasting consequences of Anne's choice in husband have consumed her to where she *is* herself the terror. Through Anne, Matheson teaches us about not only loss and the consequences of our actions, but the regret and anger than can often accompany it.

In a speech he delivered as the guest of honor at the World Fantasy Convention III in October of 1977, Matheson admitted that he never gave speeches and that this particular speech may be his "only opportunity to make a public statement about fantasy as a part of [his] life" and his personal "feelings in regard fantasy itself" (Matheson 112–113). This is obviously far from the case, as each piece of writing Matheson produced was its own statement on fantasy—albeit different facets of it that explored the wide array of human emotion and experience.

The message of Matheson's work has, more or less, always been the same and it will always be the same. Why? Because being human is timeless. To be fully human is to experience an array of emotions—this then means that grief and loss, are all too human.

Fellow writer and friend of Matheson, George Clayton Johnson (*Logan's Run*), once spoke of Matheson's writing style that resonated with so many and explained why:

> [Writers like Matheson] speak in universal symbols directly to the soul. [...]the bravest writer is one who dares to write about himself—his deepest fears, his

darkest desires, his weaknesses, his strengths, his dreams, his vision, his rationalizations and self-deceptions, his own enemy within. The writer, though cloaking himself in the guise of a story character, must look deep within himself to lovingly understand and sympathize with that character, giving him human dimension and a certain reality by the truth revealed through his telling behavior and reactions when threatened [Johnson 52–53].

In an era of "sequel-ability," mass online streaming, a twenty-four-hour news cycle, economic depression, mental depression, and constant reboots and throwbacks, the originality of Matheson's works is truly underscored but also underappreciated. Matheson's gift was taking terrifying or devastating situations and attempt to offer a way to explain them and give to them meaning where perhaps there was none and therefore, provide some comfort. Matheson's works were written with sincere love and curiosity while the timeless persistence of Hollywood studio heads, with capitalist ideals as their puppeteer, sought profit and sales.

Regardless of what genre, decade, or medium Matheson's work dabbles (there are many), his writings all share hauntological variants of an ever-present theme: an attempt to explain the inexplicable, control the uncontrollable, and make more palatable matters of loss or things of which we have no control. His *Twilight Zones*—and most of his work—offers a place for us to safely explore loss by wielding time, space, implausible science, or some combination of the three as his tools to tell his hauntings and create *A World of His Own*.

Notes

1. See Rod Serling's *The Sixteen Millimeter Shine* in Season 1 featuring the very hauntological premise of an aging movie star who spends her days re-living her younger days by watching her old films. See Charles Beaumont's *Person or Persons Unknown* in Season 2 where a man wakes up not knowing he has lost something so innate and profound—his entire identity.

2. Matheson had a deep interest in parapsychology. Speaking of a 1,000-page rejected paranormal series script that had been rejected by Hollywood executives over and over, a dejected Matheson said, "I was trying to write something that would help people [...] I've studied hundreds of books in every branch of parapsychology and metaphysics and in what I choose to call the "supernormal"—not to be confused with the supernatural. This project meant a lot to me, and it was sad to see it die" (Nolan 26).

3. Matheson often opted to reuse names of significance in his work. In *Little Girl Lost*, for example, Matheson's real wife was named Ruth and his daughter Tina; his son's middle name is Chris.

Works Cited

Genosko, Gary, and Nicholas Thoburn. "The Transversal Communism of Franco Berardi." Preface. *After The Future*. By Franco Bifo Berardi. AK, 2011.

Hawtree, Christopher. "Richard Matheson Obituary." *The Guardian*. N.p., 25 June 2013. Web. 19 Apr. 2020.

Derrida, Jacques. *Specters of Marx: The State of the Debt, the Work of Mourning and the New International*. Routledge, 1994.

Gordon, Avery. *Ghostly Matters: Haunting and the Sociological Imagination*. University of Minnesota Press, 2011.

Gorman, Ed. "Richard Matheson—A Subjective Assessment." *The Twilight and Other Zones: The Dark Worlds of Richard Matheson*. By Stan Wiater, Matthew Bradley, and Paul Stuve. Kensington Publishing, 2009.

King, Stephen. "Introduction." *Nightmare at 20,000 Feet: Horror Stories by Richard Matheson*. By Richard Matheson. Tor, 2002.

"The Last Flight," *The Twilight Zone*, written by Richard Matheson, directed by William Claxton, Image Entertainment, 2013.

"Little Girl Lost," *The Twilight Zone*, written by Richard Matheson, directed by Paul Stewart, Image Entertainment, 2013.

Matheson, Richard. "A Speech by Richard Matheson." *The Twilight and Other Zones: The Dark Worlds of Richard Matheson*. By Stan Wiater, Matthew Bradley, and Paul Stuve. Kensington Publishing, 2009. Print.

"Mute." *The Twilight Zone*, written by Richard Matheson, directed by Stuart Rosenberg, Image Entertainment, 2013.

"Nick of Time," *The Twilight Zone*, written by Richard Matheson, directed by Richard L. Bare, Image Entertainment, 2013.

Nolan, William F. "The Matheson Years: A Profile in Friendship." *The Twilight and Other Zones: The Dark Worlds of Richard Matheson*. Eds. Stan Wiater, Matthew Bradley, and Paul Stuve. Kensington Publishing, 2009. Print.

"Once Upon a Time," *The Twilight Zone*, written by Richard Matheson, directed by Norman Z. McLeod, Image Entertainment, 2013.

"Spur of the Moment," *The Twilight Zone*, written by Richard Matheson, directed by Elliot Silverstein, Image Entertainment, 2013.

Wolfreys, Julian. *Victorian Hauntings: Spectrality, Gothic, the Uncanny, and Literature*. Palgrave, 2002.

"It's simply out of my hands"

Human Nature as Illustrated
in The Twilight Zone's *"The Shelter"*

Michael Meyerhofer

Would you beat your best friend to death if it meant saving your kids from incineration? Would you abandon neighbors you'd known for years and listen to them screaming through the walls, if it meant ensuring your own family's survival? There's a classic episode of *The Twilight Zone,* appropriately called "The Shelter," that I like to assign to my college students. This is usually done in conjunction with a unit about social critique that begins with a discussion of both the Milgram Experiment and the Stanford Prison Experiment, whose societal implications are as disturbing as they are fascinating. In the meantime, suffice to say that both were highly controversial studies into human nature which offer strong evidence that while most of us generally concede that people will do terrible things in severe circumstances, it actually takes a lot less to turn us into monsters than we think.

Written in 1961, shortly before construction began on the Berlin Wall, "The Shelter" was rushed into production because Rod Serling wanted to create an episode that addressed the Cold War anxieties roiling in the minds and hearts of his audience (Perlstein). In that, the episode benefits not only from excellent writing and cinematography, but fine acting—especially in the cases of Larry Gates and Jack Albertson. Gates plays Dr. Stockton, arguably the protagonist of the story, though Alberton's portrayal of Stockton's friend, Harlowe, is just as pivotal. You might recognize Gates from the film version of *In the Heat of the Night,* where he plays Endicott, a racist plantation owner who, in a scene "…that shocked black and white audiences of the day," slaps a black detective (played by Sidney Poitier) only to be slapped back (Abele). As for Albertson, you probably caught him in *Willy Wonka & the Chocolate Factory* or the original

139

Poseidon Adventure. Both actors are at their best here. Bolstering a prime illustration of what can be accomplished when you have a socially conscious show that relies more on storytelling than special effects, Gates and Albertson portray their characters with such humanity and emotional range that watching them, you'll have a hard time believing that all this happens in less than half an hour.

At the risk of spoiling the story (if you haven't seen "The Shelter" yet, go watch it now and come back when you're done; I'll wait) I want to offer a quick synopsis of this brilliant *The Twilight Zone* episode, so that we can immediately dive into discussing some of its central themes—not the least of which is basic juxtaposition, the use of duality to make the story more engaging to an audience that ultimately senses the correctness of the episode's underlying message, even if we don't want to admit it. Basically, "The Shelter" tells the story of a close-knit community of average Americans who receive word of unidentified flying objects flying in their direction. The frequent mention of CONELRAD (Control of Electromagnetic Radiation, an emergency broadcasting service designed to warn people in the event of an attack during the Cold War) makes it clear that we're supposed to think less about flying saucers than incoming nuclear missiles emblazoned with a hammer a sickle. The government advises everyone to get to their bomb shelters (a further indication that we're dealing with nuclear missiles, not aliens).

However, it turns out that there's only one bomb shelter in the neighborhood, owned by William Stockton, the local doctor. He insists that his shelter has just enough resources to support himself, his wife, Grace, and their twelve-year-old son, Paul. That means he can't afford to let anyone else into the shelter, no matter how much he may want to. Obviously, this puts him into rapidly escalating conflict with his neighbors, who eventually form a mob (armed with a makeshift battering ram) and break into Stockton's shelter. Presumably, they do so with the intent of murdering the doctor and his family and taking their place (though obviously, given the limited space, they'll also have to turn on each other). However, just as they finally succeed in forcing the door open, word comes over the airwaves that those unidentified flying objects are just satellites. False alarm. Nothing to worry about.

Rather than cheer, everyone freezes, staring at each other in disbelief, like they just woke up from a black and white nightmare. Then, in the heady silence that follows, often punctuated by sheepish looks and nervous laughter, these average Americans reel from the fact that for all their friendship and civility, it only took about twenty minutes of mostly real time panic to dredge up their most bestial nature. That's the story, with its obvious critique of human nature, not to mention its blatant depiction of what the threat of violence can do; how fear can wreck the spirit just as effectively as bombs wreck the body. Now, let's discuss the brilliant way these themes and messages unfold throughout the episode.

"The Shelter" opens with an evening birthday party for the good Dr. Stockton, well-attended by his friends from around the neighborhood. The party takes place in his home, with fine china and formal wear. Despite clothing and attitudes that would seem stuffy and confining to a modern audience, the mood is light and jocular. In fact, right away, the episode establishes a certain tone of duality that will be maintained throughout the story and is, I contend, a primary illustration of the overall message. For example, during Stockton's party, one friend named Jerry Harlowe stands up to deliver a speech. It's obvious from their tone that the two men are great friends, yet as friends often do, they banter, trading scowls and insults often followed by moments of naked sentimentality, laughter, and handshakes. Put another way, these men are comfortable being nakedly sentimental only when their gestures are accompanied by enough sarcasm to act as insulation. After all, one must not be *too* emotional—that is, until missiles start falling out of the sky.

This scene serves another purpose, as well: Harlowe's jokes and ribbing of the good doctor's bomb shelter provide a believable and convenient excuse to detail the backstory that we, the audience, need in order to make sense of what's about to happen. By about three minutes into the episode, we have already ascertained that Dr. Stockton is a cherished and universally respected member of the community, with many of his friends being literally indebted to him for his medical services. At the same time, Stockton's friends view his bomb shelter as a silly nuisance, the forgivable but irritating act of an aging, eccentric worrywart. We also know the cultural context; there's an ever-present threat of nuclear war (though that context would have been obvious to *The Twilight Zone*'s original audience in the 60s) that most people prefer to ignore.

And perhaps most importantly, we know that all these people are old friends who possess a certain air of refinement and civilized formality. Yet the moment the warning comes over the radio, things begin to unravel at a breakneck pace that is nevertheless believable, given the circumstances. First, we see friends who had just been standing shoulder-to-shoulder, talking and laughing, splinter off and run out of Dr. Stockton's house to make preparations for the end of the world. Next, the camera shows the various neighbor-couples each running off in a different direction. That makes sense, since they obviously live in different houses, but it's also a good illustration of people always being in some sense separated from the very nexus where we choose to congregate (in this case, the doctor's literal shelter, which everyone keeps trying to enter uninvited, or perhaps even the central philosophy or attribute that unifies but does not define us).

We then cut to Grace, Dr. Stockton's wife, on the verge of panic as she tries to fill every available jar with water. While her panic is certainly believable, the fact that this episode doesn't contain a female character with anything resembling Dr. Stockton's relative sense of calm seems at first to be a black eye on the episode. However, it's worth pointing out that really, *no* character—including Dr. Stockton—is wholly in command of their senses. Even Stockton's friend, Harlowe, eventually sides with the mob against him, motivated by the selfish but very understandable wish to survive.

Still early in the episode, as panic builds and the Stockton family hurries to gather supplies, the son, Paul, asks his father if he should also gather books. The doctor immediately agrees that they'll need "books and things," since he doesn't know how long they'll have to be in the shelter. On the surface, their motivation might be one of entertainment—or more accurately, the need to maintain sanity and avoid boredom in a tiny, locked room where they might have to stay for weeks, and all this taking place decades before the popularization of video games and streaming services. However, this could also be seen as an attempt to maintain civility and order in the face of what really isn't that far-removed from what dinosaurs must have felt as they frantically tried to outrun the ejecta from an asteroid impact.

As the lights flicker and the water faucet starts losing pressure, indicating that there must be problems elsewhere (perhaps the whole neighborhood trying to do what they're doing), there's also another quick line in which Grace laments the fact that she neglected to buy lightbulbs earlier because she was waiting on a sale. This is a good illustration that no matter how hard you try to plan for disaster, you're guaranteed to miss something. This is followed by the Stockton family carrying down the last of their supplies into the shelter, only for the doctor to admit he's screwed up by forgetting to bring his toolkit. The doctor sends his son to fetch it while he attempts to comfort his wife. As they talk, Grace makes an excellent point: because they live so close to New York, a nuclear strike is bound to reach them. That means that even if they survive the initial disaster, they'll only crawl out of their shelter "like gophers" and tiptoe through "the rubble and the ruin and the bodies" of their friends.

It's both pivotal and ironic that she mentions their friends, given what those same friends are about to do. It's also interesting because it reminds us that to simply survive is not enough, or else there would be no reason for human beings to commit suicide. Rather, as social creatures, we *need* our communities to sustain certain needs that aren't necessarily physical or even readily articulable. Therefore, given the horrific world that the Stocktons may soon inhabit, a world in which their beloved community has been reduced to radioactive fallout and bomb-blistered rubble, Grace understandably asks why it's so necessary that they survive at all. In effect, she suggests that it might be better if they essentially commit suicide as a family by eschewing their carefully prepared shelter, as though a quick death with their friends might be more meaningful and less painful.

Throughout the episode, Dr. Stockton often acts with conviction, though his expression remains one of deep emotional turmoil. When he answers his wife, though, the doctor appears certain, through and through: they must stay alive for the sake of their twelve-year-old son, because even though he might only inherit a world of rubble, that's *his* world, his birthright. Neither he nor Grace have the right to deprive him of it. Grace nods, seemingly persuaded. It's also interesting that Dr. Stockton delivers his speech after Paul calls down that he's found the missing toolkit, i.e., a subtle indication that Stockton's speech (like his survivalist attitude and his entire shelter) are a necessary means to an end.

As the doctor goes back up to gather the last of the water, Harlowe knocks on the door. The doctor lets him in but insists that Harlowe should be home, preparing some kind of shelter for his own family. Harlowe answers that his modern house doesn't have a basement—hasn't *needed* a basement until now—and pleads with Stockton to let the Harlowes join them in their bomb shelter. Stockton offers to let the Harlowes use his basement, but denies them space in his shelter. "Oh, I'm sorry, Jerry. As God is my witness, I am sorry," he cries, insisting he can do no more because the air filter in the bomb shelter is only designed for three people.

Naturally, Harlowe protests: "Do you think I'm going to stand by and watch while my wife and children die in agony?" The two men struggle, only for Harlowe to apologize and plead once again for Stockton's help. Again, Stockton refuses, reminding Harlowe of all the times the good doctor urged his friends to make the same preparations he was making, regardless of how uncomfortable, expensive, and time-consuming they might be. In short, the doctor wanted his friends to face reality; perhaps to maintain their sanity because they lacked the doctor's strength and courage, they refused. Now, the doctor insists "It's simply out of my hands" as he seals himself in his shelter with his wife and son, closing the door in Harlowe's face.

One by one, other families arrive at the Stocktons' house and plead to be let into the shelter. The doctor firmly but mournfully refuses each request. One neighbor, Marty, pounds on the bomb shelter's heavy door and cries out, "You're a doctor! You're supposed to help people!" The scene cuts to the doctor's wife and son, staring at the father with looks of terror, wondering what he'll do. The implication, I think, is that Grace and Paul think they should open the door and let in their friends. After all, he *is* a doctor. But Stockton, with a ragged look on his face, mumbles, "That was a million years ago."

I won't provide a complete scene-by-scene analysis; suffice to say that as tension escalate, Harlowe initially proposes that all those locked outside Stockton's bomb shelter pool their resources and try to build a kind of shelter of their own, but his idea isn't even seriously considered. Rather, in their panic, the rest of the neighbors insist the only solution is to force their way into Stockton's shelter. This naturally leads to bickering over who "deserves" to be saved, and one of the neighbors, Frank, rants about immigrants like Marty, describing them as "pushy, grabby, semi-Americans!" Harlowe interjects, making the point that if they keep up their bickering, they won't even need a nuclear bomb after all; they'll "be able to destroy each other."

Eventually, the neighbors all gather outside the bomb shelter door, where the doctor continues to rebuff their pleas and threats. Then, something interesting happens: one neighbor suggests forcing their way into the shelter, and Frank remembers seeing heavy pipe in another neighbor's basement which they might be able to use as a battering ram. That idea is immediately vetoed, though, because it would require tipping off someone else to the shelter's existence, "...and who cares about saving him?" Ironically, the neighbors fear that if other adjacent neighborhoods learn about Dr. Stockton's shelter, they'll form a mob and try to break in—just as Stockton's friends are trying to do. His forehead damp with sweat, his eyes wide with panic, Harlowe still has the presence of mind to point out the group's hypocrisy. In that, Harlowe actually becomes something of the everyman in this episode. He frequently changes sides, and while he obviously lacks the courage and foresight of the doctor, he still glimpses through the fog of his own panic and self-preservation and sees what they are becoming. Of course, no one listens—except Marty, the "semi-American" whose protests earn him a punch in the jaw from Frank, who leads the mob outside to find a battering ram.

Back in the shelter, the Stocktons listen through the door and struggle to understand how their friends of twenty years could act this way. Meanwhile, the mob (aided by Harlowe and Frank, despite their earlier misgivings) goes and gets some of that heavy pipe after all, leaving the audience to wonder how they secured it without informing the owner what they meant to use it for. Did they just steal it? Did they knock him out? Is this simply a continuity error? We don't know. The next thing we see is a mob of men, women, and children battering down the bomb shelter door like their lives depend on it—because, from their perspective, they do. Frank is the first one through, murder in his eyes. But before things can escalate even further, an announcement from CONELRAD declares that there "are no enemy missiles approaching" and "We are in no danger" (ironic, given the bloodshed that was probably about to take place).

As couples embrace in decidedly muted celebration, Frank sheepishly approaches Marty and tries to apologize. Marty neither replies nor looks at him, and Marty slumps off. Then, as the doctor stumbles out of his shelter into a world both familiar and changed, Harlowe insists that he and the neighbors will pay for all the damages, "Anything to get back to normal." The doctor says, "I don't know what normal is. I thought I did once. I don't anymore." He starts up the steps and declares that the damages aren't just smashed doors and overturned tables, but finding out "what we're really like when we're normal. The kind of people we are just underneath the skin."

I find it fascinating that Stockton doesn't see his friends' behavior (or, likely, his own) as an aberration brought about by extreme circumstances. Rather, who we are in moments of panic is simply who we really are, like it or not. Moreover, if you swap out any of these characters—if the bomb shelter belonged to Harlowe, Marty, or Frank, for example—the results probably would have been much the same. Dr. Stockton, in his desire not just to stay alive but to protect the lives of his family, might very well have helped batter down the door, just as his friends did. That juxtaposition of compassion for one's family and cruelty toward others—even friends— is evident on the faces of all the men. It's also worth pointing out that no matter how sweaty and ragged they look, the men's ties stay on, dangling from their throats like nooses.

Stockton's final pontifications on human nature, musing that they "were spared a bomb tonight, but I wonder if we weren't destroyed, even without it," might seem a bit heavy-handed to modern audiences. However, it's balanced with Rod Serling's exiting narration: "No moral, no message, no prophetic tract. Just a simple statement of fact. For civilization to survive, the human race has to remain civilized." That lesson might seem obvious, but if you've ever seen loving, well-fed family members bicker over the material possessions of a dead relative, or wondered why scripted reality shows go to such lengths to include melodramatic betrayals and shifting alliances, you know otherwise.

The Milgram Experiment and Stanford Prison Experiment left people appalled by the extraordinary cruelty that normal human beings seem willing to inflict on one another, due to relatively mild stressors and social pressures, as well as random chance (Konnikova). Often, I ask my students to consider the obvious parallel of the Holocaust, which really only offers two possibilities: either a significant percentage of the world's most cruel and sadistic people all happened to be born at just the right time and place to become Nazis, or else virtually any human being is capable of unspeakable atrocities given the right factors. The lesson of these experiments, bolstered by virtually every history textbook ever written, is virtually the same lesson as what's offered in "The Shelter." Namely, unexamined and untested civility is an illusion, useful in times of plenty but utterly worthless in a crisis. But we need not live that way.

In his opening monologue, Rod Sterling says that this story "…is not meant to be prophetic. It need not happen." Interestingly, the children in this episode are mostly portrayed as unaware of the gravity of what's happening around them, more concerned with television and cake. Rather, it's the adults who are truly immature, even as they struggle to do what they believe in the moment to be right. Furthermore, the care placed into this episode—the juxtaposition of compassion and cruelty, primality and civility—does much to drive home its message that civility and humanity are only valuable when they've been tested.

But how does one test their civility; how do we strengthen our humanity? The answer offered in "The Shelter" would seem to be preparation; that is, by preparing for the physical event that is likely to throw your life into turmoil, you're more likely to weather said turmoil. After all, if Stockton's friends had simply taken the learned doctor's advice and built shelters of their own, much of this conflict wouldn't have happened. Yet I maintain that preparation isn't just about building shelters; it's about putting aside what you *want* to be true and examining the situation as it actually is. It's about eschewing the ego (a hard task at any time) and seeing not just the world but yourself with clear eyes. And its about having as your primary motivation something beyond self-preservation.

While it could be argued that the neighbors were motivated by desire to save their children, Stockton's desire to save his son was deeper and more sustaining because it's probably what motivated him to build that shelter in the first place, forcing his neighbors to contend with concrete trucks and the sound of ringing hammers, since no action takes place in a vacuum. In that respect, "The Shelter" is an example of truly excellent storytelling because it illustrates the intricate connections that bind every community, while simultaneously reminding us that strengthening and maintaining those connections is only possible when we acknowledge the darker aspects of humanity that prompted us to favor civility in the first place.

WORKS CITED

Abele, Robert. "The Slap Heard Round the World." *Directors Guild of America*, 2011.

Konnikova, Maria. "The Real Lessons of the Stanford Prison Experiment." *The New Yorker*, 12 June 2015.

Perlstein, Rick. *Before the Storm: Barry Goldwater and the Unmaking of the American Consensus.* Nation Books, 2009.

"The Shelter," *The Twilight Zone*, written by Rod Serling, directed by Lamont Johnson, Image Entertainment, 2011.

PART III

The Twilight Zone in the Eighties

Twilight Zone: The Meta

Interior and Epiphenomenal Elements That Frame Twilight Zone: The Movie

Kevin J. Wetmore, Jr.

Introduction

Filming of *Twilight Zone: The Movie* (*TZ:TM* from now on) began on July 5, 1982, and finished in December of that year. The project had been announced with great fanfare and anticipation, not least of which because the film brought together some of the hottest(at the time) genre filmmakers reviving a much-beloved series that had ended less than two decades before. The attachment of Steven Spielberg in particular as both producer of the film and director of one of the sequences hailed as promising great things for the film. Spielberg had, after all, cut his teeth directing an episodes of the made-for-television film that served as the pilot of Rod Serling's *Night Gallery*. Spielberg had been paired with Serling when he was twenty-two and fresh out of film school. *Night Gallery* had been his first paid directing job (Beyl). He would go on to direct another episode for the series itself, so of the four directors involved in *TZ:TM*, Spielberg was the only one who had worked directly and repeatedly for Rod Serling. When the film was announced,

Spielberg also boasted a resume that contained, to that point, *Jaws*, *Close Encounters of the Third Kind*, *Raiders of the Lost Ark*, and *E.T.: The Extraterrestrial*, among other films. John Landis had *Animal House* and *An American Werewolf in London* under his belt. George Miller had *Mad Max* and *The Road Warrior* to his credit. Joe Dante, coming out of a career working initially for Roger Corman, had *Piranha* and *The Howling*. In short, the four directors of the film had established reputations for crafting genre films of the fantastic and the dark. *TZ:TM* should have and could have been a huge cinematic experience worthy of the *Twilight Zone* legacy.

149

Instead, problems with the conflicting styles of the directors, compounded with the accident on Landis's set and the scandal that followed reduced *TZ:TM* to an interesting but inconsistent experiment that the studio released and then neglected, hoping it would simply fade from memory. The accident itself shaped public perception of the film, and continues to do so. At least two books (Ron Labrecque's *Special Effects: Disaster at* Twilight Zone: *The Tragedy and the Trial* and Steve Farber and Marc Green's *Outrageous Conduct: Art, Ego and the* Twilight Zone *Case*) and a Shudder documentary (*Cursed Films: The Twilight Zone*) have been produced about the accident.

The film version of *The Twilight Zone*, unlike the series, is problematic and perceived negatively by the critics for several reasons, both internal to the film and as a direct result of the accident and how it was presented in the media. This essay will explore the three "meta" factors that ultimately prevent *TZ:TM* from being successful as a film. First, obviously, is the on-set accident shaping the film itself and the perception of the film. Second is the uneven and inconsistent tone and emotional content due to the portmanteau format and multiple directors as opposed to the series, in which all elements ultimately fell under Serling's singular vision. Third, and finally, the meta nature of the project itself, which, by calling attention to the original as a cultural phenomenon, actually undermines the film itself. Because Landis chose to frame the wraparound segment as being about the original *Twilight Zone*, the film sets up an observable contrast in how the sequence actually does not bear much resemblance to Serling's series.

Context of the Film

TZ:TM appeared in the wake of other anthology television shows in the sixties and seventies, most notably Serling's own *Night Gallery* (1969–1973). For film audiences (and producing studios) it followed hard on the heels of George Romero and Stephen King's portmanteau film *Creepshow* (1981). *Creepshow* framed and set the stage for *TZ:TM*. Its success had demonstrated that Boomers (then in their thirties and forties) would go see films that evoked nostalgia for the fifties and sixties (such as for E.C. Comics and *The Twilight Zone*) and their children (in their teens and early twenties) were active participants in a growing genre-based pop culture as evidenced by the popularity of *Star Wars* (1977), the rebirth of *Star Trek* (1979) ten years after it went off the air, and the emergence of sci-fi/horror in children's culture.

Creepshow left cinemas after only five weeks but managed to net almost sixty million dollars in box office from an eight million dollar budget. By contrast, *TZ:TM* was a flop, making only six and a half million dollars its opening weekend and twenty-nine and a half million globally during its total run from a ten million dollar budget. Critics were equally unkind at the time, most notably due to the reputation of the film in the wake of the death of actor Vic Morrow and two Vietnamese-American child actors on set, which I shall discuss below. At the moment suffice to say the accident occurred on July 23, 1982, the film was released on June 26, 1983, and the results of the accident did not play out until long after the film had left theaters, but the knowledge of the accident hung over not only the rest of production but over the film itself when it was finally presented to the public.

The accident itself is not as relevant as its impact on perceptions of the film, and thus I will not go into details on the accident itself. Suffice to say that the details that the child actors had been working at two in the morning in violation of child labor laws, and that the director and several others on set made decisions that obviously put cast and crew in danger in order to "get the shot" resulted, even before the trial, in Landis and the film's reputations taking hits. It was hard to square *Twilight Zone*'s and Rod Serling's reputation for humanism and compassion with the events and decisions on the set. One watches the film knowing people died making it.

The National Transportation Safety Board issued its report in October 1984. Director John Landis, associate producer George Folsey, Jr., helicopter pilot Dorcey Wingo, production manager Dan Allingham, and explosives specialist Paul Stewart were subsequently tried and acquitted on charges of manslaughter in a nine-month trial in 1986 and 1987, followed by years of civil lawsuits by the families of the deceased, all of which played out in the Hollywood media (see Faber and Green; Labrecque). In other words, when the film was in theaters, and even when it was released initially on home video, the investigations into the accident and subsequent legal action were still underway or had not happened yet. The film was thus released under a cloud of tragedy and uncertainty. Virtually every reviewer at the time mentioned the accident in the review of the film, framing the film in terms of what had happened on the set (see Faber and Green).

Twilight Zone: The Meta: *John Landis, Part I*

The film consists of four sequences and a wraparound narrative. The bookending sequence, scripted and directed by John Landis, and called "Something Scary" was designed to be the introduction to the world of *The Twilight Zone*. The opening is paradoxically a metanarrative celebrating

The Twilight Zone as "something scary" but is also not at all *Twilight Zone*-esque—it fails at the ethos of Serling, not least of which because Landis constructs it first as a comedy, then as a meta-commentary on the experience of watching *The Twilight Zone*. While *The Twilight Zone* employed comedic elements, most often and notably dramatic irony, the series was not a comic one, nor was the speculative twist within most episodes ever played for laughs. Landis's primary purpose is laugher, not a sense of the mysterious or strange. His intent is obvious beginning with the casting.

Serling often cast known dramatic actors, as well as emerging ones, in the lead roles. *TZ:TM* features Dan Aykroyd and Albert Brooks, known in 1982 when they were cast solely for their comic work. Aykroyd was by that point a *Saturday Night Live* alumni, known for films such as *1941* (Spielberg, 1979), *The Blues Brothers* (Landis, 1980), *Neighbors* (John G. Avildsen, 1981), *Doctor Detroit* (Michael Pressman, 1983), and *Trading Places* (Landis, 1983), the last of which was filmed after *TZ:TM* but released before, further cementing Aykroyd's status as one of his generations leading comedic actors. A year after *TZ:TM* Aykroyd starred in *Ghostbusters*, a film he had co-written with fellow Second City alum Harold Ramis, which is the closest Aykroyd ever came to horror, and even then the film was a comedy.

While Albert Brooks did appear in *Taxi Driver* (1976), he was (and still is) known for his comedic chops—stand-up comic with appearances on the *Tonight Show* and *Saturday Night Live*, guesting on television sitcoms, and especially comedic film work as an actor, writer and director: *Real Life* (Brooks, 1979), *Private Benjamin* (Howard Zieff, 1980), *Modern Romance* (Brooks, 1981). Within the popular press of the time he was nicknamed "the West Coast Woody Allen." While the television series would occasionally use actors known for comedy, this casting is unique. Two obvious comics, known solely for their comedy, perform the introduction to the film. As a result, the opening reads far more Landis than Serling—it carries the tone and style of *An American Werewolf in London* (1981), Landis's other great work of horror comedy. The opening is played as comedy, then turns horrific, in a move which follows neither the logic of the preceding scene nor of *The Twilight Zone* itself.

The scene opens on a lonely desert highway, a single car driving in the darkness, two men in the front seat sing along with the radio. The song is "Midnight Special" covered by Credence Clearwater Revival—an interesting choice to open the film. The song is a traditional prisoner song, with the chorus offering hope that a train will come along and shine its light on the singer. The lyrics represent a desire for escape and transcendence, a recognition that one might still be stuck in a bad place, but that external events may grant one a sense of grace or wholeness. The two men sing along with soulful abandon. The moment is one of camaraderie, hinting at a sublime experience on a dark desert highway.

Brooks, the driver, asks if Aykroyd, the passenger who is hinted as being a hitchhiker Brooks picked up, wants to see something "really scary," and then proceeds to turn off the headlights and speed down the highway in the dark. "This is dangerous," the passenger says in a panicked voice, followed by, "That's scary enough." Brooks put the lights back on and the two begin to sing television theme songs, another bonding experience for those who grew up in the sixties and seventies and recognize iconic music that opens television programs. The opening of the film then becomes a meta moment celebrating famous openings. They sing or hum the themes from *Sea Hunt, Perry Mason, Bonanza, Car 54, Where Are You?, National Geographic,* and *Hawaii Five-O.* The specific choices are both iconic and nostalgic. The mood in the car is also nostalgic, which each theme proceeded by similar questions: "Hey, remember this one?"

This recognition of the significance of television themes inevitably leads to The Twilight Zone. After paying due reverence to the theme, which by this point in history had already become cultural shorthand for something weird happening, the two men begin discussing episodes of the *Twilight Zone.* "They were so good. They were so scary!" the passenger crows. They debate the merits of "Time Enough at Last," name dropping Burgess Meredith, the episode's star, who a few minutes later in the film will replace Rod Serling as the opening voice over and narrator, furthering the meta nature of the opening. Aykroyd mentions an episode in which a man receives a stopwatch that gives him the power to stop time. Brooks says that the episode he is talking about is actually from *The Outer Limits* (1963). Aykroyd reaffirms that it is an episode of *The Twilight Zone* (1959). Aykroyd is correct. The episode to which he is referring is "A Kind of a Stopwatch" (1963) from *The Twilight Zone* season five. They then discuss "The After Hours," in which Marsha White (Anne Francis) discovers she is a mannequin come to life.

This conversation does two things. First, all of the episodes mentioned frame the film—*The Twilight Zone* concerns narratives about the unexpected, the unexplained, and the moments in life when reality shifts and one enters the eponymous zone in which the experience will transform the protagonist in a meaningful way. Second, it demonstrates the iconic nature of certain episodes of *The Twilight Zone.* "Time Enough at Last," "The After Hours," "The Monsters Are Due on Maple Street," "To Serve Man," and "Nightmare at 20,000 Feet" are so well known and recognized they can be parodied on *The Simpsons, Bob's Burgers,* or *Saturday Night Live* with the knowledge that even those in the audience who haven't seen the episodes with still understand the reference. This is not true for all episodes; no parodies of "A Passage for Trumpet," for example, or "Mr. Garrity and the Graves," although both are also standard examples of Serling's storytelling and the model of a protagonist transforming due to an experience in the zone, so to speak. The irony, of course, is that "Something Scary" does not follow this model at all. It is simply a jump scare tacked onto a meta celebration of Serling's show. Aykroyd's character is transformed into a monster, but neither he nor Brooks are changed by the experience. It exists solely as a haunted house jump scare moment.

TZ:TM was marketed as a sort "greatest hits," which makes both "Time Out" and the wraparound narrative stick out as different. As will be examined below, "Time Out," like the wraparound discussed here is more of a John Landis narrative than a *Twilight Zone* one, and by foregrounding both, the film sets a jarring tone of non–Serlingesque, non–Mathesonesque stories first, then following with three remakes of iconic episodes. The tone and style clash, rendering a film less celebratory of *The Twilight Zone* and more of a comedy followed by a heavy-handed morality tale without a moral.

Closing the scene, Aykroyd then asks Brooks if he wants to "see something really scary." Brooks pulls the car over to the side of the road, Aykroyd turns away and when he turns back he has transformed into a monster, who proceeds to attack Brooks. The camera pulls back and floats up to the star-filled sky, giving way to the *Twilight Zone* opening narrated by Burgess Meredith, whose episode "Time Enough at Last" had just been name-checked by the two characters. The episode itself seems to have no specific point, other than to remind the audience of how remarkable the original series was and then give them a weird jolt, not at all in keeping with the original series.

After the four individual episodes unspool, Aykroyd returns in the final moments of the film, now driving the ambulance that is to take John Valentine (John Lithgow) to the hospital after the plane in which he is the only one who can see the goblin on the wing nearly crashes. The passenger from the beginning has now become the driver. Valentine, now on the ground and strapped to a gurney, feels much more secure and confident that he was right when the others witness the destruction to the wing. He is placed in the waiting ambulance where Aykroyd now turns and asks if he wants to see something "really scary." The callback to the opening is a clever one, and implies that the zone itself is not quite done with Valentine. It is also a problematic one, as it only exists to tie the end of the film to the beginning, implying that Aykroyd is some sort of itinerant shapeshifter, who wanders the earth seeking individuals for which he can transform and terrify. No reason is given for this being's existence; Aykroyd simply exists to scare. Such a construction could not exist in Serling's universe, as such a being would have a purpose. Aykroyd's character is pure Landis—existing solely for its own sake, for effect rather than purpose. As a result, the "Something Scary" wraparound fails as a road into *The Twilight Zone*, not least of which because the Serling formula (usually but not always) requires an exit from the zone back into normal reality at the end, even if that reality has now shifted. The film simply implies once one enters the "Twilight Zone" one is trapped there forever in a place of eternal horror. Sadly, the meta framing device does not work, setting the film up for an inconsistent and problematic creation of its assertion as the natural development of *The Twilight Zone* franchise.

Twilight Zone: The Meta: *John Landis, Part II*

Following the opening sequence comes Landis's second contribution to the film and the first full narrative, "Time Out." This is the only episode not based on an original *Twilight Zone* episode but instead was scripted by Landis in the style of Serling (except not, as I shall argue). This is also the episode that resulted in the deaths of Vic Morrow and child actors Renee Chen and My-ca Dinh Le on set. The accident not only framed reception of the entire film, the death of the lead actor with the story incomplete and the decision to include the story in *TZ:TM* anyway resulted in a truncated narrative that is not a *Twilight Zone* story in the Serling model. When one watches "Time Out" one is almost always aware of the tragedy behind it and how that tragedy changed the story one watches, thus rendering this sequence meta as well.

The segment was originally entitled "The Bigot," a story Landis claimed would retain political and social commentary of the best *The Twilight Zone* (1959) episodes. Landis scripted the episode but stated it was loosely inspired by original series episodes "Deaths-Head Revisited" and "A Quality of Mercy" without being remakes of them. The story begins with Morrow's character, Bill Connor (the name suggestive of "Bull" Connor, the Commissioner of Public Safety for the city of Birmingham, Alabama, known for his strong, violent opposition to the Civil Rights Movement) and his friends in a bar, and Bill complaining loudly about Jews, Blacks, and Asians. He contends "a Jew" got the promotion he should have received. He claims superiority to "African spear-chuckers" and "gooks." His prejudice, bigotry and hatred are laid on thick. The African American men at the next table take offense at Bill and as a result Bill's friends encourage him to leave. Bill leaves the bar and finds himself in occupied France under the Nazis, where he is perceived as a Jew. What follows is a sequence of situations in which racism leads to violence: he is a Black man, about to be hung by the Klan, he is a Vietnamese man, hunted by American soldiers. It is this trifecta of equivalence that is arguably the episode's most interesting assertion: American soldiers in Vietnam are presented as the equivalent as Nazis and the Klan. Certainly the Vietnam War was unpopular and highly problematic, and by the Reagan administration popular culture was exploring its conflicted legacy in films such as *The Deer Hunter* (1978), *Apocalypse Now* (1979) *First Blood* (1982), *Platoon* (1986), *and Full Metal Jacket* (1987), most of these films being produced by the same Hollywood cohort that made *TZ:TM*. It is interesting to reflect that had the accident not happened, *TZ:TM* would contain one of the strongest anti–Vietnam statements on film to date and posited America as a racist nation as evinced by its actions in Vietnam, a remarkably progressive political understanding of the war, but very much in keeping with Serling's own ideas about war.[1]

According to the original screenplay, the eponymous bigot was supposed to rescue the children from the Americans shooting at them, bring them to safety away from the explosions and helicopter, and tell them, "I'll keep you safe, kids. I promise. Nothing will hurt you, I swear to God." Although the only original story (other than the wraparound), this redemptive ending could be seen as Serlingesque—by experiencing violence and persecution at the hands of bigoted soldiers, Nazis and klansmen, Bill learns to empathize with people who have been historically oppressed and begins to ally with them. He would then return to the present a better human being having been transformed by his experience in the zone.

With the deaths of the performers this story could not be completed, and instead of a tale of redemption or the acquisition of self-knowledge, the story transforms into an E.C. comics tale of a horrible ending to an unlikable, one-dimensional character. Returning to Nazi-occupied France after the helicopter explodes, Bill has a Star of David pinned to his jacket and he is put on a train to Auchwitz, although the bar and his friends in contemporary America are visible between the slats of the train. He calls out to them, but they cannot hear him. The train begins to move and presumably Bill is killed in the Holocaust. This ending is neither ironic nor redemptive but vindictive. The direct result of the accident is that the filmmakers had to scrap the planned ending and construct one out of footage already made, which changed the story and the purpose of the narrative entirely. Rather than finding the time "out of joint," Bill Conner is sent to the past and then killed. End of story.

In the books about the incident, Landis comes under serious criticism and receives the lion's share of the blame for the accident (Labrecque;

Faber and Green). The sequence is also entirely Landis's, as he both wrote and directed it. Landis' filmmaking fingerprints are all over the segment, containing many elements found in his other films. In particular, Landis enjoys references to his other films in his work. The phrase "See You Next Wednesday" appears in every one of his films, for example. In the Vietnam sequence of the story, the American soldiers talk about having "fragged" Lieutenant Neidermeyer—a reference to the character from *National Lampoon's Animal House*, directed by Landis (although written by Harold Ramis and Douglas Kenney). Neidermeyer is a fascistic bully in that film, and at the end it was revealed he went to Vietnam and was shot by his own troops. The *TZ:TM* reference is to this part of *Animal House*, placing the sequence not in the "Twilight Zone" but in Landis's shared world of films. "Time Out" lives in the same world as *An American Werewolf in London* and *Trading Places*, not the other episodes of *TZ: TM*.

Inconsistent and Unironic: The Rest of the Film

The accident overshadowed the film, so that the segment in which Morrow died received a great deal of critical attention, resulting in the remaining three segments existing in its shadow. In addition to the issues of tone and emotional content, noted above, the mood of each piece was inconsistent with each other and the seriousness of "Time Out." In the wake of Morrow's death, and the audience's knowledge of it while watching the film, the sentimentality of "Kick the Can," cartoonish approach of Dante in "It's a Good Life," much closer, as noted above, to *Creepshow* than *The Twilight Zone*, and the straightforward horror approach of Miller, combined with John Lithgow's performance, neither gel together nor manage to achieve their individual effects.

As noted above, in the original series Serling's endings, whether happy or tragic, are skewered through with irony. Characters pass through a transformative experience, but we are in many ways, watching the episodes in our own homes, detached from the story—we are not in the zone, we can merely see into it. Not so the segments of this film, of which only "It's a Good Life" and "Nightmare at 20,000 Feet" retain the irony of the originals.

Part of the challenge for the film was the shift in the medium and the format. Serling offered a weekly series, which allows for small narratives separated by seven days, as opposed to a portmanteau film attempting to deliver the same experience. Many critics complain of the shift in tone and the uneven emotional content, from the meta-experience of "Time Out," watching knowing one is seeing the film Vic Morrow was killed making, to the saccharine sweetness of Spielberg's "Kick the Can," to the cartoonish and goofy "It's a Good Life," to the genuine horrors of "Nightmare at 20,000 Feet"—the film is inconsistent and imbalanced. Like a poorly made mixtape, the elements do not flow into one another to form a consistent and coherent whole with a full emotional tapestry, but rather jar the viewer from one detached experience to another. As Simon Brown observes, "In a weekly tv series, particularly one held together by the authorial stamp of Rod Serling, such variety of tone and subject matter was less problematic, but squeezed into just over 100 minutes the shifts were jarring" (92). *TZ:TM* as a singular experience created separately by four directors with different approaches, directorial styles and understandings of the material results in a film that neither holds together internally, and thus cannot overcome the external, extrinsic framing elements (most notably the accident).

Conclusion

The Twilight Zone: The Movie was sandwiched in between the original series, Serling's *Night Gallery* (1969–1973), and the 1985 reboot. The very fact that the film received a lukewarm reception at best yet less than two years later a new television series was in production speaks volumes as to the perception of the film. *Twilight Zone* on television is acceptable, even preferable, as Brown, above, observes. The film, however, remains regarded as a hot mess and an embarrassment. The film was shown on CBS (which owned the rights to the original *Twilight Zone*) in 1986 with eight of the more violent and scary minutes excised, but the film has not found a regular home on television. Mark R. Hasan, in a review of the rerelease on DVD of the film, writes, "The film's first home video release was probably locked in place long before the tragic deaths, and once those video commitments were honored, the film quietly disappeared from circulation." One can still purchase the film on DVD, but it is neither held up nor celebrated in the manner of either the original series nor any of the other reboots, especially the most recent, Jordan Peele–produced incarnation. Even Anne Washburn's play *The Twilight Zone*, in which characters who do not smoke remove a cigarette from their pocket to deliver narration in the manner of Serling, for example, more successfully delivers a meta-reading of the series.[2] Landis's attempt to make the film meta in "Something Scary" and the epiphenomena that make the film meta as a result of the accident created a film that, in the words of Shudder, seems "cursed." The film is a failure qua film, the *TZ* brand was still intact and even desirable, so long as it was on television, the ideal medium for the series. Indeed, the most *Twilight Zone* aspect of the film might just be that the film production went into a real-world form of the *Twilight Zone*, a horrific and unfortunate transformative experience, and came out on the other side as something different than it was when first conceived and created by its four directors. The end result of which, however, is not ironic, but simply tragic.

NOTES

1. See Carruther and Popiel's essay on *The Twilight Zone* and war in this volume.
2. See Bill Boles' essay in this volume for an extended analysis of Washburn's play.

WORKS CITED

"The After Hours," *The Twilight Zone*, written by Rod Serling, directed by Douglas Heyes, Image Entertainment, 2013.

Andrews, Nigel. "Golden boy howls at the moon: John Landis was feted in Hollywood for his comedies—then it all changed," *Financial Times* (August 5, 1996): 11.

Beyl, Cameron. "Steven Spielberg's *Night Gallery: Eyes* Episode (1969)" The Directors Series (November 4, 2016): https://directorsseries.net/2016/11/04/steven-spielbergs-night-gallery-eyes-episode-1969/.

Brown, Simon. *Devil's Advocates: Creepshow*. Leighton: Auteur, 2019.

Cursed Films: The Twilight Zone. Directed by Jay Cheel, Shudder, 2019.

"Deaths-Head Revisited," *The Twilight Zone*, written by Rod Serling, directed by Don Medford, Image Entertainment, 2013.

Farber, Steve, and Marc Green. *Outrageous Conduct: Art, Ego and the* Twilight Zone *Case*. New York: Arbor House, 1988.

Hanners, John, and Harry Klaman, "The McDonaldization of Horror: An Interview with George R. Romero." *George A. Romero: Interviews*, edited by Tony William. Jackson: University Press of Mississippi, 2011, pp. 88–100.

Hasan, Mark R. "DVD: *Twilight Zone: The Movie* (1983)" *KQEK.com* (2008) http://www.kqek.com/dvd_reviews/t2u/3272_TZMovie1983.htm (Accessed 1 May 2020).

"It's a Good Life," *The Twilight Zone*, written by Rod Serling, directed by James Sheldon, Image Entertainment, 2013.

"Kick the Can," *The Twilight Zone*, written by George Clayton Johnson, directed by Lamont Johnson, Image Entertainment, 2013.

"A Kind of a Stopwatch," *The Twilight Zone*, written by Rod Serling, directed by James Rich, Image Entertainment, 2013.

Labrecque, Ron. *Special Effects: Disaster at* Twilight Zone: *The Tragedy and the Trial*. New York: Scribner's, 1988.

"Nightmare at 20,000 Feet," *The Twilight Zone*, written by Richard Matheson, by Richard Donner, Image Entertainment, 2013.

"A Quality of Mercy," *The Twilight Zone*, written by Rod Serling, directed by Buzz Kulik, Image Entertainment, 2013.

"Time Enough at Last," *The Twilight Zone*, written by Lynn Venable and Rod Serling, directed by John Brahm, Image Entertainment, 2003.

Twilight Zone: The Movie. Directed by John Landis, Steven Spielberg, Joe Dante, and George Miller, Warner Brothers, 1983.

Washburn, Anne. *The Twilight Zone*. London: Oberon, 2017.

Weintraub, Robert. "A New Dimension of Filmmaking," *Slate.com* (July 26, 2012). https://slate.com/culture/2012/07/the-twilight-zone-tragedy-how-vic-morrows-death-changed-the-way-films-are-made.html.

"Where Is Everybody?" *The Twilight Zone*, written by Rod Serling, directed by Robert Stevens, Image Entertainment, 2013.

Twilight of the Vampires

The Twilight Zone, *Vampires,*
America, and War

SIMON BACON

The Twilight Zone, famous for its tales of the intersection between science fiction, the uncanny, and latterly, the supernatural curiously only featured two episodes centered on the figure of the vampire. In a further curious turn both these episodes set the vampire within the narrative framework of warfare, either during a conflict or in the difficult process of post-war reacclimatization. This essay will look at the episodes in their cultural context and in relation to the wider vampire genre to discuss what they might be saying about the undead bloodsuckers and their relationship to warfare and, as often the case with *The Twilight Zone*, American society itself.

Vampires would seem to be a necessary component, or at least the occasional guest, of any fantasy anthology television show so the surprise here is not that *The Twilight Zone* featured them, but rather how long it took the show to do so. It was not until the second incarnation of the series (1985–89) that they appeared, and then not until episodes 15, "Monster!" and 21, "Red Snow." That said, classic monsters had drifted out of favor and after the last of the Universal monster-mash-up films, *Abbott and Costello Meet Frankenstein* (Kenton, 1948)—a veritable twilight of the monsters—vampires became strictly B-movie fare seen in outings such *Blood is My Heritage* (Strock, 1957), and *The Vampire* (Landres, 1957).[1] Alongside this the original run of *Twilight Zone*, from 1959 to 1964, was far more science-fiction based and vampires did not really become acceptable fare for television series' until Dan Curtis' *Dark Shadows* (1966–71)— alongside this both *The Munsters* (Burns and Hayward) and *The Addams Family* (Levy) did not start until 1964, finishing in 1966, which also made the vampire a far more viewer-friendly item. However, by 1986 when the two episodes aired the vampire was well established in popular culture including anthology series and not just sci-fi-supernatural themed ones. Whilst *Kolchak: The Night Stalker* (Rice, 1975–75) featuring a newspaper reporter investigating supernatural murders, is an obvious example of a series where one would expect vampires to appear, more mainstream series such as *Starsky and Hutch* ("The Vampire"), *McCloud* ("McCloud Meets Dracula"), and *Fantasy Island* ("Vampire/The Lady and the Longhorn") also saw episodes centered on the undead. As well as this there was something of a vampire craze in cinemas starting at the end of the 1970s with a raft of films such as *Love at First Bite* (Dragotti, 1979), *Dracula* (Badham, 1979), *Nosferatu the Vampyre* (Herzog, 1979), *Salem's Lot* (Hooper, 1979), *The Hunger* (Scott, 1983), *Lifeforce* (Hooper, 1984), *Fright Night* (Holland, 1985), *Once Bitten* (Storm, 1985), *Transylvania 6-5000* (De Luca, 1985), *Vamp* (Wenk, 1986) and with four more *The Lost Boys* (Schumacher, 1987), *A Return to Salem's Lot* (Cohen, 1987), *My Best Friend is a Vampire* (Huston, 1987), and *Near Dark* (Bigelow, 1987) the year following *The Twilight Zone* episodes; vampires were literally in the air. The two episodes in question reference many of these films and it is often the nature of these references that add to the meaning of each. As mentioned above the war, or its shadow, features heavily in the episodes especially in relation to contemporaneous America in terms of the, then, ongoing Cold War with the Soviet Union and also the seemingly never ending fallout of the conflict in Vietnam.

The Veteran and the Vietnam War

The first episode is "Monster!" which starts very much in the mold of the teen vampire films that flourished from the middle to the end of the 1980s. Mentioned above are *Fright Night, Once Bitten, Vamp, My Best Friend is a Vampire, The Lost Boys*, and *Fright Night 2* (Wallace, 1988) all of which feature a young boy, often adolescent, living in an American suburb who often has a penchant for the supernatural[2]—usually an avid fan of horror comics and films—who realizes that vampires have moved into, or are already living in, the neighborhood. More importantly in all these it is only the young boy that can "see" the vampire. "Monster!" begins in a very similar manner as we see Toby (Oliver Robbins) playing with his father, Mr. Michaels (Bruce Solomon) who is pretending to be a monster. It transpires that both father and son are horror fanatics and constantly quiz each other over the dates of horror films. Toby is dejected as he has no one to play with since his best friend has moved away just as the summer holidays are beginning. However, his father tells him he has seen someone moving into the house vacated by the family of Toby's friend. With nothing better to do, Toby goes to investigate and it is not long before he meets the new neighbor, the elderly Mr. Bendictson (Ralph Bellemy). As they talk Mr. Bedictson tells Toby he is a vampire. Toby does not believe him saying if he is a real vampire he could not be out in the sunshine.[3] Toby leaves but is intrigued and it is not long before he returns to spy on Mr. Bendictson. Knowing he is being watched the old man lifts up his own car with one hand to clean it, and then sneaks up behind the young boy. Caught out, Toby threatens the vampire with a silver cross and garlic. Once again Mr. Bendictson just smiles and says, "Everything you think you know about vampires is rubbish" and to prove it takes Toby to an Italian restaurant for lunch with food drenched in garlic. Whilst there the old man tells him how he has travelled the world but has now returned home to die. They go back home and later that day Toby goes to Mr. Bendictson's home to look around it whilst the old man is out and discovers a cupboard under the stairs with blood bags in it. Returning to his own home, Toby is not feeling well, indeed his parents do not feel good either and it seems there is something of a "bug" going round the neighborhood. Earlier Toby's father, in an off-hand manner, had joked that it's probably from Asia, "as revenge for Vietnam." They send the young boy to bed, where, very much in keeping with lore, there is a tap at Toby's bedroom window, revealing none other than Mr. Bendictson, but rather than wanting to be invited in he wants to take the young boy out for a walk.[4] He takes Toby to the cemetery and explains to the boy that in the 147 years he's been alive this is the one place in town that has not changed. He shows the boy his gravestone and explains that he is not buried there but became ill just before he turned into a vampire but soon after had to move. Indeed, he can never stay in one place too long as the presence of vampires causes a genetic reaction in humans which makes them mutate and try and kill him. To illustrate this, he pulls Toby close and the little boy starts sneezing. They also talk about monsters, and Mr. Bendictson explains there are far scarier things in the night than him and how at midnight, the mid-point between twilight and dawn when "the night is torn between the two," the real monsters are released. However, the vampire explains that he is tired of moving and has come home to die, but before leaving he gives Toby a "gift" to remember him by in showing him the fireflies that live in the grasses around the cemetery sending a cloud of dancing lights into the night sky.

Toby returns home and due to spending so much time with the vampire is feeling quite ill. Remembering what Mr. Bendictson said, he asks his father when the middle of the night is. His father explains that, because it is summer, the midpoint between twilight and dawn would be a little after 12 o'clock, which is exactly the time that Toby has settled back to sleep on his father's lap. Suddenly the whole family begins to convulse, writhing in pain as they begin to transform. The scene cuts to an outside view of Mr. Bendictson's house, where the old man has left his front door open and sits in his living room awaiting the arrival of the human monsters that are lumbering, zombie-like, to kill him. The following day a crowd has gathered outside the old man's house where the emergency services have arrived to investigate his brutal murder. All the bystanders are horrified that such a thing could happen in their neighborhood, though no one can remember anything about him. All complain of a really bad night's sleep. Even Toby seems to have forgotten his friend, though that night he takes his father to the cemetery to show him something. Once there, the young boy disturbs the grass sending up a cloud of fireflies, which his father thinks is amazing. Just as they are about to leave, Toby sneezes; is there a vampire near or was Mr. Bendictson's gift to the young boy something more than just a light show in the cemetery?

As with many episodes of *The Twilight Zone*, its message seems to talk more of the monstrosity of humanity than a justifiable fear of the unknown, though here that would seem to be a good thing for once, or is it? The episode potentially suggests other interpretations of society's reaction to the vampire, and not just an evolutionary defense system in the war against vampires. Indeed, the theme of war floats just beneath the surface of the show and Toby's fathers mention of Vietnam is a telling one for although the last Americans had fled Saigon in 1975, the shadow of the conflict continued to fall over the United States. Not least in the repatriation of soldiers and veterans who continued to suffer the, often unrecognized, effects of war. In line with this Oliver Stone's *Born on the Fourth of July* came out in 1989 showing the ongoing issues of the veterans and survivors of war. Although the conflict is not mentioned again during the episode, Toby's father's reference to the flu-like symptoms everyone was suffered as being "revenge for Vietnam" gives the vampire itself more significance. The episode makes it clear that Mr. Bendictson[5] is not a modern vampire but more in the mold of the pre-cinema, folkloric kind, the ones that could walk in sunlight like Bram Stoker's Count Dracula. Such folkloric vampires were often associated with warfare as seen in the vampire hysteria that swept Europe at the start of the eighteenth century that was initiated but just such a circumstance. In the ongoing conflicts between the Hapsburgs and the Ottoman Empire swaths of land often exchanged hands, in this instance around Serbia and Bosnia, leaving many of the inhabitants as nomadic, changing locations as the ebbs and flow of conflict moved back and forth around them. The returning of soldiers to their homes and the arrival of strangers was commonplace and it was into this that reports of the vampire Arnold Poale began to surface in 1725, who had himself returned from foreign lands and Petar Blagojević who both reportedly came back from the dead to kill those they knew in life (Barbar 15, 16). This news spread like wildfire across Europe instigating Royal investigations and even the entry of the word "vampire" in the *Oxford English Dictionary* in 1733 (Ruickbie 21–58). Even Stoker's Dracula extols how he was born of conflict and that the blood of the fallen runs through his veins (Stoker 31). Mr. Bendictson then returns to his hometown as a veteran and one who is vastly different from the man that left. His experience of the world has changed him, and although we do not know whether he visited the Far East, or if that is where he has most recently returned from, once home, like many other veterans, it is not long before he realizes he does not fit in there anymore and that his being there causes uncomfortable reactions from those that live there.[6] The monstrosity of the neighborhood then is the aspect of it that instinctively expels intruders and those that are different. Constructing these outsiders, even if they were originally from there themselves, as dangerous others and points of pollution and disease that threaten the "body" of the neighborhood—the notion of contagion is confirmed in the flu-like symptoms caused by the very presence of the vampiric outsider.

The Enemy from the East

The next episode, "Red Snow," retains both the historical moment and the connection to older forms of vampire lore, though shifts the location to the Soviet Union. Here we see KGB officer Colonel Ulyanov (George Dzundza) arresting a dissident who has been in contact with western agents. Later, when meeting his superior, a minister in the Party, Ulyanov recommends sending the dissident to a gulag but his, unnamed, colleague insists on an execution as an example to others. The Minister (Rod Colbin) concurs with execution and then warns Ilyanov about his colleague as he "has connections." As if to prove Ulyanov's friendless state within the Party, the Minister then sends him to a town in Siberia to investigate the mysterious deaths of two party officials there. Unable to refuse, Ulyanov leaves for the small town in the middle of nowhere. Upon arrival he makes himself known to the town's inhabitants in a bar, which also seems to double as the Party headquarters. He warns them the peasant music they are playing is not allowed by Moscow, but after a few moments tense silence, continues that they "better not play it in Moscow!" Signaling that he is maybe more a Russian than a Soviet—the first born of tradition and the other an ideology—a distinction that is important within the episode. The locals relax somewhat but Ulyanov reminds them he is still in charge and orders one of their number, Comrade Polvin (Barry Miller), to make sure all records for the victims are on his desk first thing in the morning.

After looking at the files Ulyanov is intrigued that both of the bodies were drained of blood. He tells Polvin he needs to see the bodies so they leave to go and get Mayor Titov (Vladimir Slomavrosky) who can arrange it, but as they walk into the street they encounter a woman, Valentina (Victoria Tennant) that looks strangely familiar to Ulyanov. As he racks his memory he realizes she looks just like a woman exiled by Stalin fifty years previously, but she looks far too young to be the same woman. Before Ulyanov can question the woman further, Polvin interjects that this Valentina is a descendent of the one Ulyanov remembers. The men join the Mayor at an abandoned church outside of town to look at one of the bodies that is still encased in ice. As they do so the sound of wolves howling outside gets nearer and it sounds like one of them is being attacked. Ulyanov goes outside to investigate and discovers Valentina over the body of a slain wolf, drinking its blood. However, before the Party official can react, he is knocked unconscious. Upon waking he demands to go back to the church where there are now many empty coffins and as he looks at them Valentina and Polvin appear from the shadows. It transpires that, because the town cannot rely on the Party for protection, they turned to vampires and allowed them to live in the town in return for their protection from criminals and wild animals. This has attracted many vampires to the region, though here they are called wurdulaki. Wurdalacs (or wurdulak, or verdilak) are vampires from the Slavic tradition (Garza 2014)—in Slavic vălkolak, volkodlak, volkolak, vukodlak, wurdulak, in Romanian *Vârcolac* and in Greek *Vrykolakas* some of which can also apply to werewolves—though vampires are more commonly called upir in Russia. The more strict Russian appropriation of the word came in Alexander Pushkin's poem called "Wurdulac" from 1836 in his *Songs of the Western Slavs* cycle. Alexie Tolstoy's *The Family of the Vourdalak* (1839), though written about Serbian vampires, gave the Russian vampire the characteristic of drinking the blood of its loved ones to convert its entire family. And indeed, something of this spills over into "Red Snow" where the vampires are part of the community, and actually seem to be more one big family than two separate species. More so, this purposely links the vampires not just to traditional Russia and its people but more specifically to a Russia before the Soviet Union.

Back in the church Valentina and Polvin argue over whether to kill Ulyanov or not when the Colonel grabs the Mayor and runs out of the building. They are attacked by wolves and Titov is killed. Ulyanov surrenders to the vampires and Valentina decides that maybe he can help them as well as stop any unwanted suspicion from central command in Moscow.

The scene then cuts to the office of the Minister that sent Ulyanov to Siberia and the Colonel has submitted his report blaming Titov for murdering the two officials. Happy with the results the Minister congratulates Ulyanov and walks past him out of the office. Ulyanov looks at his superior's back as he passes and smiles, revealing two large fangs.

The ending is interesting on many levels. Throughout the story Ulyanov is portrayed as vaguely sympathetic character, at least in his dealings with fellow Russians—when searching the dissident at the start of the episode he confiscates a letter to the man's mother which Ulyanov later posts for him, and there was also the scene regarding peasant music mentioned earlier. In this sense he is cast as more a servant of Russia than the Soviet Union, even though he works for the KGB. His being made a vampire then reinforces the idea that the wurdulac are somehow on some level the true Russians and almost an evolutionary defense against the monster of communism. Not that Russia was any less driven by colonial endeavor when an Imperial regime rather than being a Communist one,[7] but in the 1980s it seems to be cast more in the light of "my enemy's enemy is my friend." Indeed, the episode's stance on communism is interesting and worth looking at in the light of the wider vampire genre.

During the years of the Cold War Russia was seen as America's "Great Satan" (Donald 2014) and American President Ronald Reagan called the Soviet Union the "evil empire" in 1983 (Voices of Democracy) which would seem the perfect set-up to depict it as a nation of vampires, yet rarely this did not happen, at least not before the "Red Snow" episode—Dan Simmons was one of the first to say this about Communism, though he was speaking about the regime in Romania under Nicolae Ceaușescu in his 1992 novel *Children of the Night*. In fact only a few films in the west had directly mentioned the Communist regime in Russia or Eastern Europe; *Dracula pére et fils* (Molinaro, 1976), *Zoltan, Hound of Dracula* (a.k.a. *Dracula's Dog*; Band, 1977), and *Love at First Bite* (Dragoti, 1979)—oddly *Transylvania-6500* (De Luca, 1985) though largely meant to be taking place in contemporaneous Romania makes no reference to Communism in its plot. All of the films focus on Romania under communist rule rather than Russia and involve the vampire fleeing from their homeland.

Dracula pére et fils is the least relevant here as the vampires flee Romania for London and Paris, though interestingly they are forced from their home by a cross made from a hammer and sickle. Zoltan would seem an odd one to include here but curiously the plot is driven by family ties, which is very in keeping with Tolstoy's idea of the wurdalak. Communist troops are setting off explosive charges in the environs of the Dracula family castle. In doing so they disturb the graves of an old family retainer and the family pet; a hell-hound known as Zoltan.[8] The dog is compelled to find its nearest surviving family—descendants of Count Dracula—and so travels to America to find Michael Drake and turn him into a Master vampire. Whilst not specifically anti–Soviet the dog does then embody a kind of ideological infection from the East once he is in America.

Something similar occurs in *Love at First Bite,* but there is far more criticism of the Soviet Union than in the other films. Here it is the People's Cooperative (the Soviet version of the angry mob) that pushes Dracula (George Hamilton) from his castle with the Commissare (a woman Dracula continually mistakes for a man) telling him "Either you spend the rest of your life in an efficiency apartment with seven dissidents and one toilet, or you gather your aristocratic shit together and split!" This is far more a popular vision of Soviet Russia than it is of a Romania under Ceaușescu and it sees the Old-World vampire fleeing his homeland, which without him will be as exciting as "Bucharest on a Monday night." Curiously, whilst in Romania Dracula is both older and "newer" than the communist environment around him, being an Old-World aristocrat but also decadently Western. However, once in New York he is decidedly foreign and an outsider. Whilst the film casts a rather jaundiced and "traditionalist" eye over what it sees as the New World embodied by New York liberalism where women prefer sex rather than commitment and the men are so wracked with self-doubt they will all be "homosexual by the 21st century," it is still a place where Dracula manifests a dangerous, aggressive, ideology. One could even argue that the New York men in the film embody the "broken male bodies" post the Vietnam war as described by Susan Jeffords (37–8, 118) that are no match for the violence and aggression seen in the undefeated masculinity from the East. Dracula here then is a danger to the future of America itself (Bacon 60–1), and one which is given supporting evidence as he flies away with his American bride that he as "stolen" from her American fiancé; he is quite literally stealing the future of America itself.

Undead Traumas of War

These films rather complicate the ending of both *The Twilight Zone* episodes. For "Red Snow" it shows that Communism and vampirism do not mix. Indeed, one could argue that vampirism is the more natural manifestation of capitalism, as argued by Karl Marx himself, and latterly Franco Moretti, quoting Marx (91). In that sense it is the inherent Westernism of the vampire that makes it anathema to Soviet Russia—maybe also explaining why post-communism vampires are far more prolific in Russian literature and film[9]—making its flight to the eastern side of the Iron curtain almost inevitable. Red Snow, seemingly, goes against that, at least initially. The wurdalacs seem to want to only protect themselves and their vampiric family. They seem at home in the almost perennial darkness of the Siberian wastelands—not unlike the vampires in *30 Days of Night* (Slade, 2007)—though it is not made clear whether Tolstoy's vampires are killed by sunlight or just happier when it is dark—sunlight was never fatal to vampires until Murnau's *Nosferatu* as mentioned earlier. However, sending Ulyanov back to Moscow is a curious turn. Although it does prevent further investigation and interest from the central Party headquarters, the now vampiric Colonel seems keen to share his newfound belief in traditional Russian family values rather than keep it to himself. Even the lighter climes of Moscow do not deter him. This opens up the possibility seen in both *Zoltan* and *Love at First Bite* where the wurdulac, once gaining safety from their former Soviet oppressors wanting to reunite with family descendants further afield. And the wurdulac do not seem to cause the same kind of allergic reaction in humans in their vicinity leaving the "soft bodies" of America open to their advances. In a curious way this sees the vampire as equally a victim of war, in many senses suffering at the hands of the traumas of conflict and resultantly being made a stranger in their own homes, as well as an expression of that war, where they reenact its violence and trauma on those they later encounter; they literally infect their victims with "war."

This brings us back to "Monsters!" which could then be read in the light of *Love at First Bite*. The film, as with the "Monsters!" episode is arguably a narrative underpinned by war; both the after effects and the ongoing conflict of Vietnam and the Cold War respectively. Mr. Bendictson, the veteran, returns home to his hometown in America that is now full of the "soft bodies" of the defeated masculinity since Vietnam, yet another revenge of the lost war. Their inherent softness revealed in their inability to even contain the monstrosity within them further exampling their porosity and penetrability by outside forces. The vampire then romances the most vulnerable part of this broken community, its youth, in the figure of Toby. As with Count Dracula, Mr. Bendictson visits his intended at his bedroom window, leading him into a world of darkness and revealing the life that rises from the cemetery. At stories end the vampire has departed but Toby sneezes, as though he too might now be infected (his father does not sneeze), destined to come down with the same illness that Mr. Bendictson described as leading to his new, undead, existence. Toby has now been infected with the trauma and violence of war, fated now to spread it within the suburban heart of America itself.[10]

At first glance then these two episodes would seem to offer a sympathetic view of the vampire, indeed one that was increasingly popular from the late 1970s with the huge popularity of Anne Rice's novels *The Vampire Chronicles* (1976–2018). In "Monster!" they are more afraid of us than we are of them and in "Red Snow" they provide the means of defeating the red menace from within. However, on further reflection and contextualization they reveal themselves to be rather more sinister than at first thought. That once they, and the infection of war they embody, has been invited in there is no way to escape the twilight zone of its unending trauma and undead afterlife.

Notes

1. Alongside this, Richard Matheson's influential novel, *I Am Legend* (1954), and subsequent film, *Last Man on Earth* (Ragona and Salkow, 1964) took the classic figure of the vampire in very different directions.

2. Interestingly in earlier vampire films where women are seen to "invite" the vampire in to their home, town, nation—*Dracula's Daughter* (Hillyer, 1936) and *Son of Dracula* (Siodmak, 1943)—they are blamed for having a "morbid" obsession, fascination with the occult.

3. Count Dracula and vampires before F.W. Murnau's *Nosferatu* (1922) could walk in the daytime without spontaneously combusting.

4. The period within which the episode was made suggests no hint of pedophilia in the relationship between the old man and young boy.

5. The vampire's name is of interest here as Bendictson can be translated at "son of a blessing" and a "benediction" is a blessing itself. Whether this speaks of the "blessing" of the vampire in the show is questionable, though it certainly forced Mr. Bendictson to leave the "monstrosity" of the suburbs when he was much younger. This reading is less convincing if one interprets the giving of the vampiric "gift" as one that is inherently abusive and traumatic (see Claudia in *Interview with the Vampire* [Rice, 1976, and Jordan, 1994] for example).

6. For descriptions of the difficulties suffered by Vietnam veterans returning home see Scurfield 61–84, and Scott 29–49.

7. For pre-revolutionary Russia and Imperialism see Plokhy.

8. Zoltan is a Doberman pincher which was the hell-hound representative of choice in the 1980s.

9. *Day Watch* (Bekmambetov, 2004), *Day Watch* (Bekmambetov, 2006), *Guardians of the Night* (Velyvis, 2016), and *Ghouls* (Ginzberg, 2017) being a few examples.

10. Something of this fear is realized in films such as *The Day After* (Meyer, 1983), and *Testament* (Littman, 1983) where the Soviet Union drops nuclear weapons on towns in America. Though retrospectively even more clearly seen in the communist infiltration of small-town USA in *Stranger Things* (The Duffer Brothers, 2016–present) which is based on a nostalgic look at 1980s America.

Works Cited

Bacon, Simon. *Dracula as Absolute Other: The Troubling and Distracting Specter of Stoker's Vampire on Screen*. Jefferson, NC: McFarland, 2019.

Barbar, Paul. *Vampires, Burial, and Death: Folklore and Reality*. New Haven: Yale University Press, 2010.

Donald, Ralph. "America's 'Great Satan' Then and Now." *American Studies Today*. Online. 20 February 2014. http://www.americansc.org.uk/Online/Great_Satan.htm. Accessed 11 July 2017.

Garza, Thomas J. *Slavic Blood: The Vampire in Russian and Eastern European Cultures*. San Diego: Cognella Academic Publishing, 2014.

Jeffords, Susan. *Hard Bodies: Hollywood Masculinity in the Reagan Era*. New Brunswick, NJ: Rutgers University Press, 1993.

"McCloud Meets Dracula," *McCloud*, written by Glen A. Larson, directed by Bruce Kessler, Universal Television, 1977.

"Monsters!" *The Twilight Zone*, written by Robert Crais, directed by B.W.L. Norton, CBS, 1986.

Moretti, Franco, *Signs Taken for Wonders: Essays in the Sociology of Forms*, trans. Susan Fischer, David Forgacs and David Miller. New York: Verso, 1988.

Plokhy, Serhii. *Lost Kingdom: The Quest for Empire and the Making of the Russian Nation*. New York: Basic Books, 2017.

Reagan, Ronald. "'EVIL EMPIRE SPEECH' (8 MARCH 1983)." Voices of Democracy: The U.S. Oratory Project. N.d. http://voicesofdemocracy.umd.edu/reagan-evil-empire-speech-text/. Accessed 14 July 2017.

"Red Snow," *The Twilight Zone*, written by Michael Cassutt, directed by Jeannot Szwarc, CBS, 1986.

Ruickbie, Leo. "Memento (non)mori: Memory, Discourse and Transmission during the Eighteenth-Century Vampire Epidemic and After." *Undead Memory: Vampires and Human Memory in Popular Culture*, edited by Simon Bacon and Katarzyna Bronk. Berlin: Peter Lang, 2014, pp. 21–57.

Scott, Wilbur J. *Vietnam Veterans Since the War: The Politics of PTSD, Agent Orange, and the National Memorial*. Norman: University of Oklahoma Press, 1993.

Scurfield, Raymond Monsour. *A Vietnam Trilogy: Veterans and Post Traumatic Stress 1968, 1989, 2000*. New York: Algora Publishing, 2004.

Simmons, Dan. *Children of the Night* [1992]. New York: Griffin, 2012.

Stoker, Bram. *Dracula* [1897]. New York: Signet Classics, 1996.

Tolstoy, Fodor Alexis. *Vampires: Stories of the Supernatural (The Vampire; The Family of a Vourdalak; The Reunion after Three Hundred Years; Amena)*. Stroud: Hawthorn Books, 1973.

"The Vampire," *Starsky and Hutch*, written by William Blinn, directed by Bob Kelljan, Mill Creek Entertainment, 2014.

"Vampire/The Lady and the Longhorn," *Fantasy Island*, written by Daniel B. Ullman, directed by Arnold Laven, Shout! Factory, 2012.

If You Dream It, They Will Film It

Paul Chitlik

In 1985, my writing partner at the time, Jeremy Bertrand Finch, and I had just come off working on an intense, but amazingly bad "reality" series where we each wrote one criminal or civil trial re-enactment per day. The show was cancelled (thankfully), after an initial run of sixty-five episodes in thirteen weeks, and so we were looking for work. Through a friend of Jeremy's who was working on Courtney Cox's first show on NBC, *Misfits of Science* (1985–1986), we got a pitch on the Universal lot with the executive producer of that show and his staff.

The pitch did not go well. We had great stories, according to the staff, though the executive producer spent most of the time reading a magazine, so he just nodded when Don Todd, a producer on the show who later worked on *Ugly Betty* (2006–2007), *Sleepy Hollow* (2014–2105), and *This Is Us* (2016–2017), said, "Great stories, but not for us. You should pitch them to *The* new *Twilight Zone.*"

Though we were disappointed that our first network show pitch had gone so poorly, we decided to see if we could get into *The TZ* offices to pitch. In those days, you could get onto a studio lot by just saying you were going to visit somebody working on a show, so we lied our way onto the CBS Studio City lot in the San Fernando Valley of Los Angeles where, we had found out, *The* new *Twilight Zone*'s offices were located. The series had been brought back to network television by CBS and was looking for stories.

We strolled into the offices and found Harlan Ellison, the science-fiction writer par excellence, lounging in the reception area. We chatted with him for a while and discovered that, unusual for its time, *TTZ* was going to be helping writers prepare to pitch for their show at a Writers Guild of America picnic the following weekend. We said we'd see him there.

We weren't, however, WGA members yet as the program we first worked on was non-union. But that didn't stop us from finding out where the picnic was, asking our girlfriends to come with us, and showing up at the site bright and early. We listened to what *The* new *Twilight Zone* was looking for, made contact with some of the writers on the staff, and were invited to set up an appointment to pitch.

Great. What to pitch? Here's where dreams come in. We worked up a bunch of what we thought were *TTZ* stories, including one which had come to me in a dream about a young man who met a much, much older woman on the Venice Beach boardwalk who he wished were younger so they could have a romantic relationship. That suggested a way to make the woman keep her soul but look much younger, which turned into a story about an aging model who used "aqua vita" (think fountain of youth in bottled water) to stay young looking so as not to age out of her job. Don't ask how that evolved, that's just the way things sometimes work.

We prepared the pitch, but I came down with a very nasty case of the flu, which included laryngitis, so we had to send Jeremy in to pitch on his own. They bought the idea in the room, though Jeremy said he wasn't exactly sure what they said, when he reported it to me on the phone, after he heard the words, "We'll buy that."

Our new agent negotiated the contract, and we set to work on the story, now titled "Aqua Vita." We conceived it as a metaphor for cocaine: once you drank the water, you were hooked. You had to have it to maintain your youthful looks, and the water deliveryman gave you the first bottle free, but the ones after that were costly. And if you stopped drinking it, you would age quickly beyond your years. Okay, fine. But the season was over by the time we turned in the story, and they weren't sure of a pick-up for the fall, so they put the story on hold.

By the time they got back to us it was the summer of 1986, and we were looking for work in sitcoms. We got a pitch on a Monday for an episode of *Brothers* (1986), the Showtime comedy featuring a gay man who came out on his wedding day to his very straight brothers. It was a great pitch, with another buy in the room, and we spent the day on the Paramount lot beating out the story with the executive producer and his staff. When I got home, there was a message on my machine (we had answering machines in those days) telling me *TTZ* wanted a first draft of the script by Friday. The *Brothers* script was also due by Friday. So, we put our heads down and wrote. You don't say no when you're just starting out.

TTZ messengered over the revised story, and we were surprised to find out that the model had turned into a television news anchor struggling to hang onto her job. The revisions had been made by George R.R. Martin, whom we didn't know at the time. But they were damn good revisions, and we didn't object. We turned in both scripts by deadline and waited.

Brothers called to say they wanted us on staff. We accepted. *TTZ* called to say they wanted a second draft and could we come in for notes?

That notes session was one of the strangest and most intimidating notes sessions of my career. First of all, there were eleven people in the meeting. The late Phil DeGuerre was in nominal charge, though he kept ducking out for short breaks of an undisclosed nature. One of the others was not supposed to contribute in a notes meeting due to Guild rules (he was a staff writer), so he had to go out into the hall when he had something to say, usually with George, who then would come back into the room and say he "just got an inspiration" and would then give us the note. But the room was chaos. We got eleven different opinions, and Phil did not tell us which ones to take. At the end of the meeting, he threw our script into the trash and said, "Next."

Not the best way to end our first network notes meeting. In the car, we just sat and looked at each other for a couple of minutes trying to absorb what just had happened. Then we asked ourselves which notes to follow and decided to use just the ones we thought helped the story. Turned out to be one of our favorite scripts and a touching love story.

Some weeks later, we took some time off from *Brothers* to watch the filming of "Aqua Vita." They filmed the episode on the same lot where we had first pitched the story, and they spent heavily on it, reportedly a million dollars for the half hour, which was a fortune at the time. While on set, we were approached by one of the actors, Chris McDonald (later Thelma's husband in *Thelma & Louise* [1991], among other things), who wanted to talk with us about how to play his role as the water delivery man. As freelance writers, we had no say on set, and so we referred him to the director, though we loved his take. All in all, we were wowed by the production detail and looked forward to seeing the finished product in the fall. Then we went back to *Brothers*, though we did later pitch another idea to Phil et al. that came out of a conversation Jeremy and I had over lunch. They bought it, but it was never made, because CBS cancelled the show after that season.

The story in "Aqua Vita" comes to a crisis point when the protagonist, who has been hiding her addiction, accidentally spills a glass of it and tries desperately to mop it up so she can reverse her sudden aging. Her husband discovers her, and she explains that she has to drink it or she'll look like an old hag. We then see him pour some of the water into a glass, and we are left to wonder if she drinks it. Then there's a final scene in a park.

One thing that has always bothered us about the way the episode was edited was that scene. We had put a very specific note in the script so that the reveal would be, after seeing a young couple in a wide shot—intimating that her husband had also taken the water and become young—we would see an aged couple on a park bench and learn that he had taken the water and then stopped so that he could age like her. Touching love story, right? But instead of starting the scene with a voiceover of the couple talking, seeing the younger couple in wide, they started close on the older couple, undercutting the full effect of the *TTZ* twist at the end. Still, it was a beautifully shot episode.

We lasted one season on *Brothers* before the executive producer who had brought us on got into a pissing match with the boss, and we were not picked up by the new EP. Then, in the spring of 1987, I read that CBS and MGM were going to bring *The* new *Twilight Zone* back to complete a package for syndication. They were going to shoot thirty more episodes in Canada. Our agent knew nothing about it, but I found out who the executive producer was (Mark Shelmerdine) and called him up out of the blue. He asked what episode we had written. When we told him "Aqua Vita," he said it was one of the only ones from CBS's latest that he thought had a complete story. We met with him, and before long we became story editors on the new show, along with J. Michael Straczynski, who had just come off *Captain Power and the Soldiers of the Future* (1987–1988), a CGI loaded sci-fi series. Joe later went on to create *Babylon 5* (1993–1998).

Having been the executive story editor on my first show, and a staff writer on *Brothers*, I wanted to be upped to producer on *The* new *Twilight Zone*, but, because of Canadian content rules (the show was to be shot in Canada where there were cheap crews, cheap actors, and tax incentives), none of us could have a producer title; however, we did what supervising producers do on most shows: hear pitches, help decide which ones to buy, rewrite freelance episodes, and suggest casting. We weren't happy with the title of story editor, but we were really excited about the opportunity to work on the iconic show.

Thus, began one of the most creative and free-thinking periods of my writing life. Shelmerdine was not a writer, so it was up to us to come up with a new bible for the show so that we had a format we could all agree upon and which we could share with prospective writers. We were planning to have at least half of the episodes written by freelancers. So Straczynski came up with some ideas for the bible, and we came up with others. We discussed back and forth until we came to agreement, along with Shelmerdine, what would become the guiding precepts for the show: get to the magic early, no "I'm a ghost/robot/alien but didn't know it stories," ordinary people in extraordinary situations, and try to say something meaningful in each little morality play.

Shelmerdine had rented offices on Hollywood Boulevard, right in the middle of crazy town. At the time, it wasn't yet full of tourists, but, as we used to say, there was one of everything on Hollywood Boulevard. Lots of story inspiration in the streets.

Shelmerdine asked us what we wanted in our office. Our requirements were simple: two computers that could be linked up (still a new thing in Hollywood), desks facing each other, and two couches. Ever since I had lived in Spain, I liked to have a siesta after lunch, and while working at *Brothers*, Jeremy picked up the habit, too. Besides, all pitches were heard in our office, so with Shelmerdine, Straczynski, Jeremy, and me, we needed the seating area, especially when teams came in to pitch.

Every writer in Hollywood wanted to pitch the show or submit a *TTZ* script they had written on their own. Though we shared the bible with freelancers before they came in to tell us their ideas, we often heard stories we had specifically asked not to hear. Jeremy and I called in writers we knew, including D.C. Fontana (from the original *Star Trek* [1966–1969]), Al Brenner (*McMillan & Wife* [1972]), and Lynn Barker (of the previous season of *TTZ* [1985]); and Straczynski called in writers he knew, while agents called us directly and pitched their writers over the phone. We even got a spec script (meaning he had written it without being commissioned to write it) from Frank Darabont (*The Shawshank Redemption* [1994], *The Green Mile* [1999]), with whom I'd worked on his first film (*The Woman in the Room* [1984]). We saw everyone except one writer who would not come in to pitch to us—Harlan Ellison. He insisted we come over to his house for dinner instead.

We brought Chinese takeout to his house, decorated in gargoyle re-creations of, I believe, members of the Nixon cabinet, just off Beverly Glen in Los Angeles. Harlan and his wife, Susan Toth, greeted us warmly, and we were let into their little kingdom. There were sci-fi *tchotchkes* everywhere, including a cove where a 3D *Star Trek* chess game was set up. Before dinner, we played a little snooker pool in his den, which had an embossed copper ceiling. Now, Jeremy is a tall man, and he held his cue up high while eyeing a shot, and put a dimple into the ceiling, which did not endear him to Harlan. But we continued on and eventually convinced him to let us look into using one of his *TTZ* scripts that had been bought by CBS. He wasn't going to write a new one for us. There was one he really wanted us to use, but it was too grim. We did, however, shoot one that turned out fine, "Crazy as a Soup Sandwich" (1989).

Eventually, we heard pitches from about seventy-five freelance writers, probably a record for one season on one show. We would pitch Shelmerdine our own story ideas, and he would generally say yes, though sometimes with minor modifications. The only other person we would get notes from was the executive at MGM, Mark Massari. His notes were also generally minor, though we did have one or two disagreements that were easily resolved. Mark went on to create *Real Stories of the Highway Patrol* (1996), calling me in after their first season to be their coordinating producer, supervising all their re-enactment stories (265 of them!).

Back to the *Zone*. Where did our original ideas come from? Again, dreams.

I dreamt that cave paintings of hunters and animals came off the walls at night and morphed into living and breathing beings. That became "The Hunters" (1988). I dreamt that a political prisoner could transport himself out of a prison cell by thinking hard enough. That became "Room 2426" (1989). I dreamt that a man pointed at a deer and it froze in its tracks. That became "Stranger in Possum Meadows" (1989). Jeremy dreamt that a mysterious steamer trunk that could grant wishes was left in a cheap motel room. That became "The Trunk" (1988). I thought of my father, the man that God could not kill even though he was a diabetic, had suffered many mini-strokes, and had congestive heart failure. I thought, "what if," which was the question we asked our outside writers to start thinking about, "What if he had every organ replaced by a mechanical one, even his brain? Would he still be human?" That became "Father and Son Game" (1989), an episode that was nominated for a Writers Guild Award that season.

Our workdays were intense. We made our own schedule, usually working from 10 a.m. to 7 p.m. During this time, I became engaged and started planning the wedding with my first wife. Actually, she and her mother did most of the planning, as I was consumed with working on the show. Like most grooms to be, all I did was taste cake and approve of color schemes and venues. We got married during the writing season and postponed our honeymoon until the following December, because I couldn't take the time off.

But all was not puppy dogs and rainbows on the show. For one, Straczynski never let us forget that we had been sitcom writers and not true sci-fi writers like he was. Of course, that missed the point. *The Twilight Zone* was all about "what if" situations, something that sitcom writers work with every day. And who's to say that you can't write across genres? Rod Serling certainly did. Straczynski insisted that we not meddle with his stories, and we agreed, so long as he didn't meddle with ours. So there was no rewriting by anyone other than us on our scripts until filming began at around the same time that the WGA strike did. In the end, some episodes had some minor rewrites, usually for economy, done in Canada by unknown parties, though we suspected that some scripts were touched up by a scab writer who shall go nameless.

Once the strike was over, and the first option of our contract came up, the scripts for the season were virtually completed, so we left the show; and Shelmerdine hired us to develop a British sitcom he had optioned for U.S.

production. Straczynski went off to work on *Jake and the Fatman* (1987–1992), and we continued in the sitcom world with *Small Wonder* (1988–1989), *Who's the Boss?* (1987), *Perfect Strangers* (1990), and *Amen* (1987). It always bugged Straczynski that one of our episodes and one of the freelance episodes were the only ones of that *TTZ* season to be nominated for WGA Awards, but he soon got over that.

I have gone on to work on other shows as a writer, coordinating producer, field producer, and director, including a science fiction movie (the first found-footage movie) for television called *Alien Abduction* (1998) for the now defunct network, UPN. And though I have written three novels and a dozen films since then, including a science-fiction novel about cloning almost thirty years ago, I have yet to have the kind of creative stimulation and freedom as I had that season on *The* new *Twilight Zone*.

My "If She Dies" Diary

A Writer's Personal Journey
into The Twilight Zone

DAVID BENNETT CARREN

On a bright, sunny day in February of 1984, I walked from my house in Venice, California, to the beach. I was a lonely 32-year-old freelance screenwriter whose most notable credit was an episode of *Buck Rogers in the 25th Century* (1979–1981), and I was frustrated, confused and a bit depressed. The opportunities available for me at that time, upcoming pitch sessions with *Hart to Hart* (1979–1984) and *The A Team* (1983–1987), simply did not excite me. I knew that I was fortunate to have any avenue to pursue my chosen profession but these projects simply did not touch my soul. Despite credits in instant trivia questions like *Beyond Westworld* (the first television project based on the *Westworld* feature film that aired only three episodes in 1979), or major hits like *Knightrider* (1982–1986) or cartoon series such as *GI Joe* (1983–1986), and even comic books (I had just written a story for *Alien Worlds*), I still considered myself an artist.

I was also a realist; I needed to make a living at my craft, and, even though this was still relatively early in my career, I had already learned that the vast majority of my future credits were destined to be for commercial assignments offering little or no personal expression. But that day, Washington's Birthday, would gift me with one of my most satisfying creative endeavors, one that would remind me why I became a writer in the first place. I would record as much in my diary....

MONDAY, FEBRUARY 20, 1984: Was depressed and lonely. What else is new? But it was a truly gorgeous day, and I enjoyed the walk anyway. On the way back, saw a bed for sale at a church rummage sale. It made me cry. The next thing I knew I had a beautiful story that had to be written—a rarity. I do have something in me—even if it does come out of pain.

The bed I had seen in the front yard of that church was small and child-sized; it had driven me to tears because a sudden, strong feeling had overcome me; a conviction that the last child to sleep in that bed had died in it. Now this was probably not true at all, just call it an inspiration, a sensation, an idea. Whatever it was, it drove me to my home office to write the story that became "If She Dies," the title of which was inspired by the child's prayer, "If I die before I wake, I pray the Lord my soul to take." The process of creating the story over the next few days could only be described as a pure joy....

TUESDAY, FEBRUARY 21, 1984: Worked on "If She Dies," which will be a comic book, I hope. It went very well. Wrote it with almost ridiculous ease. But that was because it was one of those rare times I had the whole story.

I had already written a couple of pieces for Bruce Jones, the creator and editor of two very adult graphic anthologies, *Alien Worlds* (1982–1984) and *Twisted Tales* (1982–1984). My "If She Dies" was a ghost story and highly visual; which meant it could work for Bruce. Which quickly proved true.

TUESDAY, FEBRUARY 21, 1984: I wrote all day. "If She Dies" is the easiest job I've had in I can't remember when. The rewrite flowed as gently as the story line. Even the proofing and revisions were painless. Can't remember when writing was this pleasant.

In this case, I was writing a comic script in which every angle or shot, every caption or sound effect, as well as the characters' dialogue, must be delineated in each panel. It's a wonderful format in which a writer plays director, sound designer, and storyboard artist all at once. When it's married with a story like "If She Dies," the process can be beyond satisfying.

Writing is work, writing is hard, but sometimes—when it comes directly from the heart, the soul, the whatever—it can be almost transcendent.

Here is the plot of the script I wrote those two days in the February of 1984:

A desperate and distraught Paul Molano is leaving the hospital after visiting his comatose daughter who was seriously injured in the car wreck that killed his wife. Defeated, bereft and aggrieved; he knows his child is not long for this world. However, as Paul walks down a street, he looks through the window of an antique shop and sees a child's bed. For no reason he can understand, he starts weeping uncontrollably. Driven by these feelings, he enters the store to learn the bed was stored for many years in the basement of an orphanage, Saint Amelia's, which has been torn down recently. Now it's available for sale. Even though he knows the decision makes no discernable sense, Paul impulsively buys the bed and has it delivered to his home.

That night, the pale, white ghost of a child, a little girl named Sarah Brannigan, comes to him, looking frantically for "Toby" who she can't sleep without. When Paul has no idea where Toby is, the phantasm asks him to escort her back to bed. Paul takes her hand, which startles him, it's cold as ice, and guides her to the haunted bed in another room, where he tucks her in and kisses her good night. Then she vanishes into thin air.

Understandably intrigued, Paul hunts down the only person who can reveal to him the history of the bed—an aged nun living in a retirement home. Sister Carmella tells him that Toby was Sarah's stuffed teddy bear, which the nun has kept as a memento of the girl, an orphan who died in a fire at Saint Amelia's. As young Sarah lay in the bed fading away, the nun and the child prayed together. "Now I lay me down to sleep, I pray my Lord my soul to keep. If I die before I wake, I pray the Lord my soul to take."

Sister Carmella tells Paul that Sarah went to sleep that night and never woke up. The other children would have nothing to do with the bed after that so it was placed in the orphanage's basement. Decades later, Saint Amelia's was torn down, and the bed ended up in that antique shop.

Carmella offers Paul the stuffed teddy bear Toby. If Sarah's ghost returns to him tonight, seeking Toby once again, it's only right she have him back.

Paul's reaction to this is a bitter one. What kind of God abandons the soul of an innocent child in a forsaken bed for so many years? Why didn't He take her spirit to Heaven as the Sister so fervently wished and prayed?

Carmella smiles and says, "Perhaps the Lord knew she had another destiny ahead of her."

Taking the hint, Paul checks his dying daughter out of the hospital, transports her home, and places her in the bed. He spends the night beside Kathy, watching her sleep, holding Toby, hoping for he knows not what.

Finally the morning comes, and his daughter is motionless in the bed, seemingly dead. Paul crosses to a window, holding Toby, telling himself he dreamed it all. He never talked to Sarah, there are no ghosts, and there is no God.

Then he hears his daughter call to him. "Daddy? Can I have Toby back?"

The final panel of the graphic story depicts Paul seated on the bed, his arm around Kathy as she holds Toby with the caption "Is this my daughter or is it Sarah? I do not care. She died before she woke; the Lord did not her soul take. He gave her to me."

I mailed the script to Bruce Jones the next day, and he offered a contract to buy it within the week. There were no notes, which is highly unusual. There are always notes.

"If She Dies" was published in the last edition of *Twisted Tales*, #10, December 1984. The art was by Attillio Micheluzzi, coloring by Ron Courtney. And that should have been that. Comic books, or graphic novels as they are often currently called, usually possess the shelf life of a magazine or even a newspaper. However, the story had an unexpected and quite satisfying future that would present it to a much larger audience.

That fall, a good friend of mine, Alan Brennert, had been hired as the executive story consultant of *The Twilight Zone*, the first reincarnation of the original series, which would eventually air on CBS from 1985 to 1989. Now this was when television shows had small staffs, just a story editor or a consultant and two or three producers, and freelancers wrote the great majority of the episodes produced. Today a series will have a dozen producer writers who will script all the episodes themselves, and it's as difficult to secure a freelance television assignment, as it is to sell an original feature screenplay.

But this was not the case on Saturday, December 8, 1984, when I met Alan over lunch and pitched him some ideas, including "If She Dies." He liked what I had to offer and set a meeting for me with the show's producers on a cold, windy....

WEDNESDAY, DECEMBER 12, 1984: I'm in shock. Very tense, hands actually shaking went to CBS Fox to pitch to Phil DeGuere, Jim Crocker, and Alan Brennert. To my complete astonishment sold two stories, the nuclear war comedy and "If She Dies." The sale of "If She Dies" blew me away. Walked out of there in a daze ... a dream come true.

First off, even though this was a time when television series accepted freelance submissions, booking a legitimate pitch where someone is in the room with the immediate power to buy a story was not an everyday occurrence. Second, I had never sold an idea as personal and precious to me as "If She Dies," and the moment felt momentous; well beyond any ordinary professional considerations. I knew that, if I could do any justice to the teleplay, this would be a powerful creative experience.

However, there were challenges ahead, and, before I launch into what they were, I need to bring Aristotle and Joseph Campbell into this. If it wasn't for the advice and creative support of a Greek philosopher, dead for over two millennia, and a college professor, who died in 1987, I could not have pulled off the adaptation of "If She Dies" from its comic book origins to the teleplay. A short review of these great men's work is advisable.

The vast majority of the narrative fiction produced, published, or aired today employ the basic Aristotelian tenants of drama. As he defined in his *Poetics* in 335 BC, a properly developed story has a clearly established protagonist or hero who must face a strong antagonist whose singular aim is to block the protagonist in his mission or journey. This is the mythic hero's journey, with which Aristotle, living in a world where myth defined almost all of his day's philosophy yet alone all of the period's religions, was deeply familiar.

Joseph Campbell took these concepts further in his work, defining or clarifying that the protagonist has a want that drives them through the plot on a quest or a mission, usually after an inciting incident changes their world for the worse. As the protagonist pursues their goals, they acquire important allies; hopefully a father figure or mentor, and they encounter obstacles, reverses, and surprises, many of them created by a strong antagonist or villain, or at least difficult and demanding circumstances.

While the protagonist travels on his hero's journey, an ally, usually the mentor, dies; there are a series of confrontations or battles, which rise in intensity along with the action until the hero defeats the villain or opposition. As a result of this journey, the hero's world is set right and he or she experiences a strong change and thereby becomes the best possible person they should be. They may or may not achieve their "want" but they will gain what they really need, a need they were not aware of or even desired at the beginning of their journey. In addition, the entire narrative will support or illustrate a strong and accessible theme.

It sounds simple but it is actually quite difficult to create a satisfying story with a solid theme and an interesting hero with a fresh want and need in an appealing or interesting world. In theatrical terms, playwrights like William Shakespeare, Arthur Miller, Tennessee Williams, and Sophocles met these challenges brilliantly in their respective plays *Macbeth*, *Death of a Salesman*, *A Streetcar Named Desire*, and *Oedipus*.

But it must also be made clear that these foundational concepts of drama also apply to television and movies, which are simply photographed theater. *Citizen Kane* (1941) is an Elizabethan tragedy presented within an American milieu. *Star Wars* (1977) is a coming of age story set in space (Lucas has freely acknowledged the influence of Joseph Campbell's work on his interstellar mythic epic). And in television projects, especially serialized series like *The Walking Dead* (2010–present,) *Game of Thrones* (2011–2019) and *This Is Us* (2016–2022) strong characters travel on the hero's journey, facing the same obstacles, reverses, surprises, and antagonists that any similar character would experience in a good play or movie.

These creative challenges are compounded when a writer approaches the process of adaptation. All literature can be the source or subject of adaptation. Whether it's *The Tragical History of Romeus and Juliet* by Arthur Brooks that provided the storyline for William Shakespeare's *Romeo & Juliet* or Akira Kurosawa's film *Seven Samurai* (1954) that inspired the plot of *A Bug's Life* (1998), one story can feed another in any conceivable genre, presentation or period.

In this process, the authors of the adaptation will often recreate or reinvent the story's medium or message but also its characters, theme, and basic narrative, even the nature of the genre itself. However, the best adaptations will employ key elements from its source material to not only transform the material but also maintain the dramatic components that enriched and informed the original piece.

The foundational tenets of Aristotle and Campbell, a proactive hero pursuing their goal after an inciting incident changes their world in a tale that displays a strong theme, must also be supported throughout this process. As has been already noted, this is no simple or easy task.

As we examine how the version of "If She Dies" published in *Twisted Tales* was adapted into an episode of *The Twilight Zone* franchise, we will see how its plot and key characters were radically altered while still preserving the original intention, heart and soul of its source.

However, mention must also be made of how *The Twilight Zone* also had its own moral and dramatic code that needed to be honored and implemented as well. Rod Serling's own original, iconic television series (1959–1964) was ambitious and striking, even unique. It was extremely filmic with locations, special effects, and concepts that often matched or even exceeded the theatrical cinema presentations of its day. It was presented in an anthology format with fresh stories and characters every week, which presented enormous challenges in creating dependable production values and appropriate narrative concepts.

The series also tackled difficult and controversial subjects such as the Holocaust, nuclear war, and racism with these themes masked behind their genre elements for better audience acceptance. Despite often middling ratings and network interference throughout its original run, the series has been staunchly durable, its original black and white episodes continually in syndication, while also spawning a feature film and three television reboots, including the Jordan Peel version that recently aired on CBS Access.

In fact, the series has become part of the international zeitgeist. How many people in this world are not capable of humming its jarring and distinctive Marius Constant theme?

Despite the wide variety of stories presented, whether they could be defined science fiction, supernatural, fantasy or horror, consistent elements were maintained. These fundamentals included high concepts; twist endings, empathetic themes and shocking reversals. However, the particular theme that supported and defined a multitude of episodes, the most prevalent and pleasing, was the protagonist being offered a second chance. As the audience experienced the hero receiving a the great gift of reinventing their life, they would not only enjoy the tale on its merits but could revel in the idea that their own lives might also present them with the same gratifying option; if not necessarily through fantastical, super-natural, or science fictional means.

When I was offered the opportunity to create an episode of the first series reboot I understandably leapt at the chance. A zealous fan of the original show, I knew that "If She Dies" was a good fit for *The Twilight Zone*, as it was a supernatural piece with a twist ending that featured a second chance for its protagonist. It was also a ghost story, a concept not at all alien to *The Twilight Zone* and quite compatible with the series' basic dramatic mission: to intrigue, surprise, and reveal.

Within "If She Dies," we also have the classic hero's journey as Campbell would have outlined it; a secular disbelieving Paul is launched on a search for the truth that leads him to a religious mentor, Sister Carmella, and eventually to what he wants, a second chance with his daughter. At the same time he receives what he really needs, a spiritual reawakening. What's more, "If She Dies" contains a dramatic and dark story bridge with which Aristotle would have been fully familiar. As in the Greek tragic myth of Orpheus, the character of Paul, in his quest to save his daughter, literally speaks with the dead.

In any case, after my successful pitch, I immediately launched into work on my two stories for *The Twilight Zone*. The nuclear war comedy never got past a first draft, which is not surprising when one considers that only Stanley Kubrick has ever really licked that kind of material. However, after I turned in my first draft of "If She Dies" on December 17, the story found initial approval with Alan and the producers and I proceeded through a series of rewrites. It was a difficult process as you can see....

FRIDAY JANUARY 4, 1985: The day started our horribly. Alan calls to tell me Phil (De Guerre, the executive producer) hated the script.... Alan came by and we drove to the meeting together ... not half as bad as expected but still wearing stuff. Phil wants all the talk cut out or cut down. Which leads to a big problem on the Sister. She can't be a real character this way. Actually fought back on this ... and Phil won. He won anyway ... a big chunk of the story won't work because the sister won't work. That's television.

By the way, Phil was right and I was wrong. Just because a writer feels passionately about a particular element, line, moment, or character in his work doesn't necessarily mean he or she is on the right path. Sometimes it really helps to get an outside, unvarnished view of things. Which I realized later as I rewrote the script....

SUNDAY JANUARY 6, 1985: I think I found the script again. The Sister is a stock character but the whole thing will move a lot more simply and quietly—a lot less talk.

See what I mean? Important and productive changes had to be made.

In the script and in the final filmed episode, the story opens with Paul and his daughter Kathy sharing a pleasant moment at breakfast where we establish their close and loving relationship. We also learn that Kathy's mother, Paul's wife, died less than a year ago. In the next scene, we witness the inciting incident that changes the world of the protagonist for the worse—a car crash that seriously injures Kathy.

After a scene at the hospital where Paul talks to his comatose daughter and her doctor tells him Kathy's prognosis is dire, the distraught father leaves for home. As he crosses to his car parked at the curb, he sees the pale, ethereal ghost of Sarah standing on the roof of Saint Amelia's orphanage, which is now located across the street from the hospital as opposed to already torn down in the *Twisted Tales* version.

In another important change, Sister Carmella (now named Sister Agnes,) is physically at the recently shuttered orphanage, selling the items taken from the building's basement. When the ghost, now seated on a swing, directs Paul to the bed, he buys it and takes it home. The next few scenes— Paul meeting Sarah, escorting the ghost to her bed, tucking her in, and the ghost vanishing—are very close to the original story. However, when Paul seeks out Sister Agnes, he already has a plan in mind when she introduces him to the stuffed teddy bear Toby. It's his notion, not the Sister's, that he can use Toby to save his daughter via the ghost of Sarah in the bed.

After Sister Agnes reluctantly gives him her precious memento, Paul takes his comatose daughter home, places her in the bed and waits out the night by her side. The ending is again very similar to the one in the graphic story. Sarah asks her Daddy for Toby, receives the stuffed bear, and smiles as she hugs it. Freeze frame.

Why were these changes instituted? For one thing, television and film are immediate, visual projects. In the original *Twisted Tales* version, by beginning the story in the hospital, we're never offered an opportunity to observe Kathy and Paul's close, loving relationship. We also don't witness the accident, and we're almost half way through the piece before we meet Sarah. The haunted bed is introduced in an antique store, not a very interesting location, and the salesman is not a very intriguing character. Joining Kathy and Paul earlier in their story and watching the impact of the accident was a much stronger beginning to the piece both dramatically and visually.

Having the orphanage, the nun, and the bed across the street from the hospital not only offered the possibility of striking images of the phantom Sarah standing on the building's roof and seated on a swing; this obviated the need for a wordy explanation for where the bed came from. We see the orphanage, the bed, and the ghost, and we visually connect them all together. We also meet a key character, Sister Agnes, earlier in the plot.

In the story in *Twisted Tales*, Paul is not motivated to save his daughter when he seeks out the Sister for answers to Sarah's ghostly presence. He's simply curious to solve a mystery. It's the nun who gives him the idea that this situation might present other possibilities, which leads Paul to placing his dying daughter in Sarah's bed. This means Paul is not being proactive with a plan to fulfill his want; he's reactive to what the nun implies he should do.

In *The Twilight Zone* production, Paul is introduced to the bed and the nun in a much more satisfying, spooky and visual fashion. He's also pushing the story more dynamically, seeking out the history of the haunted bed in an energetic and focused manner.

An active hero always makes for a better story. Paul has a plan and he pursues it even over the protests of the nun, who does not want to give up Toby. If there is an antagonist willing to provide any conflict in this story, it's the nun. If she's not, then the opposition is death itself.

From *Twisted Tales* to *The Twilight Zone*, the plot is basically the same but much stronger, immediate, and visual with a more active and directed protagonist. These are all elements necessary for not only a strong *The Twilight Zone* story but for any tale that honors the fundamental doctrines of Aristotle and Campbell; a determined and motivated hero should be launched on a difficult journey to satisfy a want and need.

Beyond these basics of drama, a writer must also understand and respect their story's genre. Whatever piece a writer is trying to produce— whether it's a drama, comedy, science fiction or horror—he or she should do her homework and know the genre they are working in so they don't just copy or misinterpret, they revive and revisit.

"If She Dies" is a ghost story, which requires haunting images and spooky moments. The best ghost stories also have a strong emotional underpinning or center; they don't just scare and shock, they affect the heart. The writer's knowledge of this genre was vital to the proper development of the story. A successful and productive process in creating any piece in any genre is acknowledging and properly employing the set pieces familiar to that particular genre, such as the car chase in a heist thriller, the street shoot out in a western, or the katana fight in a samurai drama. In a proper ghost story, the dead haunt the living. "If She Dies" couldn't have functioned without that moment where Sarah Brannigan's wraith visits Paul Molano in the dark of the night.

In June of 1985, after the rewrites were completed, my script entered the production process. John Hancock, who directed *Bang the Drum Slowly* (1973) amongst many other projects, was hired to helm. Andrea Barber, who later starred in *Full House* (1987–1995), and Jenny Lewis, who eventually became a successful singer, were cast as Kathy and Sarah respectively. The talented Tony Lo Bianco, who I had worked with previously on a series called *Cliffhangers* (1979) was cast as Paul. In all these cases I was fortunate; the actors and director were excellent.

Sets were built at the CBS Fox studio in Studio City and locations secured around Los Angeles. I was allowed to visit the stage where they shot the interiors, which was highly unusual. Most writers find sets boring, even when it's their own material being shot, and directors are loathe to allow writers to hang around, offering a potential source of trouble or creative interference. But neither circumstance was the case here….

THURSDAY, JUNE 20, 1985: …drove up to the Studio Centre to watch the shooting of "If She Dies." They did the hospital stuff. John Hancock was distant, trying to be cordial. I was very happy with what I saw done … a truly great day.

I especially enjoyed talking with the lady who played Sister Agnes so superbly. Nan Martin, a vastly experienced performer with credits dating back to *Ben Casey* (1961–1966) and even the original *The Twilight Zone*, would sit in her chair, dressed in her nun's habit, chain-smoking Marlboro Lights, regaling me with tales of what it was like to work with Robert Stack on *The Untouchables* (1959–1963).

FRIDAY, JUNE 21, 1985: Spent entire day on Stage 11. Some of the scenes were wonderful. But they ran out of time on the kids, and they raced through the Sarah stuff, it killed me. The show was just under scheduled. I know I was lucky Hancock got as good as he got, but I was depressed as hell anyway.

I was referring to a scene—lifted almost word for word from the original comic book piece—where Paul would have walked down a hallway in his house, holding hands with Sarah while her feet floated over the floor. They had even built the set of the hallway and had the harness in place to "fly" Jenny Lewis, but they ran out of time and couldn't film this material. As you can see from my diary entry, I was devastated.

But for people who watched the episode; what they never saw didn't matter. The episode worked perfectly well without this scene. The point is that writers will always have their darlings, by which I mean dialogue, scenes, or even entire characters they dearly cherish, but it's not necessarily a terrible thing when some of them are cut or don't get shot.

After the show was filmed, it went into post-production. I didn't have a chance to see the finished product for several months but was not disappointed with the final result….

THURSDAY, OCTOBER 3, 1985: Drove to Studio City to see a tape of "If She Dies." It made me cry. It's turned out beautifully even with all the cuts and changes.

The episode mattered to me because the story, basically unchanged in its significant events, characters, and intention, was the same. From the moment I conceived this tale that day in Venice when I saw that child's bed at that church rummage sale I really cared about Paul Molano and his daughter Kathy and that ghost Sarah Brannigan. That passion had carried me a very long way; from a comic book relatively few people read to an episode of *The Twilight Zone* that millions have seen.

Another important, more academic point; the story worked because it possessed an active character with a clear, desperate want to save his daughter, and a powerful need; to trust in a loving God. Aristotle, Joseph Campbell, and the power of myth still matter.

I must offer a final, personal note about my *The Twilight Zone* experience. I was so proud of the episode I invited all my closest friends to a party at my house to watch its premier.

FRIDAY, OCTOBER 25, 1985: Was very tense all day about the party.... Went very well. About 30 people showed up. That was fine ... but the show. I was so nervous about the show. It was wonderful ... my first real television. I got drunk on the sheer pleasure of it. I finally have a piece of good work to point to; something past money or credit. And everyone truly loved it. I got calls from friends. It was great. So great, I was scared of dying.

In conclusion, as we can see in this examination of this particular episode, and in this review of both its graphic anthology source material and the television adaptation, we have clearly established that, while Aristotle may have shown the way in the fourth century BC, and Joseph Campbell in the twentieth century, today's writers can still create new and exciting ways to explore and re-invent the power of myth, legend and heroes no matter the medium or message they pursue. With a clear understanding of these precepts, and with a true commitment to his or her craft, any dramatic writer, no matter the discipline or intention of their story, no matter the genre, source material or inspiration, or whether their project is a play, film, or television show, can produce work that lasts and matters.

Bottom line, a story's character must overcome obstacles and reverses to achieve the necessary change to achieve their goals or to become the best person they can possibly be. Which is not that different from the way we all need to live our lives, isn't it?

And it helps; it really helps, if you love the story you are writing as much as you can love anything else.

Works Cited

Aristotle. *Poetics*. Penguin, 1997.
Campbell, Joseph. *The Hero with a Thousand Faces*, 3rd. ed. New World Library, 2008.

Carren, David, writer, Attillio Micheluzi, art, Ron Courtney, colors. *If She Dies, Twisted Tales, Vol. 1, No. 10*, Independent Comics, December 1984.

_____. Revised Production Draft, *If She Dies, The New Twilight Zone*. PROD. # 0310-906-0027, 17 June 1984.

"If She Dies," *The Twilight Zone*, written by David Bennett Carren, directed by John Hancock, Paramount, 2017.

PART IV

Comparative Zones

Strange Realities

Twilight Zone-*sploitation*
in Encounter with the Unknown

Nicholas Diak

> To walk this bridge is to accept all kinds of possibilities, especially the most exciting possibility of all: the possibility of impossibility.

These are the words of Rod Serling, creator and presenter of the influential television program, *The Twilight Zone* (1959–1964). Though the statement sounds like it was lifted from the television series, one would be hard pressed to determine from which episode. This is because the dialogue is from *Encounter with the Unknown* (Harry Thomason, 1973), a curious entry in Serling's filmography, late in his career when he was providing voice work for a variety of projects. *The Twilight Zone* left an enduring legacy, and not just with its revival incarnations and 1983 film, but inspiring and influencing numerous other programs and becoming a pop culture phenomenon. *Encounter with the Unknown* is such a post–*Twilight Zone* film that greatly exhibits the series' influence. However, unlike shows such as *The Outer Limits* (1963–1965) which sought to capitalize on *The Twilight Zone* formula, *Encounter* went even further in its emulation by employing Serling to provide narrations in his recognizable style, recreating that distinct *Twilight Zone* vibe.

This essay posits that *Encounter with the Unknown*, by leveraging distinctive and iconic attributes of *The Twilight Zone*, specifically Serling's narrations and visual cues, becomes both a multiplicity and an exploitation film derivative of the original *Twilight Zone* series. After a plot synopsis of *Encounter with the Unknown* along with text of Serling's narrations as they will be referenced in subsequent sections, this essay will define what exploitation films and multiplicities are and how they allow *Encounter* to continue the textual tradition of the original show. Afterwards it will be demonstrated precisely how *Encounter of the Unknown* exploits *The Twilight Zone* through emulation of the aural and textual aspects of Serling's narrations and repurposing the show's iconic imagery onto home releases of the film.

Synopsis and Serling's Narrations

Encounter with the Unknown is an anthology film divided into three stories, similar in structure to the episodes of Serling's own *Night Gallery* (1970–1973). An unknown and uncredited non–Serling narrator opens the film by referencing studies of unusual deaths, seemingly related by all being interred in twenty three cemeteries, by a fictitious scientist named Jonathan Rankin. A textual crawl coincides with the narration, but the text of the crawl does not verbatim match the narration. Aside from an attempt at giving *Encounter* a modicum of authenticity, this non–Serling narrative truly exists only to pad the running time of the film, as will be demonstrated at the film's conclusion. Serling himself only provides opening and closing narration for each of the individual stories in *Encounter with the Unknown*.

The first story opens with a funeral procession for Johnny Davis (John Cissne) with Serling ominously setting the mood:

> There are few things as strange as reality, for reality comes to us wearing many faces, disguised as all manner of things. What is reality and what is illusion? Some things we think are real may be merely wisps of smoke from our minds. And some things we think illusion are merely cloaked in that guise, so they may play their parts without knowing what they really are [*Encounter with the Unknown*].

Once the procession stops and the characters gather around Johnny's grave, Serling proceeds with the story's introduction proper:

> Did these events happen by coincidence or by an unknown and unknowable calculation? Let's start by populating this day's stage with some of the characters. Dave Terrell. Frank Cameron. Randy Powell. Three young men, college students, all the "boy next door," all people we've known before. Brother Taylor, a well-meaning and God-fearing man. Johnny Davis, the one who holds the rather dubious place of honor at this gathering. And this is Camille Davis, Johnny's mother, the seventh daughter of a seventh son. Does she have anything to do with our story? Perhaps. Let's unfold it [*Encounter with the Unknown*].

Johnny is the unfortunate victim of a prank gone awry. His friends, Dave (Tom Haywood), Frank (Gary Brockette), and Randy (John Leslie) set him up on a date with a nonexistent woman, however when Johnny arrives at the address given, he is accidentally shot by the lady of the house. Blaming the trio for her son's death, Johnny's mother Camille (Fran Franklin) curses the lot with a spell that will be repeated many times through *Encounter with the Unknown*: "Listen you well to my word. One by land, two by sky. Look to the heptagon for it is there. Seven times around go the three of you and may your reward be just and true" (*Encounter with the Unknown*).

The rest of the story unfolds mostly in flashback with Frank on an airplane recounting his ordeal to Father Duane (Robert Ginnaven), revealing that seven days after the funeral, Dave was accidentally hit by a car, and now as he sits on the airplane, it is seven days later. Upon disembarking from the plane, Father Duane witnesses Frank's plane crash. Seven days later, Duane attempts to call Randy at his college, only to find out that Randy is away from the campus for the day as he is out skydiving. Serling closes out the story over scenes of skydivers:

> So, Randy Powell went skydiving. What was it that woman named Camille said? One by land and two by air? Didn't Frank say that he found a heptagon to be a seven-sided figure? And didn't Dave die seven days after Johnny's funeral and Frank fourteen days after? What is the reality and what is the illusion? Our story doesn't tell us, but I wonder if Randy knows that it is the twenty-first day? [*Encounter with the Unknown*].

The second story begins with verdant shots of a trees and ponds while Jess (Kevin Bieberly) and his pet dog Lady frolic around. Serling opens with:

> It is tradition that ghosts and ghouls and various other citizens of the grotesque wrap themselves in malevolent mists of deep darkness. Horror is a condition existing most often when morning seems farthest away. So, it would seem unlikely that this bright, spring day in 1906 would begin a horror that, to this day, haunts a small community in southern Missouri. A boy and his dog chase dreams and butterflies back and forth across Saturday. Observe one man-child and one man-child's dog on their way to a uniquely soul-shattering rendezvous with darkness, a terrifying encounter with the unknown [*Encounter with the Unknown*].

Jess loses his dog in the woods and happens upon a deep hole with strange groans and wails emanating from it. Speculating his dog has fallen into the hole, Jess informs his parents. Eventually the mysterious hole garners the attention of the menfolk of the town and they converge upon it. Jess' father Joe (Robert Holton) volunteers to be lowered into the hole. Once inside, he bellows a horrible scream and is pulled out, unconscious. Upon coming to he becomes frantic, screaming and running through the woods while his son and the rest of the onlookers give chase. Serling closes by revealing the fate of Joe:

No one knows what happened down in that cave. Joe was a strong, intelligent man who had lived his entire life close to the earth. Never before had he intruded upon the affairs of that godless society that dwells deep within the bowels of the Earth. But he did leave them. After a manner of speaking. Somehow, through this wild experience, he had lost his mind. He was insane and spent the rest of his life a state insane asylum [*Encounter with the Unknown*].

The third and final story opens with scenes of a truss bridge over a gently flowing river. Serling introduces the folk-ghost story as follows:

There is a bridge in our mind that leads through time and memory from what we know to shores beyond knowing. It sways high and darkly dangerous above the canyons of our disbelief like some spectral span spun by devils for us to tread. To walk this bridge is to accept all kinds of possibilities, especially the most exciting possibility of all: the possibility of impossibility. Some tales of the impossible so capture the imagination that they quickly spread over much of the country. "The Girl on the Bridge" is such a tale. Countless variations of this story are told and retold. In North Carolina it is the "Lydia Story." In Illinois it is the "Spectre of the Mists." And in Texas it is called "The White Rock Lady." Dozens of interviews and hours of newspaper research trace the story's origins and consequent spread across the country from central Arkansas beginning in 1929. Come now and explore the possibility of the impossible. Come stand beside the girl on the bridge [*Encounter with the Unknown*].

As with the first story of *Encounter with the Unknown*, this segment is also mostly told through flashback: young flapper Susan (Rosie Holotik) is unable to get her miser father's (Gene Ross) approval of her beau due to his lack of wealth. The couple, very much in love, take off in their car to be secretly wed, only to wind up crashing into the river at the truss bridge. Decades later, an Arkansas senator (Michael Harvey) and his wife (Judith Fields) encounter Susan as they drive over the bridge. Susan asks to be taken home, which the senator obliges. They arrive at the house and encounter Susan' father who informs the senator that his daughter died long ago. Upon returning to his car, the senator finds Susan has vanished, leaving her bouquet of flowers in the backseat. The story ends with Susan's ghost back at the bridge while Serling's narration closes out the tale:

It has been said that our lives are merely bridges through time. But what of death? We know where death begins, but across what does it span? Where does it lead? These are questions Susan could easily answer if we could befriend her. And this too is possible for dozens of people, including the senator, say she still stands upon the bridge, waiting, perhaps for you, to pass her way once more [*Encounter with the Unknown*].

The film ends with the non–Serling narrator recapping the three stories, underscoring the occult and paranormal themes in each. Without this unknown non–Serling narrator, *Encounter* clocks in at a scant seventy-six minutes of running time. It can be deduced that the film needed to increase its running time to the standard ninety minutes and that Serling was no longer available (or affordable, or both) to record additional narrations. In a true exploitation film fashion this was solved by re-using the scenes from the film and overlaying a new narrator over them to bookend the film. The end result is roughly two minutes and twenty seconds of padding used as the film's intro and eleven minutes of rehashed scenes used as the conclusion.

Exploitation Films and Multiplicities

From *The Last House on the Left* (Wes Craven, 1972) to *Faster, Pussycat! Kill! Kill!* (Russ Meyer, 1965), from *The Texas Chainsaw Massacre* (Tobe Hooper, 1974) to *The Exterminator* (James Glickenhaus, 1980), exploitation and grindhouse films play an important counterpart to Hollywood and mainstream cinema. Exploitation cinema is a realm of gory horror films, sleazy erotic imports, low budget genre fare, and ambitious independent filmmakers operating outside the traditional industry structures. In *Nightmare USA: The Untold Story of the Exploitation Independents*, Stephen Thrower dives deep into the realm of 1970s and early 1980s exploitation cinema and defines such films as:

> independently made non-studio films produced either: (a) to exploit the financial possibilities of a popular genre; (b) to respond quickly to current interest in a contemporary topic; or (c) to milk an existing market success [Thrower 12].

With this definition in mind, *Encounter with the Unknown* can be classified as an exploitation film because it meets each one of the criteria proffered by Thrower: it situates itself within the horror anthology genre, it takes advantage of pop culture interest in the occult and paranormal, and it attempts to capitalize on the success of *The Twilight Zone*.

Genre-wise, *Encounter* is ostensibly a horror film, though it lacks the blood, gore, and sex that saturated the exploitation films of the period. However, in regard to specifying a genre formula that the film unabashedly apes, *Encounter* is a horror anthology film, a niche genre made up of shorter horror films, oftentimes linked with themes or characters. *Creepshow* (George A. Romero, 1982) epitomizes the format: it contains five short stories that replicate the feeling of 1950s EC horror comics, and it is tied together with a prologue and epilogue about a young boy (Joe King) being disciplined by his father (Tom Atkins) who receives his comeuppance at the film's end.

The horror anthology format, also known as the portmanteau film, has seen periodic cycles of success. Examples of horror anthologies that were released in the 1960s before *Encounter with the Unknown* include *Twice-Told Tales* (Sidney Salkow, 1963), *Black Sabbath* (Mario Bava, 1963), and *Tales of Terror* (Roger Corman, 1962), the latter two both being released by American International Pictures. Across the sea, Britain's Amicus Productions released a slew of horror anthologies during the 60s and 70s: *Dr. Terror's House of Horrors* (Freddie Francis, 1965), *Torture Garden* (Freddie Francis, 1967), *The House that Dripped Blood* (Peter Duffell, 1970), Asylum (Roy Ward Baker, 1972), *Tales from the Crypt* (Freddie Francis, 1972), *The Vault of Horror* (Roy Ward Baker, 1973), and *From Beyond the Grave* (Kevin Connor, 1974). *Encounter of the Unknown* is an early 1970s entrant of the genre, subsequently being followed by the infamous *Trilogy of Terror* (Dan Curtis, 1975), *Dead of Night* (Dan Curtis, 1977), and *The House of the Dead* (Sharron Miller, 1978). *Encounter*, along with these other films, would help usher in a renaissance of horror anthology films in the 1980s that include the aforementioned *Creepshow* and its 1987 sequel, *Twilight Zone: The Movie* (1983), *Nightmares* (Joseph Sargent, 1983), *Cat's Eye* (Lewis Teague, 1985), *Deadtime* Stories (Jeffrey Delman, 1986) *From a Whisper to a Scream* (Jeff Burr, 1987), and *After Midnight* (Ken and Jim Wheat, 1989).

The second point of Thrower's definition is that an exploitation film is often produced in response to a contemporary trend. In the case of *Encounter with the Unknown*, this would be an interest in the occult, supernatural, paranormal, new age, extraterrestrial, and metaphysical that was occurring in the late 60s through the 70s. This was a time period where Erich von Däniken's book *Chariots of the Gods? Unsolved Mysteries of the Past* (1968) had just been turned into a commercially successful documentary and Danbury Press published a twenty-one volume set of books called *The Supernatural* which would pave the way for Time-Life Books releasing a similar series of books called *Mysteries of the Unknown* in the 80s. The 1970s would see the broadcasting of the popular television series *In Search of...* (1977–1982) which featured Rod Serling narrating the first three episodes, *In Search of Ancient Astronauts* (1973), *In Search of Ancient Mysteries* (1973), and *The Outer Space Connection* (1975). Of note, narration duties of *In Search of ...* would be handed off to Leonard Nimoy, who in addition to portraying the iconic *Star Trek* role of Spock had also previously appeared in the season three *Twilight Zone* episode, "A Quality of Mercy." The end result would be that *In Search of ...* was banking on the marquee currency of both *The Twilight Zone* and *Star Trek* simultaneously.

In regard to cinema, per Thrower, "Swelling the ranks of the supernatural horror film, at least numerically, are those concerned with the occult.

After the smash success of *Rosemary's Baby* (Roman Polanski, 1968), and the even greater commercial and cultural impact of *The Exorcist* (William Friedkin, 1973), tales of sorcery and Satanism were, if you will, legion" (Thrower 39). Interest in the occult and supernatural were certainly capitalized on by films such as *Blood on Satan's Claw* (Piers Haggard, 1971), *The Wicker* Man (Robin Hardy, 1973), *Beyond the Door* (Ovidio G. *Assonitis and* Robert Barrett, 1974), *The Devil's Rain* (Robert Fuest, 1975), and *The Omen* (Richard Donner, 1976) and its sequels. Folk horror scholar Howard David Ingham notes the pervasiveness of this subject matter: "There is something oddly prosaic about the way the occult was presented in the 70s. It always seemed close, part of the public realm, and crucially not the preserve of the privileged classes" (Ingham 7) and "occult, astrology, and spiritualism were not central in our culture, but their iconography was present enough in the 1970s that they needed no introduction. And it infected our pop culture" (Ingham 13). All in all, the time period in which *Encounter with the Unknown* was released in was experiencing a surge of interest in these occult topics and the film took advantage of this trend and in the process, wound up contributing to it as well.

Finally, to Thrower's third point, *Encounter with the Unknown* fits the definition of an exploitation film because it attempts to cash in on the success of *The Twilight Zone*. In addition, *Encounter* can also be said, to use the definition put forth by Amanda Ann Klein and R. Barton Palmer in *Cycles, Sequels, Spin-Offs, Remakes, and Reboots*, to be a multiplicity of *The Twilight Zone*. For Klein and Palmer, texts (films) are not self-contained entities, but are "joined by various bonds to other texts" taking on forms such as "adaptations, sequels, remakes, imitations, trilogies, reboots, series, spin-offs, and cycles" (1). All these various forms of textual continuations and re-imaginings can be folded up under the umbrella term of multiplicities. Multiplicities create a "connection between texts" that "afford the opportunity for complex forms of aesthetic enjoyment" allowing consumers "to appreciate the new in the context of the familiar and already approved, sanctioning readings that crisscross textual borders" (Klein and Palmer 1). The existence of the successor texts also "volatilize the original by underlining its insufficiency, by announcing that there is a 'more' that the urtext does not contain and likely does not anticipate, in the process revealing that there is a desire for continuation or repetition that the original cannot satisfy" (Klein and Palmer 4).

With this in mind, viewers of *Encounter with the Unknown* (new text) are able to find enjoyment because of the familiar elements the film lifts (exploits) from *The Twilight Zone* (original, approved, sanctioned text), which in effect, also creates the linkage between both texts. This linkage, essentially in the form of imitation, causes *Encounter with the Unknown* to become a multiplicity of *The Twilight Zone*. This puts *Encounter* in the same camp as the many *Twilight Zone* revivals and the 1983 film which are multiplicities because they are reboots and remakes of the original text. The sheer existence of *Encounter* (along with the TV reboots, films, and so on) also demonstrate that the original text of *The Twilight Zone* is still an open book, and that stories, ideas, concepts, and so on that were not present in the original can be found in the successor and derivative texts.

How exactly does *Encounter with the Unknown* capitalize on *The Twilight Zone* and in the process become a multiplicity of the show? Two attributes of Encounter that accomplish this feat include mimicking Serling's *Twilight Zone* narrations and recreating iconic *Twilight Zone* visual cues for the home video releases of the movie.

Voices and Images

By the early 1970s, *The Twilight Zone* had been off the air for many years, yet Serling was still much in demand. The early 1970s saw the airing of Serling's successor series, *Night Gallery*, and what followed during and after this endeavor was a variety of audio work. Aside from *Encounter with the Unknown*, Serling lent his vocal talents to the previously mentioned *In Search of …* episodes, the radio program *The Zero Hour* (1973–1974), narrating the introduction the Brian De Palma's cult classic *Phantom of the Paradise* (1974), narrating *The Undersea World of Jacques Cousteau* (1968–1975), and many other films, documentaries, and programs.

Undeniably, Serling's voice had currency. In his review of *Encounter of the Unknown*, Brett Gallman at *Oh, The Horror!* stated:

> One can argue that Boris Karloff's booming, gravelly dialogue is just as distinctive as his often monstrous facial features; likewise, who would mistake Lugosi's Hungarian accent or Price's velvety voice for any other? While Rod Serling's face might not have been as famous as these titans of horror, his voice is arguably just as recognizable, as it haunted television audiences for a couple of decades as the host of *The Twilight Zone* and *Night Gallery* [Gallman].

In her book, *As I Knew Him: My Dad, Rod Serling*, Anne Serling expounds:

> My father's voice has many different intonations and pitches. There is the tight, clipped *Twilight Zone* or *Night Gallery* host voice introducing that week's episode. There is his regular Dad-speaking voice. There's the voice he uses for his *PBS* narrations or commercial spots, all of his different and funny dialects and accents, and, finally, his playful voice [Serling 206].

It is this iconic "tight, clipped" hosting voice that Serling uses that puts him in the same pantheon as the aforementioned Karloff and Lugosi in

Gallman's observation, and it is the same voice that *Encounter with the Unknown* channels in order to harness Serling's *Twilight Zone* marquee value.

In addition to Serling's hosting voice, the text of Serling's narrations in *Encounter of the Unknown* draw heavily from the text of the narrations in *The Twilight Zone,* making similar similes and references. For example, in the opening narration to *Encounter with the Unknown*, Serling's narration asks, "what is reality and what is illusion" (*Encounter with the Unknown*)? Similar statements, challenging the viewers to question the duality of reality, are found in abundance in *Twilight Zone* episodes, such as in "Perchance to Dream" ("They say a dream takes only a second or so, and yet in that second a man can live a lifetime. He can suffer and die, and who's to say which is the greater reality: the one we know or the one in dreams, between heaven, the sky, the earth in the Twilight Zone" ["Perchance to Dream"]), "A World of Difference" ("But in just a moment we will see how thin a line separates that which we assume to be real with that manufactured inside of a mind" ["A World of Difference"]) and "Shadow Play" ("We know that a dream can be real, but who ever thought that reality could be a dream? We exist, of course, but … but how, in what way?" ["Shadow Play"]).

The matter-of-fact way characters are introduced in *Encounter*'s first segment mimics similar introductions in "One for the Angels" ("Man on a sidewalk named Lew Bookman, age sixtyish. Occupation: pitchman" ["One of the Angels"]) and in "Walking Distance" ("Martin Sloane, age thirty-six. Occupation: vice president, ad agency, in charge of media" ["Walking Distance"]).

In the introduction to the second story of *Encounter*, Serling's narration mentions idyllic scenes of a young boy playing with his dog and muses on the nature of the horror and the grotesque before mentioning how a small town becomes besieged with something horrible. These musings have parallels in "It's a Good Life" ("They have to think happy thoughts and say happy things because once displeased, the monster can wish them into a cornfield or change them into a grotesque, walking horror" ["It's a Good Life"]), "Third from the Sun" ("Quitting time at the plant. Time for supper now. Time for families. Time for a cool drink on a porch. Time for the quiet rustle of leaf-laden trees that screen out the moon. And underneath it all, behind the eyes of the men, hanging invisible over the summer night, is a horror without words" ["Third from the Sun"]), and especially in "Valley of the Shadow," an episode that also has a disappearing dog and a small town with something sinister going on:

> You've seen them. Little towns, tucked away far from the main roads. You've seen them, but have you thought about them? What do the people in these

places do? Why do they stay? Philip Redfield never thought about them. If his dog hadn't gone after that cat, he would have driven through Peaceful Valley and put it out of his mind forever ["Valley of the Shadow"].

The ghostly references about the lady on the bridge that begins the third story in *Encounter with the Unknown* is tonally similar to the opening narration of "The Mighty Casey" ("What you're looking at is a ghost, once alive but now deceased" ["The Mighty Casey"]). This especially poignant as both narrations are over scenes of abandoned and deserted places: the bridge in encounter and the empty stadium in "The Mighty Casey." The similarities in the narrations between *Encounter with the Unknown* to the narrations from *The Twilight Zone*, all delivered in the same style of voice from Serling, is quite telling. If the audio narrations were divorced from their visual counterpart in *Encounter*, they would certainly be indistinguishable from those used in *The Twilight Zone*.

Serling's narrations, both aural and textual, were not the only aspect of *The Twilight Zone* that *Encounter with the Unknown* sought to capitalize on. Iconic visual imagery from the television show found its way into promotional aspects of the film in order to entice viewers, promising them a *Twilight Zone*–esque experience.

The movie poster for *Encounter with the Unknown* only makes a modicum of capitalization on Serling and *The Twilight Zone*: it simply shows a frame from the burial scene of the film's first story depicting Mrs. Davis staring at the three youths while a "Narrated by Rod Serling" appears above the film's title. It is not much, but potential consumers of the film are still informed that the film contains narration from Serling, which would certainly evoke memories of his intro/extros from *The Twilight Zone*.

The home video market, however, greatly leveraged as much Serling and *Twilight Zone* aspects as possible in order to promote the film. The first VHS release of *Encounter with the Unknown* was in 1988 by InterGlobal Video Promotions Limited, a mere year after the original series of *The Twilight Zone* found new life through mail-order VHS releases by Columbia House. Perhaps in response to these *Twilight Zone* VHS releases, but definitely capitalizing on the television show proper, the artwork on the InterGlobal Video Promotions Limited release contains a plethora of Serling/*Twilight Zone* connections. Serling's head floats in the exact center of the cover art, behind an open door, while a large key is aimed at said door. Serling's disembodied head looks exactly as he did during his *Twilight Zone* years. The open door on the cover art recalls the opening sequence of the last two seasons of *The Twilight Zone* which depicts a floating, opening door in space. The floating key aimed at the door is a visual representation of Serling's title sequence narration where he states, "You unlock this door with the key of imagination." The VHS box boasts, in a *Twilight*ian fashion, "Is it real? Or only an illusion? Rod Serling of '*The Twilight Zone*' is your guide." In essence, the box art of this release is both a re-imagining and a capitalization of the iconic season four and five openings of the original series. The exploitation elements are further compounded by the fact that the film's title on the VHS box art is in a font that closely mimics *The Twilight Zone*'s logo. Of note, the entire layout, font, and artwork of the InterGlobal release of *Encounter with the Unknown* was reused verbatim for their VHS release of the aforementioned Serling-narrated *The Outer Space Connection*. InterGlobal would reuse the artwork for a third time in a two-tape set that contained both films.

The VCI Home Video VHS release of *Encounter with the Unknown* also exploits Serling and *Twilight Zone* elements, though not as brazenly as the InterGlobal release. As with the InterGlobal version, the VCI box art displays a floating Rod Serling head, though it is a picture of an older Serling that looks to be from the early 70s. The font of the film's title is the same as the InterGlobal release, showing reuse and recycling of shared resources between the two distributors and other companies. The background of the VCI release depicts a horizon at dusk: the top of the box is dark and slowly transitions to a dark red before terminating at a mountainous horizon, mimicking a sun that has just set. The visuals here bear resemblance to one of *The Twilight Zone* commercial bumpers that was used by CBS during the series' original run. This bumper used images from the season one introduction superimposed over each other: a flat landscape with rocky outcroppings, a hard horizon with twinkling stars about, and *The Twilight Zone* logo in the center. The VCI cover attempts to make an overt connection between the film and the television series by stating "Rod Serling takes you past the '*Twilight Zone*' into *Encounter with the Unknown*." The covers of both VHS releases of *Encounter with the Unknown* reimagine and emulate many of the distinguishable images from *The Twilight Zone*. These visual components, combined with Serling's narrations that mimic his intros and outros from *The Twilight Zone*, come together in *Encounter* to create an overtly exploitative and derivative film.

Conclusion

Critical assessment of *Encounter with the Unknown* has not been positive. *The Bloody Pit of Horror* website calls the film predictable and redundant while stating Serling's narration is unnecessary but that it "at least lends this low budget regional picture a little class" (*The Bloody Pit of Horror*). Brian Holcomb at *Kinetofilm* seconds that the film is predicable and "too amateurishly made to give any real credit," but does cede that the film is "entirely unique and once seen can never be forgotten" (Holcomb). Stephen Thrower equates Serling's narration to that of Criswell from the beginning of *Plan 9 from Outer Space* (Ed Wood, 1959) and states that the film is repetitive and fails to "generate much of a shudder" (Thrower 448). It can be deduced that *Encounter* fails at being scary or suspenseful because it so repetitive: from the final segment of the film with the non–Serling narrator that recaps the entire film to the recycling of Camille's heptagon curse that is both overused and overplayed. The alternation between the non–Serling narrator and Serling proper only adds to the amateurish quality of *Encounter*.

Such assessment, however, is typical of exploitation fare, which often suffer from low production values and inept filmmaking (which would help explain its repetition problem). Exploitation films often exhibit charm or other enduring qualities through other avenues, and for *Encounter with the Unknown*, that would be its mimicry of *The Twilight Zone*. Though the original series had ended nearly a decade prior, there was still demand for *Twilight Zone* adjacent product. Per Klein and Palmer, "Entertainment now includes the promise that pleasure does not have to end after the lights go up or the series finale airs, that limits can always be exceeded by what the immediate future will bring if only the viewer will return" (5–6). *Encounter with the Unknown* stepped in to attempt to fulfill the audience need of want of more *Twilight Zone*. The film was not as successful as it could have been, but regardless, it remains an intriguing entry in both *The Twilight Zone* canon and Rod Serling filmography. *Encounter* demonstrates just how absolute *The Twilight Zone* was in its influence, not just at the mainstream level, but down into the realm of exploitation films as well.

WORKS CITED

"Bumpers & Noted Variations Guide." *Time and the Twilight Zone*, 30 Jul. 2010, http://timeandthetwilightzone.blogspot.com/2010/07/bumper-variations-list.html.

"CBS Video Library." *The Twilight Zone Wiki*, https://twilightzone.fandom.com/wiki/CBS_Video_Library. Accessed 9 May 2020.

Cochran, Robert, and Suzanne McCray. *Lights! Camera! Arkansas! From Bronco Billy to Billy Bob Thornton*. University of Arkansas Press, 2015.

De Palma, Brian, director. *Phantom of the Paradise*. Performances by William Finley, Paul Williams, and Jessica Harper, Twentieth Century Fox, 1974. DVD.

"Encounter with the Unknown." *Critical Condition*, http://www.critcononline.com/encounter_with_the_unknown_1973.htm. Accessed 22 Mar. 2020.

"Encounter with the Unknown." *The Rod Serling Archive*, https://www.rodserlingarchive.com/encounter-with-the-unknown. Accessed 5 Mar. 2020.

"Encounter with the Unknown (1973)." *The Bloody Pit of Horror*. http://thebloodypitofhorror.blogspot.com/2012/12/encounter-with-unknown-1973.html. Accessed 15 Apr. 2020.

Gallman, Brett. "Encounter with the Unknown." *Oh, The Horror!*, 22 Mar. 2011, http://www.oh-the-horror.com/page.php?id=790.

Grundhauser, Eric. "The 1980s Book Series That Literally Claimed It Had to Be Read to Be Believed." *Atlas Obscura*, 22 Sep. 2015, https://www.atlasobscura.com/articles/the-1980s-book-series-that-literally-claimed-it-had-to-be-read-to-be-believed.

Holcomb, Brian. "Encounter with the Unknown (1973) Film Review." *Kinetofilm*, 1 Feb. 2010. http://kinetofilm.blogspot.com/2010/02/encounter-with-unknown-1973-film-review.html.

"In Search of..." *IMDB*, https://www.imdb.com/title/tt0074007/. Accessed 6 Apr. 2020.

Ingham, Howard David. *Secret Powers of Attraction: Folk Horror in Its Cultural Context.* E-Book, Room 207 Press, 2018.

"It's a Good Life," *The Twilight Zone*, written by Jerome Bixby and Rod Serling, directed by James Sheldon, Image Entertainment, 2005.

Klein, Amanda Ann, and R. Barton Palmer. "Introduction." *Cycles, Sequels, Spin-Offs, Remakes, and Reboots*, edited by Amanda Ann Klein and R. Barton Palmer. University of Texas Press, 2016, pp. 1–21.

"The Mighty Casey," *The Twilight Zone*, written by Rod Serling, directed by Alvin Ganzer and Robert Parrish, Image Entertainment, 2005.

"One for the Angels," *The Twilight Zone*, written by Rod Serling, directed by Robert Parrish, Image Entertainment, 2005.

"The Outer Space Connection." *VHS Collector*, https://vhscollector.com/movie/outer-space-connection. Accessed 22 Mar. 2020.

Parisi, Nicholas. *Rod Serling: His Life, Work, and Imagination.* University Press of Mississippi, 2018.

"Perchance to Dream." *The Twilight Zone*, written by Charles Beaumont, directed by Robert Florey, Image Entertainment, 2005.

Serling, Anne. *As I Knew Him: My Dad, Rod Serling.* Citadel Press, 2013.

"Shadow Play," *The Twilight Zone*, written by Charles Beaumont, directed by John Brahm, Image Entertainment, 2005.

"Third from the Sun," *The Twilight Zone*, written by Rod Serling, directed by Richard L. Bare, Image Entertainment, 2005.

Thomason, Harry, director. *Encounter with the Unknown.* Performances by Rod Serling, Robert Ginnaven, Fran Franklin, and Rosie Holotik. Centronics, 1973. Blu-ray.

Thomason, Harry, director. *Encounter with the Unknown.* Performances by Rod Serling, Robert Ginnaven, Fran Franklin, and Rosie Holotik. Centronics, 1973. VHS.

Thrower, Stephen. *Nightmare USA: The Untold Story of the Exploitation Independents.* FAB Press, 2007.

"The Twilight Zone—All Openings (1959–2002)." *YouTube*, uploaded by Tardis & Beyond, 7 May 2018, https://www.youtube.com/watch?v=tJj9nvk0AgY.

"The Twilight Zone: Valley of the Shadow, Quotes." *IMDB*, https://www.imdb.com/title/tt0734688/quotes/. Accessed 14 Apr. 2020.

"Walking Distance," *The Twilight Zone*, written by Rod Serling, directed by Robert Stevens, Image Entertainment, 2005.

"A World of Difference," *The Twilight Zone*, written by Richard Matheson, directed by Ted Post, Image Entertainment, 2005.

Get Out of *The Twilight Zone*

The Original TV Series and Newest Reboot Juxtaposed

David Melbye

This essay restricts itself to a cultural juxtaposition of the original series with the current reboot's first season, in order to provide some insight into the latter's awkwardness in contemporary television. Unintentionally toward this end, I wrote the recent study *Irony in The Twilight Zone: How the Series Critiqued Postwar American Culture* (2015). In its introduction, I contextualize my personal relationship to the original series, declaring myself among the "Twilight Zone Generation," simply for the fact that during my impressionable adolescence, syndication of the original series' episodes appeared daily on local Los Angeles network KTLA Channel 5, back-to-back at noon, and then once again at midnight, in addition to recurring "marathons" over holiday weekends—a tradition scooped up by the Sci Fi Channel in subsequent years. Rather conveniently, then, I could digest nearly all of *The Twilight Zone*'s 156 episodes—an opportunity baby boomers of a similar age could scarcely have enjoyed when the series first aired on CBS. By the time I found myself ready to transform these leisure hours into cultural research, I discovered what seemed to me a "dearth" of academic material on the topic. My hard-won insight might have striven to be interventional in what should have been, by then, a fertile continuum of productive discourse on a television show still persistent in mainstream culture as atypically blank-and-white Netflix fodder. Instead, I may have only intervened by protesting the also-persistent presence of Marc Scott Zicree's *The Twilight Zone Companion*. And I pointed out that his tendency to condemn episodes rather than to identify virtues or larger correspondences made this aged reference guide less of a "companion" than it intends. I do not need to rehash that fairly thorough literature review here, and, anyway, there

206

just was not and still is not an abundance of scholarship out there about the show. It might have seemed systematic enough for me to embark from a "corrective" monograph toward encouraging other scholars to collate our insights—in the form of an edited volume. But feeling I had heaped enough attention on the topic, I went in other directions. Five years or so later, I am pleased to find myself contributing to a forum for those ideally having some overdue insight into *The Twilight Zone* and its legacy.

Where I am apt to find fault with the categorical logic and would-be cohesiveness of the typical edited volume as a productive instrument for research, in this case, the topic's subdivision is implicit at least as far as *The Twilight Zone*'s screen permutations: the original series, as such, the 1983 film *Twilight Zone: The Movie*, and the three subsequent series revivals with roughly fifteen years between them. And, of course, in imagining such a volume, I would anticipate a section on "*The Twilight Zone* marginalia" covering any/all franchise-oriented media and merchandise appearing over the years. In other words, an edited volume on the larger cultural trajectory and/or impact of *The Twilight Zone* as an idiosyncratic narrative paradigm makes sense, and, from the outset, would promise some immunity to arbitrariness and academics inviting their colleagues and friends to contribute chapters for the sake of convenience and camaraderie. And, what's more, my assigned function here in considering the current revival series in the light of the original in this context allows me to leave questions applied to anything within the larger interim of *The Twilight Zone* media to others. I intend no further "juxtapositions" with the previous revival series, the film, etc., appearing in the wake of the five Serling-hosted seasons.

Rather, this essay will be a stark "then-and-now" analysis for its own sake, partly to do with a reasonable although inconclusive assumption of far less influence taken from these other media products in order to generate the first season's worth of episodes and beyond. Also, though, I freely admit of my limited fandom and exclusive dedication to the original series, however dated it may be now and however flawed it already was according to Zicree's *Companion*. I have turned my attention to the current CBS revival as an academic exercise only, rather than for anything to do with *The Twilight Zone*'s legacy and/or more contemporary forms of cultural hype. In the latter context, for example, I expect many viewers have been drawn to the series not only because the "Twilight Zone" reference ignites at least some expectation of interesting and alternative narrative content, but also because it is happening within what many embrace as American television's new "golden age." And this consideration, alone, distinguishes my juxtaposition of these two collections of *The Twilight Zone* episodes from other comparisons. *Any* comparison of the original series to one of its revivals or even that of the revivals themselves in the larger "Twilight Zone" context inherently compels us to acknowledge distinct cultural periods, delineated only vaguely by the decades we have assigned to them. But, in this case, we are also compelled to compare two "golden age" moments in popular television culture and consumption, and ideally arrive at a newly informed perspective thereby. While I am assuming this responsibility, as such, I can also admit no such anticipation of "quality" ever magnetized my spectatorship in this case. Nor did Jordan Peele's presence, as the would-be "Serling" host/provocateur, compel me toward the new series. And yet Peele's presence and its own ideological ramifications are critical to this discussion, even if that presence may be closer to a form of preemptive *branding* than a governing vision, per se. I shall address these concerns in due course.

I am going to be relentlessly systematic in my "then-and-now" analysis. Accordingly, I believe the best place to begin is with the culture of American television. Why does popular sentiment perceive the current climate of content-streaming as a new "golden age"? Television's original Golden Age was televised theater, a merely visualized extension of what had become a mainstay on the radio—live performances written by respected writers like Paddy Chayevsky, Reginald Rose, and, eventually, Rod Serling himself. And when such craftsmen began to write specifically for television itself, their work was referred to as a "teleplay" (as opposed to "screenplay"). At that time, the suppliers or, rather, commodifiers of the new suburban lifestyle sponsored these programs, advertising in name only by simply branding the production, as with *Kraft Television Theatre* (1947–1958), *The Chevrolet Tele-Theatre* (1948–1950), or *The Philco-Goodyear Television Playhouse* (1948–1955). Increasingly, though, sponsors inserted live advertisement segments for their products at the end of the program, in the middle, or both. In any case, the narrative tendency of these teleplays emerged in a postwar climate of social consciousness, especially with the influx of European films after the Paramount Decision took down Hollywood's vertical integration in 1948. The influence of Italian Neorealist filmmaking should not be underestimated, and especially *Bicycle Thieves* (1948), with its sentimental account of a common laborer in Rome succumbing to theft to support his family—a refreshingly modest and unpretentious little story nevertheless drenched in a classical Hollywood film score. This Academy-Award-winning film would find its American analogue in the 1955 film *Marty*, starring Ernest Borgnine, about a lonely butcher living with his mother in the Bronx and struggling to find a spouse. Although the film garnered several Academy Awards and the Palme d'Or at Cannes, it had already impressed popular audiences as Chayevsky's teleplay for *The Philco-Goodyear Television Playhouse* two years earlier, in 1953. But, really, this particularly profitable moment of confluence and cooperation between Hollywood and American television was atypical at this time, when they were ostensible competitors. The means by which the cinema strove to lure suburban audiences away from their fuzzy black-and-white TV sets and back into movie theaters downtown are immediately palpable in terms of spectacle, or, rather, sensorial emphasis. These means included color filmstock, widescreen formats, 3-D, and even experiments like *Smell-O-Rama* and *Smell-O-Vision*. And spectacular aesthetics compelled spectacular narrative contexts, often in the form of Biblical and historical epics shot overseas in locations American audiences would perceive as exotic, such as Egyptian deserts in *The Ten Commandments* (1956) or Norwegian fjords in *The Vikings* (1958). Television, on the other hand, could only rely on the power of good storytelling—and within extremely modest production circumstances. Social consciousness narratives probing the uglier sides of postwar American culture became desirable for middleclass audiences, especially finding themselves at a comfortable suburban distance from the mostly urban subject matter, as in *Marty*. At the same time, these narratives were amenable to television sponsors compelled to minimize costs. And, of course, since everything was televised live, actors needed a theatrical level of expertise in their craft. They could not reshoot their lines or simply memorize small segments independently, one shot at a time. In other words, these teleplays were usually a single "long take." So, if motion picture storytelling ever deserved to be condemned as merely "canned theatre," it was in this postwar television context, except it was precisely everything inherent to the craft of playwriting for the stage that made these teleplays so absorbing for the home audience—and sufficiently so to make Hollywood studios panic.

Seventy odd years later, the picture has changed rather dramatically, and so readopting the notion of a "golden age" could be misleading. First of all, the "teleplay," as such, no longer exists in the vastly expanded universe of television content. The last of the live TV drama programs, *Playhouse 90* (1956–1960), where Rod Serling really honed his writing prowess, ended its four-season run in 1960. After the three major networks began producing their own content during the 1950s, a shift away from socially conscious toward more escapist fare ensued, deriving mostly from mainstream radio genres like western, crime, and comedy. And the concurrent rise of the science fiction genre, oriented around popular American fears of nuclear holocaust and/or Soviet invasion spawned narratives of laboratory experiments gone afoul and hostile aliens arriving in flying saucers. As TV sets became more affordable, networks sought to create a diversity of content less targeted at educated, middleclass adults and more broadly intended for everyone in the family and regardless of economic status. Advertising slots were sold to companies seeking to promote their products, and, understandably, these slots only multiplied as television evolved, finding their most saturated degree in cable networks of recent decades. Enter the era of paid streaming. Escapist, genre-oriented television has persisted, although the cost of production has now been transferred to the consumer. Of course, the evolution from cost-free, televised content to a purified subscription television is more complex, having its roots in On TV, Select TV, HBO, Showtime, and Cinemax, all of which screened only pre-released films initially. Meanwhile, cable television expanded the range of channels and the content associated with them exponentially, while mostly persisting with advertising slots just as CBS, NBC, and ABC had been doing all this time. Many of these cable networks began to produce their own content, and so, predictably, the surviving premiere networks arrived at a logical profit-maximizing strategy: self-produced subscription content. Only recently has the original trio of television networks begun to introduce their own subscription content—completing a historical cycle from television's "teleplay" roots to the current era of "premiere" network streaming, or, rather, from one "golden age" to the next.

But the narrative content itself only began to shift noticeably toward its "goldenness" with the arrival of *The Sopranos* (1999–2007) on HBO. And it is this series that has become far more paradigmatic for the surplus of "quality" television content right now than *The Twilight Zone*, regardless of the latter's steady stream of revivals and still-syndicated presence on Netflix. At first glance, it would not seem to require a great deal of insight to account for the explosive reception won by *The Sopranos*. For some years previously, *The Godfather* (1972) had supplanted *Citizen Kane* (1941) on "best film" lists, such as AFI's, appearing all over the internet. And *The Godfather*, along with its first sequel, had become almost ubiquitous on cable television, especially on AMC, TBS, TNT, and similar retro movie channels. And other "mafia family" films appearing in the wake of *The Godfather*, especially Martin Scorsese's also-celebrated *Goodfellas* (1990), only reinforced the legacy of Coppola's 1972 classic. And, put succinctly, *The Godfather* had done something groundbreaking, not merely by perpetuating the trajectory of antihero characters from Godard's *Breathless* (1961) to the seminal counterculture films *Bonnie and Clyde* (1967) and *Easy Rider* (1969), but moreover by extending the antihero characterization across *several* family members. In this way, the primary sympathetic locus of Hollywood storytelling, the (white) nuclear family, could *also* function as a countercultural force of resistance toward the American establishment. This emerging narrative paradigm no longer required a "Benjamin Braddock" character to rebel against his cocktail-generation parents and their suburban neighborhood friends, as in *The Graduate*

(1967). Now, the larger family entity could potentially take up the cause, although mostly in the spirit of revenge *as allegorical resistance. The Godfather's* baptism climax famously uses crosscutting to indicate Michael Corleone's hypocrisy, but the countercultural subtext here encourages us to ignore Michael's presence and, instead, to revel in the graphic montage of poetic justice against all those characters inhibiting or doing violence to this "American family," as such. And so, it suffices to affirm *The Sopranos* essentially *serializes The Godfather*, where the film had proven not quite able to do so successfully on its own, across its two sequels. As a television series, the HBO show expands the mafia family narrative by developing its characters to a much greater degree of complexity, and, according to a much older cinematic tradition of the cliffhanger strategy, with such silent-era progenitors as *The Perils of Pauline* (1914) or even 1960s television's *Batman* series (1966–1968). That is, each episode leaves us with a burning question of what happens next, and how these more human-like protagonists will resolve their immediate predicaments. We are irresistibly compelled to pursue the next installment in order to find out. *The Sopranos'* widespread popularity and universal acclaim would, of course, usher in a deluge of willfully "premiere" serial content, whose complex characters and serpentine narratives have mostly maintained this standard of "quality" or, rather, this would-be formula for guaranteed immersion. Another seminal crime family series within this tendency, of course, was *Breaking Bad* (2008–2013), about a high school chemistry teacher (Bryan Cranston) tempted into manufacturing and dealing crystal methamphetamine to provide for his family in the aftermath of his imminent demise from cancer. And the paradigm of the antihero-family, per se, would eventually find its most complex fruition in the globally celebrated *Game of Thrones* (2011–2019), whose array of family strongholds are pitted against each other across a seven-season span of episodes sufficient to manipulate audience sympathies in the opposite direction, as we discover hidden personal motives for actions previously seeming malevolent, especially in the case of the Lannisters. So far, this recent entry represents the apex of television's new "golden age," having its paradigmatic roots in both *The Sopranos* and *The Godfather*. And it might be more productive to understand this "premiere" paradigm as "*The Godfather* meets *Dynasty*," or rather "violent family melodramas." Beyond the inner politics of family hegemony, the complexity of human psychological and emotional relations is explored more intensively, mainly through elaborate dialogue. *Game of Thrones*, for example, only pursues a green-screen *façade* of an action-oriented spectacle, with its bloody sword fights and pornographic content. So it would be a misunderstanding to categorize this series' episodes among, for example, AMC's "Movies for Guys Who Like Movies."

Game of Thrones is actually closer to a soap opera. Although he dedicates most of his energy to Rod Serling's personal history, Brian Murray finally speculates on the writer's "legacy" in this current "high-quality" climate of television, opining, "Perhaps Serling, with his wish to use television as a vehicle for artistic expression on pressing moral and political issues would fit right in."

Nevertheless, *The Twilight Zone* series depended on a different narrative paradigm altogether, and this difference illustrates a larger cultural discrepancy between these two "golden" eras of American television. Instead of a soap opera format, pursuing the same principal characters week after week, *The Twilight Zone* and its live teleplay predecessors were drama *anthology* series. Each episode presented new characters and situations. In some cases, these programs really did behave like literary "anthologies" of popular stories for middleclass Americans reading in the evenings, and were pre-filmed adaptations of canonical short stories rather than live, dedicated teleplays. The first of these was NBC's *Your Show Time*, airing for one season in 1949, and featuring half-hour adaptations of stories by Guy de Maupassant, Charles Dickens, Arthur Conan Doyle, Victor Hugo, Robert Louis Stevenson, Frank Stockton, Mark Twain, and many others. At the same time, there were anthology or "portmanteau" films appearing in movie theaters, such as *Quartet* (1948) and *Trio* (1950), both featuring stories by W. Somerset Maugham, and *O. Henry's Full House* (1952), screening five adaptations of the latter author's stories. Often, these programs included an onscreen host, a male of authoritative and erudite demeanor, who would typically introduce the episode and would then return at the end for some form of closing afterword or insight. For example, *Your Show Time*'s host Arthur Shields appeared in a mockup library and would pull volumes down from shelves to introduce that week's episode. And Maugham himself even appeared on camera, as if at his own writing desk, to introduce his stories in the two aforementioned anthology films, as did John Steinbeck to introduce O. Henry's stories in the latter film. Here, again, was an atypical moment of confluence between cinema and television, where they appeared to be almost equivalent media, at least in their approaches to visual storytelling. In any case, these film and TV harbingers established a palpably highbrow context for television content in subsequent years, to be perceived as visualized literature hardly different from reading the source material itself. These anthology programs also provided a rationale for a TV writer, on the strength of recent fame for "Requiem for a Heavyweight," his Emmy and Peabody Award–winning teleplay for *Playhouse 90*, to also step in front of the camera to host a new anthology series, just as Alfred Hitchcock, the increasingly celebrated film director, could now host his own anthology series, *Alfred Hitchcock*

Presents (1955–1965), on television—even if each of them did not necessarily write or direct all the episodes. Although the live, social consciousness dramas had all but disappeared by the late 1950s, these genre-oriented anthology series, by retaining their charismatic hosts, preserved an illusion of continued "quality," if nothing more.

According to the larger cultural context for the original *The Twilight Zone* anthology series, then, the current *The Twilight Zone* reboot could be embraced as a means to "bridge" these "golden eras" of television. On the other hand, the reboot could simply rehash a historical TV format long since abandoned. Already, *The Twilight Zone*'s anthology series approach would appear to defy the greatest source of momentum for current trends. Such episodes cannot attempt to flesh out a limited range of characters across several seasons, and, accordingly, such characters are unavailable to dangle precariously from the edge of cliffs at the end, compelling us to crave the next installment like a heroin fix. And, of course, what is even more effective about the typical "premiere" series' cliffhanger is that it is less action-oriented and more psychological, where suspense derives from complex social predicaments central characters find themselves in, again, akin to popular nighttime soaps of the 1980s. So if anyone binge-watched the new *The Twilight Zone* episodes, it would not be for any reason to do with suspense, per se. But, even if the anthology format is an anomaly in the current television climate, it has already proven to be a viable alternative. Specifically, the British series *Black Mirror*, commencing in 2011, has already set a precedent for an anthology format revival, and moreover in having been celebrated as "the new Twilight Zone," with obvious similarities in terms of genre and thematic agenda. To consider the reasons is outside the scope of this analysis, however. Whether or not the current reboot of *The Twilight Zone* took encouragement from *Black Mirror*, it goes a step further in the spirit of revivalism by faithfully integrating a series host, in Rod Serling's stead. This is its first mistake. There is simply no cultural relevance for a drama series having a host (or "narrator") in the current television climate—except in referencing the original postwar format. Certainly many conventions of visual storytelling persist on our flat-screen TVs, but the attempt to sophisticate the television atmosphere with a solemn and articulate male introducing and/or reflecting on the narrative content was only revived briefly in Serling's case, on *Night Gallery* (1969–1973), because his charismatic onscreen presence was undeniable, regardless of the genre shift to horror. But, more generally, anthology dramas and their astute hosts faded out just as fast as genre series replaced them across the sixties. So, unless one really embraces the reboot of *The Twilight Zone* in a pure spirit of nostalgia, the nondiegetic appearance of a commentator at the advent and close of episodes seems officious, if not contrived. At the same time, the program's producers deserve some credit here in positioning one of American entertainment media's most currently relevant provocateurs as the would-be "Serling," at least categorically.

Like Jordan Peele has been of late, Serling was also a provocateur in his time, although network executives stifled his aggressive agenda for social consciousness long before it ever reached its full expression. His intended narrativization of the 1955 Emmett Till murder, for example, as the 1956 *Playhouse 90* entry "Noon at Doomsday," was ultimately sanitized for mainstream American television. Serling's racist scenario in the South, with an African American victim, ended up taking place in New England, with the same "victim" character reconfigured vaguely as a "foreigner." American popular culture has changed dramatically since then, in terms of censorship, at least, and this is nowhere more evident than in the "premiere" streaming content of recent years—something the reboot of *The Twilight Zone* is less able to take advantage of, on CBS. As for white racism toward African Americans, Peele's sketch comedy and controversial debut feature *Get Out* (2017) have boldly suggested otherwise. According to Ryan Poll's analysis of the writer-director's film, "To be Black in America, *Get Out* suggests, is to be trapped within an unending narrative of racialized terror." For this reason, Peele would seem the ideal choice to assume the function of what Serling had been—the host and visionary of an anthology series drawing attention to America's most immediate social problems through the guise of escapist TV genre fare. From this mindset, a manifold array of shortsightedness has unfolded across this current revival series' first ten episodes. First of all, Peele has already positioned himself as a comedian and satirist, mostly as a result of his work on Comedy Central's *Key & Peele* (2012–2015). Even if his subsequent two films assume a more sober tone, especially within their horror trappings, his screen presence hasn't yet established the dramatic range necessary to leap into Serling's role so abruptly. He is palpably awkward, and particularly when he decides to raise his eyebrows after closing his "Twilight Zone" commentary, almost as if his comedic, tongue-in-cheek impulse is impossible to suppress. Or he is simply not taking himself seriously, which is of no service, of course, to the program's larger intentions, at least according to its legacy. Also, and this has been a rampant cultural misunderstanding of *The Twilight Zone* in its wake, the original series, even in its overarching agenda for social consciousness, was extremely eclectic. It is not merely a "science fiction" program, as even Peele himself remarks in the season finale "Blurryman" (2019), and to reduce it to such not only constricts the range of its story directions, but also misguides the means by which these narrative trajectories ultimately arrive in the same place. The science fiction film genre could have developed from as far back as Melies's silent

Trip to the Moon (1902), but really only burgeoned in the postwar era, as I mentioned, as a response to Cold War fears of nuclear holocaust and/ or Soviet invasion. As a result, conventions of the genre formed around imagined technologies, often to be found in a dystopian future, or simply the means by which invaders arrived from outer space to wreak havoc on Earth. Serling's series certainly exploited the popularity of these narratives across the 1950s, but moreover to point to their implicit McCarthyist paranoia. And such episodes only made up a portion of the series' content, which also included western, war, fantasy, domestic, and other contemporary dramas. Each of these genres, of course, has its own narrative conventions distinct from science fiction and from each other. And, of course, in *The Twilight Zone*, genres may be hybridized. When imagined technologies are not at work, in any case, what connects nearly all of the remaining original episodes is a *metaphysical premise*—allowing for circumstances and events to behave outside of human understanding. This is not science fiction, per se, but if anyone preferred to restrict consideration of postwar anthology series to that genre, I would point them to *The Outer Limits* (1963–1965), a series completely dedicated to space invaders and technology gone wrong. Even if the reboot of *The Twilight Zone* only perpetuates this misunderstanding of science fiction, its conventions, and its cultural context, the series nevertheless adopts the original's metaphysical premise as a narrative option beyond imagined technologies and/or futures. At the same time, it has yet to expand into other drama genres the original series explored. Its first season, at least, has restricted itself to the immediate present and impending future. Furthermore, if Peele's presence is to be embraced according to Serling's own agenda and legacy, I would point out his own parameters of social critique have been restricted to issues of *race*. In appropriating *The Twilight Zone*'s anthology format, then, the new series should offer a broader exploration of genre than it has so far, just as its assumed social consciousness agenda should not be framed around a media personality whose own agenda has been so specifically targeted.

Once the original "Twilight Zone" formula can be understood as in no way dependent on imagined technologies, futures, or outer space scenarios, it remains to affirm precisely what becomes paradigmatic across all five seasons. If anything, Serling's prologue suggests these narratives derive from "the dimension of imagination," or what he initially referred to as the "fifth dimension." Peele's prologue, on the other hand, lazily swaps out the definite article by dubbing the Twilight Zone "*a* dimension of imagination," thus dispensing with any notion of that which exists beyond what is measurable within the "four" dimensions of sensorial perception. In any case, outside of the original series' many science fiction scenarios, even a metaphysical premise is not an essential alternative. In the final season's episode "The Jeopardy Room" (1964), for example, about a defecting KGB man (Martin Landau) forced to search for a hidden explosive in his hotel room, there is no science fiction element or metaphysical phenomena whatsoever. Nevertheless, the episode delivers on the series' consistent pattern of ironic circumstances, in this case, as the typical twist ending. The protagonist outwits his would-be assassins by barely escaping their gunfire, awaiting their investigation, and finally ringing them up on the booby-trapped telephone they had intended him to answer in the first place. In my monograph, I argue that narrative irony induces a contemplative state in the television consumer, thereby increasing the probability of reception for the intended social critique. Of course, this is only theoretical, and many or most mainstream American consumers of the show may never come away with any raised awareness of postwar problems in American society. But this was Serling's own attempt at a "compromise" between his former "angry man" agenda for social consciousness on television and the broader shift in consumer demands toward escapist genre programming. This precedent on irony across a range of genres is readily affirmed with the initial run of original teleplays of which only the first and last of seven in a row are science fiction—before the first adapted story appears, and then Charles Beaumont's first contribution after this. And, according to the persistent presence of irony, instead of categorizing *The Twilight Zone* narratives according to genre, I detect a range of ironic categories across the series, namely: "technological" irony (i.e., robots, computers, and other "future" technologies, as well as already present "haunted" technologies), "invasive" irony (i.e., astronaut and alien narratives), "martial" irony (i.e., World War II, previous, and future wartime soldier/civilian contexts), "sociopolitical irony" (i.e., Cold War politics and socialization), and "domestic" irony (i.e., courtship, marriage, and family situations). To address these categories in more detail is well beyond the scope and purpose of this essay, but another crucial formulaic aspect I probe across these narrative divisions is the overarching presence of a *moral universe*. Essentially, I argue, the original series becomes an aggregate system for social critique, wherein always-ironic circumstances either "reward" or "punish" characters according to their proven degrees of socialization. For example, in the celebrated episode "Time Enough at Last" (1959), starring Burgess Meredith, about the four-eyed bookworm's thwarted expectations of endless reading opportunity, the common interpretation finds an existential or cynical comment on the "unfairness" of life. Yet in the context of affirming *The Twilight Zone*'s larger narrative paradigm, this episode's ironic outcome points to his deficiency as a team player on the worksite and as an attentive husband. In other words, he proves both unwilling and unable to contribute to his own human ecosystem.

To be fair, the current reboot of *The Twilight Zone* does engage with an agenda for social consciousness, but, again, within diminished parameters, particularly in terms of genre. Within the first season, current American issues such as date rape, media hype, illegal immigration, gun possession, and, of course, racial stereotyping and intolerance are explored. And ironic circumstances also serve to imply a moral universe in these episodes, accordingly "correcting" manifestations of social deviance and/or moral turpitude. Nevertheless, these are consistently flawed narratives, and by saying so, it would seem I am—ironically—assuming Zicree's predisposition. Allow me to consider the first season's debut episode as an example. The metaphysical premise for "The Comedian" (2019) starring Kumail Nanjiani, reveals a standup protagonist's acquired ability to erase the existence of anyone he mentions in his act. In confronting his own narcissism, he eventually erases *himself*. Such a logline promises an interesting and original "Twilight Zone" narrative, although two fundamental problems emerge. First, the comedic onstage content on which the realism of the episode depends, especially according to the notion his act becomes increasingly hilarious, is never remotely amusing. If my evaluation sounds immediately subjective, I shall put it another way: the depicted audience's response *overstates* the narrative intention here, and these scenes are anything but convincing. For instance, while the audience is stone-faced toward his "second amendment" rant, his desperate turn toward scatological anecdotes about his dog prompts laughter all too artificially. If the episode had intended its metaphysical universe to make unfunny content funny, that would be different. But, here, his previous Faustian bargain with an idolized comic (Tracy Morgan) at the bar only anticipates his new emphasis on "personal" experiences. And so a pattern of unconvincingly hilarious references to everyone he ever disliked ensues, culminating in a non sequitur, where he references *himself* deliberately in a catharsis of self-loathing. But, in this moment, his audience is still laughing at a presence supposedly erased from ever existing at all. The narrative logic breaks down here. Also, his own "narcissism," referenced at one point by his girlfriend (Amara Karan) before she, too, is eventually erased, is never established through any initial action. He never behaves selfishly, per se, before metaphysical events begin to transform his personality from what had seemed normal, gentle, and even kind. So this pilot episode's formulaic moral universe ends up "correcting" its protagonist for a social deviance he would only appear to develop *as a result of* his newfound powers, rather than as an aspect of his nature.

An unfortunate pattern of narrative *contrivance*, wherein characters' behavior would also seem conveniently pliable according to metaphysical or outlandish circumstances, persists across the first season's remaining nine episodes. To clarify further, the original series typically introduces metaphysical circumstances or science fiction in order to manipulate characters into confronting their true natures, or, if not, then to at least enable the audience to see into these characters' true natures. Here, on the other hand, metaphysical circumstances do not necessarily account for what are often peripheral characters' abrupt shifts in their attitudes. For example, in the fourth entry, "The Traveler" (2019), about a young policewoman (Marika Sila) encountering an alien invasion in Alaska, a well-dressed man (Steven Yeun) inexplicably "materializes" inside one of the police station's jail cells. How this individual appeared in the cell in the first place is just as inexplicably "overlooked" by the protagonist and her superior officer (Greg Kinnear) until only after the man is "pardoned," according to the police station's Christmas tradition, and released. Such behavior on the part of these law enforcement characters undermines the episode's credibility. In the subsequent episode, "The Wunderkind" (2019), a presidential campaign manager (John Cho) dedicates his media talent to an outspoken, eleven-year-old boy (Jacob Tremblay), who is eventually "spoiled" by his presidency and so waxes tyrannical. The entire scenario demands a generous suspension of disbelief, but the problem is that no metaphysical element is provided to explain everyone's brainless devotion to the boy, amidst the protagonist's increasing disillusion. In the seventh entry, "Not All Men" (2019), on the other hand, it is a sudden meteor shower and its strange glowing meteorites accounting for widespread violent aggressiveness among the local male population. Nevertheless, this latter episode also falls prey to contrivance, although more in terms of plot assemblage, as the female protagonist's first-offending date (Luke Kirby) suddenly reappears to accost her again in a completely different corner of the city, just after she (Taissa Farmiga) has arrived in the absolutely perfect instant to save her brother from his murderous companion. And further contrivances abound in subsequent entries. In "Point of Origin" (2019), a wealthy middleclass matriarch (Ginnifer Goodwin) is ultimately discovered by government agents to be an "imposter" from another dimension, but this is no way explains her husband's absolute estrangement and unsympathetic disposition toward her in this moment. And "The Blue Scorpion" (2019), about the metaphysical presence of a handgun able to literally "select" and then possess its series of unfortunate owners, reveals several artificial elements, such as a local gun-shop owner explaining the entire "legend" of the weapon, only to be echoed redundantly by a ghost suddenly appearing in the protagonist's home. Also, at one point, the protagonist (Chris O'Dowd), a college professor, is visited by a student (Luisa d'Oliveira) in his office who just happens to be doing her project on "animism" and so believes even her shoes have "personalities of their own."

Finally, Peele's sage epilogue pointing at people "loving *objects* more than other people" is inconsistent with the protagonist's own behavior, since he, after all, never invited the gun into his life. Rather, it forced itself on his father first, "never" having owned a gun, and then on him and his conscience, in turn. So what were these characters really guilty of? Materialism? If so, such a premise is not clarified sufficiently before the gun arrives. Even the emphasis on issues of race, in no less than three of the season's ten episodes, seems artificially imposed on the *Twilight Zone*, per se, when compared to the merely two such episodes in the original series. And compounded by Peele's own agenda in his two films and comedy sketches, this implicit, if not ostensible fixation only makes the inclusion of so many minority characters in the other episodes seem less than incidental or natural.

Beyond its many forms of contrivance, the current reboot of *The Twilight Zone* also sets itself apart from the original series in another significant way—its shameless compunction for cultural nostalgia. And this should not be taken as inherent to reviving a cultural artifact, per se, if that artifact can be recontextualized sufficiently to avoid any trappings of its own milieu. I have already provided the historical context for Serling's role as series host, and how such a role feels completely inappropriate for the present times, even if the anthology format itself manages to achieve tolerance within the otherwise "golden" ubiquity of the serial narrative and its complex characters. What becomes in Jordan Peele's role an implied nostalgia for Serling himself, then, does not stop here, or perhaps leave open the potential for Peele's own idiosyncratic presence to reorient the new series toward the present. Disappointingly, many of the episodes only bask in their assumed audience's nostalgia for the original series and other media references mostly only Gen-X viewers would catch. First of all, there are "narrative" cases, such as the first season's second entry, "Nightmare at 30,000 Feet" (2019), immediately referencing the campy original of similar name, "Nightmare at 20,000 Feet" (1963), wherein William Shatner's signature theatrics redeem the cheap pajama-like costume intended to provide convincing ambiguity as visiting nemesis or neurosis. But promisingly, the new version completely reimagines the plot, only retaining the premise of a passenger's unreliable experiences during his flight. To echo my previous paragraph's point, this episode nevertheless also forfeits credibility, this time, by depending on an audiobook mp3 player that just happens to appear in the backseat pocket, with an inauthentic-sounding "story" about a passenger sabotaging a commercial flight. There may also be narrative mashups of the original episodes, although this is purely speculative. For example, "Replay" (2019), about a video camera that "rewinds" time and whose use eventually becomes a vicious cycle of the protagonist's repeated attempts to thwart her son's death, could appear to be an imaginative conflation of "A Most Unusual Camera" (1960), about a camera that photographs the future, and "Shadow Play" (1959), about a condemned man's perpetual "nightmare" cycle of his trial's events and sentencing. And then there are literal "iconographic" references to the original series, as in "The Traveler" with its various Christmas tree ornaments and objects citing specific episodes. Additionally, there are references to other popular media of the Gen-X television experience, such as the oft-rescreened Clint Eastwood crime film *Dirty Harry* (1971), when, while holding the Blue Scorpion, the protagonist says, "Ya gotta ask yourself. Did he take six shots or only five?" Of course, if there were any doubt as to this particular reboot's adherence to the increasing nostalgia for America's cultural past, also to be found in the 2017 *Blade Runner 2049* sequel, for example, its series finale builds its reflexive plot about one of its own writer's studio soundstage universe waxing metaphysically bizarre—until Rod Serling himself makes a CGI-cameo, as if this were the "inevitable" culmination of such events. Ironically, the intended effect of both surprise and welcome nostalgia fails, thanks to the noticeable veneer of digital effects combined with an execrable attempt at Serling's vocal inflections. Of course, this first season's culmination of narrative contrivance and desperate nostalgia do not bode well for an improved, although imminent, second round.

All told, the complex artificiality of the new series establishes its *unintentional* irony, as an anthology series seeking to wield the once-impressive "Twilight Zone" narrative paradigm for social critique. With all of its dated special effects and retrofuture trappings, the original series holds up for the quality of its teleplays, not only in the imaginative breadth of their scenarios, but in the potency of the dialogue itself regardless. What characters actually say to each other in these episodes, reinforced through their noticeably superior acting prowess, such as in the case of Jack Klugman's appeal to God (or the Twilight Zone) for his dying son in "In Praise of Pip" (1963), invokes a greater emotional response than the more action-oriented narratives offered so far in the current reboot— and especially the season finale, with its desperate fanfare of CGI-driven spectacle. But to simply notice an "inferior quality," which may, indeed, be just as noticeable in the previous revival series, is shortsighted to the larger cultural context for Rod Serling's agenda and the obstacles he faced within *that* era of television. If the studios hadn't shifted away from social consciousness toward more widely popular escapist fare, Serling would have conceived a very different series, more probably akin to the quotidian scenarios found in *Playhouse 90*. Today's television culture is much more open toward social critique in the media, however controversial. The persistent issue of racism and violence toward African Americans, for example, does not need to be veiled in narratives sans any black characters. And Jordan Peele has certainly shed light on the less ostensible ways in which this racism is still perpetuated in white middleclass American culture through his previous film and television work, although the marriage of this agenda to the classic "Twilight Zone" paradigm only inflects audience reception, for example, by forcing us to acknowledge so many minority characters and even interracial intimacy we might otherwise take for granted in other current shows. In other words, Peele's presence as anachronistic series host merely makes these characters and their situations all the more artificial and deliberate. What should be believable circumstances *within* scientifically or metaphysically impossible narrative contexts becomes itself a forced element. And so, again, the new series fails thereby. Rather than greeting the current reboot as an unfortunate cultural continuum, I want to be optimistic it will be the last attempt to revive a television show whose steadfast legacy requires no such gesture or homage. Really, these reboots are a disservice to *The Twilight Zone*, Rod Serling, and the many other contributors to its moment. Otherwise, we'd also be witnessing *their* legacy on Netflix.

WORKS CITED

"Blue Scorpion," *The Twilight Zone*, written by Glen Morgan, directed by Craig William Macneill, CBS All Access, 2019.
"Blurryman," *The Twilight Zone*, written by Alex Rubins, directed by Simon Kinberg, CBS All Access, 2019.
Booker, M. Keith. *Monsters, Mushroom Clouds, and the Cold War: American Science Fiction and the Roots of Postmodernism, 1946–1964*. Greenwood Press, 2001.
Booker, M. Keith. *Strange TV: Innovative Television Series from* The Twilight Zone *to* The X-Files. Greenwood Press, 2002.
"The Comedian," *The Twilight Zone*, written by Alex Rubins, directed by Owen Harris, CBS All Access, 2019.
Edgerton, Gary R. *The Columbia History of American Television*. Columbia University Press, 2007.
Gerani, Gary. *Fantastic Television*. Harmony Books, 1977.
"In Praise of Pip," *The Twilight Zone*, written by Rod Serling, directed by Joseph M. Newman, Image Entertainment, 2011.
"The Jeopardy Room," *The Twilight Zone*, written by Rod Serling, directed by Richard Donner, Image Entertainment, 2011.
May, Elaine Tyler. *Homeward Bound: American Families in the Cold War Era*. Basic Books, 1999.
Melbye, David. *Irony in* The Twilight Zone: How the Series Critiqued Postwar American Culture. Rowman & Littlefield, 2015.
"A Most Unusual Camera," *The Twilight Zone*, written by Rod Serling, directed by John Rich, Image Entertainment, 2011.
Murray, Brian. "The Enduring Legacy of *The Twilight Zone*." *The New Atlantis*, no. 48, Winter 2016, pp. 90–112.
"Nightmare at 20,000 Feet," *The Twilight Zone*, written by Richard Matheson, directed by Richard Donner, Image Entertainment, 2011.

"Nightmare at 30,000 Feet," *The Twilight Zone*, written by Marco Ramirez, directed by Greg Yaitanes, CBS All Access, 2019.

"Not All Men," *The Twilight Zone*, written by Heather Anne Campbell, directed by Christina Choe, CBS All Access, 2019.

"Point of Origin," *The Twilight Zone*, written by John Griffin, directed by Mathias Herndl, CBS All Access, 2019.

Poll, Ryan. "Can One Get Out? The Aesthetics of Afro-Pessimism," *The Journal of the Midwest Modern Language Association*, vol. 51, no. 2, 2018, pp. 69–102.

Presnell, Don, and Marty McGee. *A Critical History of Television's* The Twilight Zone, *1959–1964*. McFarland, 1998.

"Replay," *The Twilight Zone*, written by Selwyn Seyfu Hinds, directed by Gerard McMurray, CBS All Access, 2019.

Sander, Gordon F. *Serling: The Rise and Twilight of Television's Last Angry Man*. Dutton, 1992.

Sconce, Jeffrey. *Haunted Media*. Duke University Press, 2000.

"Shadow Play," *The Twilight Zone*, written by Charles Beaumont, directed by John Brahm, Image Entertainment, 2011.

Spigel, Lynn. *Make Room for TV: Television and the Family Ideal in Postwar America*. The University of Chicago Press, 1992.

"Time Enough at Last," *The Twilight Zone*, written by Rod Serling, directed by John Brahm, Image Entertainment, 2010.

"The Traveler," *The Twilight Zone*, written by Glen Morgan, directed by Ana Lily Amirpour, CBS All Access, 2019.

"The Wunderkind," *The Twilight Zone*, written by Andrew Guest, directed by Richard Shepard, CBS All Access, 2019.

Zicree, Marc Scott. *The Twilight Zone Companion*. Silman-James Press, 1989.

PART V

Staging the Zone

From Curator to Co-Author

*Examining the Narrative and Political Choices
in Anne Washburn's Stage Adaptation
of* The Twilight Zone

William C. Boles

Imagine if you will that a small, award-winning, and influential theater in the toney London neighborhood of Islington decides that its holiday show during the 2017–2018 season will be an adaptation of a popular American anthology series from the 1960s. Tapping Anne Washburn, an American playwright, best known for her post-apocalyptic play *Mr. Burns, A Post-Electric Play* (2012), the award-winning director Robert Jones asks her to transport the show and its various trappings into a theatrical showcase. She does so, and due to its financial, but not necessarily critical, success at the Almeida Theatre, it transfers in 2019 to the West End, London's Broadway, enticing ticket buyers to once again enter *The Twilight Zone* (2017), but, as we will see, with narrative and political twists not found in the series itself.

The Almeida Theatre's foray into performing *The Twilight Zone* was not the first attempt to transfer Rod Serling's television show to the stage (and, no doubt, it will not be the last). In fact, *The Twilight Zone* (1959–64) has been a regular presence on the stage ever since the television series went off the air in the mid–1960s. While Marc Scott Zicree details in *The Twilight Zone Companion* of the multiple, problematic, and ultimately failed attempts by producers, writers, and directors to reboot cinematic and television versions of *The Twilight Zone*, he notes that the theater has been "more successful" in replicating the vitality of the original show and that theatrical productions of various episodes have been "ubiquitous" over the years (454). Theatres across the country including those in "Los Angeles, St. Louis, Baltimore, and Rod's hometown of Binghamton, New

York" have been home to successful theatrical offerings of Serling's work (454). Some of the more successful episodic transfers to the stage have been "The Monsters are Due on Maple Street" (1960), "Five Characters in Search of an Exit" (1961), and "Will the Real Martian Please Stand Up?" (1961). One of the longest running performative connections to the television series was to be found in Seattle, where Theater Schmeater, starting in the 1990s, offered late night performances of individual episodes. Their show was abruptly cancelled by CBS, as the company withdrew the rights in 2019 (Zara). Why would the corporation rescind permission after more than two decades of successful late-night presentations? While some internet chatter presumed Jordan Peele's upcoming reboot for CBS's streaming service was the reason, it was actually Washburn's stage adaptation and its transfer to the West End, which prompted Manhattan producers to consider the possibility of a Broadway production and with it the lucrative profits to come from potential ticket buyers attracted by the familiar brand. Therefore, CBS, wanting to protect its property and the possible riches to be had, felt it necessary to take away the rights, even from a small West coast theater that only performed episodes for its late-night crowd. The rise of Washburn's adaptation into a possible theatrical moneymaking juggernaut makes it an intriguing addition to *The Twilight Zone* canon of material and a piece worth studying in more detail. Specifically, for this volume I am interested in two aspects of the production: the narrative choices made by Washburn in adapting the series to the stage and the incorporation of the rhetoric of Donald Trump's presidential campaign into "The Shelter" (1961), which Washburn identified as the centerpiece story of the play. In both cases, London theater reviewers found the choices made by Washburn to be problematic to the success of the production, and yet, Washburn's choices were driven by her recognition that 50 years on from the initial broadcast of *The Twilight Zone* audience expectations around narrative and political animus across the aisles had dramatically changed. A reimagined adaptation, incorporating both fronts, was necessary.

The Final Eight: Washburn's Process of Selection

When Washburn was first approached by Richard Jones to create a stage version of the iconic show, she initially wondered about the success of transferring a series so reliant on visual components to the stage space. Upon further contemplation, she recognized that "the original writers all [came] from theatre. So many of the scripts have a heavily theatrical quality, and also the theater is a very spooky place. Because it's physical and it's ambient, and you're trapped in the shadows, and there's the offstage space. Who knows what's going to emerge? There's a very tangible spook-iness" (Longo). Convinced about the theatrical possibilities and ability to stay true to the tone of the show, Washburn set about to watch all 156 episodes from its five-year run. While viewing, she kept an eye out for those episodes that have continued to stay part of our cultural consciousness. Part of her process in honing down the list of viable options was asking of everyone she met: "What *Twilight Zone* episode traumatised you as a small child?" (Trueman 14). From their answers she recognized that "Everybody had a *Twilight Zone* shaped scar somewhere in their heart" (Longo). What episode scarred Washburn? "I was most traumatised by that one, where the bomb landed and the man broke his glasses. It was heartbreakingly unfair, and I refused to watch it again" (Appleyard). Washburn describes "Time Enough at Last" (1959), where Burgess Meredith plays a survi-vor of a nuclear attack who makes his way through the devastation and finally comes to the town library, where he realizes he now can read all the books he wants without interruption. His joy is suddenly shattered when his glasses fall and break into pieces. For Washburn the attractiveness of revisiting Serling's television show was also due to its incredibly powerful comment on the state of the American mind: "*The Twilight Zone* is about America dreaming—or America's nightmares" (Trueman 14). Despite her recognition of the power of the series as a whole, Washburn revealed in interviews that she was not a big fan of the show, so her role in transform-ing Serling's vision to the stage would be "curatorial more than creative" (Gilbert).

After watching all the episodes in the New York offices of CBS and processing the results of her informal poll, she whittled the possible options down to 20 or 30 episodes that she then shared with Jones. "There was one episode that I thought you could not do on stage, which is 'Eye of the Beholder' but which Richard kept holding on to it and found an alter-native way of bringing it in" (Longo), which was to jettison the episode's theme about conformity and just focus on the surprising reveal that the bandaged patient's face is beautiful, but in the eyes of her medical team and fellow citizens, all of whom have deformed facial features, she is hid-eous. Washburn, working with Jones, ended up deciding to include eight episodes in her adaptation, including "Eye of the Beholder" (1960). From Season One, they selected "Perchance to Dream" (1959; written by Charles Beaumont) about a man who visits a doctor's office believing that if he falls asleep he will die; "And When the Sky Was Opened" (1959) about three astronauts, who, upon their return to earth, begin to question the truth of their own existence; and "Nightmare as a Child" (1960) about a teacher who returns home to find a young girl on her doorstep who has in-depth knowledge about the teacher's past, which revolves around a traumatic event. In addition to "Eye of the Beholder" from the second season, they also selected "Will the Real Martian Stand Up?," which details the investigation of two police officers as they hunt for an alien in a diner filled with stranded bus passengers. Season Three had two episodes featured: "The Shelter" about a group of neighbors who batter their way into a neighbor's nuclear shelter during a missile threat and "Little Girl Lost" (1962; written by Richard Matheson) about a young girl who has entered an alternative reality through the wall next to her bed and her parent's attempt to rescue her. Finally, one episode from Season Five was included "The Long Morrow" (1964), where a deep space astronaut about to embark on a mission of forty-five to fifty years long discovers love with a co-worker. Opting not to be cryogenically frozen during the journey, he returns an old man to discover that his love has opted to freeze herself so she will be the same age when he returns.

Crafting the Play: Washburn's Narrative Decisions

After deciding upon these eight episodes the next question involved the actual process of transferring them to a theatrical form. In her role as curator Washburn opted to take a different route from previous stage versions, which essentially enacted each episode in its entirety. Instead, she chose an unconventional narrative approach in retelling the stories by Serling, Matheson, and Beaumont. Rather than having each episode played in its entirety, she cut out extraneous scenes from the episode and then divided the remaining story into segments, which she then interspersed amongst other episodes, also segmented, throughout the play, creating an effect of the audience channel surfing through The Twilight Zone. (The set designed by Paul Steinberg reinforced the idea of watching television, as the frame around the playing space was shaped like a huge television screen and before the play began and during the intermission the CBS logo was projected onto a scrim.) Her decision to cut the episodes into segments makes sense when one considers the play's running time. Each episode had a run time of 25 minutes, meaning if all were performed in their entirety, then the play would have had a three hour and twenty minute run time *before* the inclusion of an intermission. Such an offering would rival Shakespeare's tragedies in its length. So cutting each episode down was to be expected in such an endeavor.

To provide an explanation of how Washburn's adaptation intercut the shorter segments of the episodes together, let me describe briefly the narrative structure of the first half of act one. "Will the Real Martian Stand

Up?" opens the play with all the travelers from the stranded bus gathered in the diner waiting for the bridge, which was closed due to a heavy snowstorm, to open back up, so they can resume their travels. The majority of Serling's dialogue from the episode is used as Washburn conveys the growing tension between the various stranded passengers faced with the possibility of an alien in their midst, but there are slight changes as Washburn has to make the episodes jibe with her limited number of cast members, who play multiple roles throughout the performance. (For example, a little girl travelling alone is now one of the passengers. Instead of two police officers, there now is only one doing the investigating.) The travelers eventually leave to get back on the bus. The surprise conclusion to the episode is not shown to the audience for another thirty minutes, as Washburn then introduces snippets from the birthday party section of "The Shelter" played on a television monitor in the back of the diner; parents being awoken by their crying child in "Little Girl Lost" and discovering her absence from her bedroom; the entirety of "Nightmare as a Child" is played out through three scenes interspersed between the other episodes; the characters in "And When the Sky Was Opened" are introduced and their confusion about who was actually on the mission occurs over a few intermingled scenes; the main conceit of "Perchance to Dream" is introduced by the patient to the doctor as well as short scenes that takes us into his actual dream at the carnival; and a brief snippet of "Eye of the Beholder" floats across the stage as the face of an unseen nurse begins to take bandages off of a covered face, before the action once again returns to the diner. In total, seven of the eight episodes are introduced between the opening and closing scene "Will the Real Martian Stand Up?" Only "The Long Morrow" is missing, and it does not appear until the second act.

Clearly, such a narrative organization demonstrates that Washburn is not interested in maintaining the narrative purity of each episode. (As mentioned earlier, "Eye of the Beholder" is reduced just to the surprise reveal of the woman's face beneath the bandages.) Instead, one might compare the production to a tasting menu, where the audience has the experience of sampling various morsels over the evening and eventually, by the close of the show, they would have experienced an eight course meal of episodes. From one perspective, the disrupted sequencing works because of the distinct difference between all the chosen episodes. When one looks at the entirety of *The Twilight Zone*'s episodes, many of them overlap in sharing similar themes and settings, but Washburn has selected a cross section of story lines and character types so that no overlap exists. And when an overlap does exist, she separates storylines by the two-act structure of the play. Precisely for this reason is why "The Long Morrow" does not appear until the second act, so that no confusion exists between its space going astronaut with the returning astronauts from "And When the Sky Was Opened." Perhaps more pressing for Washburn though was a recognition that audiences in the twenty-first century have a much different expectation when it comes to storytelling than they did back in the early 1960s, and the narrative technique of *The Twilight Zone*, which, at the time, was groundbreaking, was now a familiar device in television and the movies. As she thoughtfully argued, she broke the episodes up "because they were written for a different pace of attention. People now are just so fast on the narrative curve. You can give them things much quicker and I think if you look at the original episodes, they'd spent a long time looping around and preparing you for the shock and then taking you through it carefully because it was so new" (Longo). In essence, the narrative format was crafted with an audience in mind that had long grown accustomed to multi-tasking as well as keeping straight the narrative threads and multiple characters in television sagas, like *Game of Thrones*. This was *The Twilight Zone* for the YouTube generation.

And yet, how well did her curatorial skills of re-jiggering the episodes actually work when it came to the performance of the piece? A sampling of the critical response to the play by London theater reviewers reveals that cutting up the episodes was not an asset to the production. Sophie Gilbert was not a fan of the disrupted narrative technique. She argued that one of the strengths of *The Twilight Zone* was "the moral framework Serling was able to disguise in stories about faraway worlds that somehow exactly reflect our own." Washburn's "splicing different episodes together in a spoofy, winking package … generally misses the acute imaginative insight of the original." Dominic Cavendish called the production a "vortex of diminishing returns" and he laid the errors at the narrative framework, which produced "a disjointed, stilted tone" (33). He noted that as the audience begins to get involved with one story and its characters "other tales start to intrude" (33). Henry Hitchings also found the narrative structure problematic because "to weave the stories together rather than present them separately reduces their suspense" (33). Along the same line, Benedict Nightingale noted that "the narrative jerks, jumps and somersaults" made the audience more confused and the play confusing. Clearly, the resounding feeling among the critics was that they disagreed with Washburn's choice to disrupt the narrative, as it proved to be a hindrance to the flow and feeling of the piece. Audiences, though, did not agree, and the full houses at the Almeida Theatre and the ensuing financial success of the production indicated that even with its narrative bumpiness the attraction of *The Twilight Zone* itself overcame any structural weakness in Washburn's curatorial presentation, testifying to the strength of the original material that still managed to shock, provoke, and entertain almost 60 years removed from the series premiere. Washburn's imprint on the theatrical adaptation of the series though was not finished. While she originally attested to merely being a curator of the material, we will see in the next section that when it came to "The Shelter," Washburn removed her curatorial title and became a co-author with Serling, updating the episode to reflect the political conversations of 2016.

The Political Zone: The Influence of Trumpian Rhetoric

While she was working on *The Twilight Zone* in London, Washburn found that it was impossible to avoid conversations with others about presidential candidate Donald J. Trump and the improbable rhetoric of the election season. She revealed that "It was all I was thinking about and all I was talking about. That dialogue was just ringing in my head so it felt kind of dishonest to write about anything else" (Trueman 14). While in workshop with the play, Washburn found herself "writing page after page after page of political discussion"—not for any purpose, just "to get it out of my system. It felt like I was sort of doing my part" (Trueman 14). The result of the writing and daily discussions about Trump would be *Shipwreck* (2019), her follow up play to *The Twilight Zone*, which also premiered at the Almeida. What is pertinent to this discussion is that those Trump inspired scenes that would become *Shipwreck* also found their way into the adaptation and, more specifically, into her reworking of "The Shelter," which details what happens to a seemingly happy and normal neighborhood gathering of friends for a birthday celebration when an impending missile attack is announced and only one of the four couples has the foresight to construct a bomb shelter with only enough room for their immediate family members. While working on the draft of the play during the 2016 campaign, she was befuddled by what she was watching daily on and in the news. She soon realized that Serling's "The Shelter" would provide a perfect conduit for her to engage with the current state of an American subconsciousness run amuck with hatred and divisiveness.

The similarity between "The Shelter" and "The Monsters Are Due on Maple Street" has been noted by many commentators, as the latter depicts over a day the growing disruption to a shady, idyllic suburban street, as neighbors begin suspecting one another of being an alien that has infiltrated their neighborhood, leading to a disastrous and deadly turn of events. Critics have deemed "The Monsters Are Due on Maple Street" to be far superior to "The Shelter," especially when it comes to the depiction of mob rule and neighbor turning against neighbor. Brian Murray observed that the earlier episode "also recalls, even more explicitly, the mob-driven irrationalities that fueled the rise of Nazism, still fresh in the public mind in the 1950s, and the subject of several other *Twilight Zone* episodes. The threat of barbarism, Serling repeatedly suggests, never ends; the margin between order and murderous chaos is thin." The strength of the episode has led it to be taught in high school classrooms around the United States as well as being a popular choice for performance on stage. Its poorer cousin has not found the same level of appreciation. Lamont Johnson, who directed "The Shelter," thought it was too preachy due to "Rod [being] in one of his messianic moods" (Zicree 216). Zicree felt that the characterizations relied on a "rather too-obvious and heavy-handed manipulation" by Serling. Other commentators shared similar dismissive observations about the quality of the episode from it being "a bit too didactic" (Mortensen 71) and "too uptight with its own self-righteousness" (Johnson qtd. in Zicree 216). Ultimately, "The Shelter" was "one of the show's weaker efforts" (Mortensen 60).

Not everyone though so easily criticized the episode. Gilbert offers a contrary position, arguing of its value within *The Twilight Zone* canon:

> When "The Shelter" aired on television, Serling's infamous closing narration downplayed the episode's power. "No moral, no message, no prophetic tract," the voiceover read. "Just a simple statement of fact: For civilization to survive, the human race has to remain civilized." But the drama is one of the more searing indictments of American society, and how "neighborly" affects and niceties often inoculate people from confronting the uglier strains of racism and resentment they secretly feel.

No doubt, in deciding to include "The Shelter," Washburn shared Gilbert's minority view about the dramatic power of neighbor pitted against neighbor. In fact, for Washburn, the episode would become "the centerpiece of the show" (Longo). Recognizing that the episode was "a little outdated," she added a black couple to the dinner party, which was not the case in the original, which had "much more of Italian and Jewish foreigners as the focus of it" (Longo). While she shared the same view that the episode was preachy, she felt that the narrative structure of the piece offset Serling's moralizing. She explained that "it's just such a great tense setup. It's just such a clear discussion. And it's completely plausible, it's utterly plausible. It's exactly what happens. People are fine, they're fine, they're fine, they're fine, and then something happens, and they freak out" (Longo).

What becomes immediately noticeable about Washburn's version of "The Shelter" is that she jettisons her curatorial touch, which lightly made changes to the other seven episodes, as she did minor editing, renamed characters, and switched or rewrote lines for the sake of context and clarity due to the intermingled format and the limitations of the cast size. In contrast, "The Shelter" contains newly written material by Washburn that expands the episode into a political discussion about American identity, as she spied an opportunity to include those conversations she was having with others about Trump's candidacy and eventual presidency. While it is well documented that Serling's political perspectives influenced the writing of *The Twilight Zone* episodes, Serling relied upon aliens and alternative universes to make his political points. Washburn, though, is far more direct and overt than Serling was, placing the episode directly within our own world where Trump's policies and ideologies fracture relationships between next door neighbors.

The scenes from "The Shelter" featured in the play follow fairly closely to the original script until the neighbors begin trying to formulate a plan to get into the Stockton's already sealed bomb shelter. In Serling's script Marty Weiss suggests that they do some kind of lottery to see which family should be let into the shelter. Frank Henderson accuses him of wanting his own family to be saved, Marty responds, "Why not?" since he has an infant child. Henderson spews in response: "That's the way it is when the foreigners come over here. Pushy, grabby, semi-American" ("The Shelter"). The potential for Henderson's xenophobic insult to develop into a larger explosion of words and castigations dissipates as a fighter jet zoom over the house, reminding the inhabitants of the oncoming threat from foreign missiles. The on-the-verge-of-fracturing group puts aside the insult and goes in search of a battering ram to attack the shelter's door. It is this moment where Washburn diverges from the episode's narrative track, as she offers her own interpretation of what the dialogue would have been if Henderson's attack on Weiss was allowed to continue. No doubt, the xenophobia latent in Henderson's comment from over 50 years ago struck Washburn as accurately echoing the political tenor of America's rhetoric in 2016, where Donald Trump's long shot campaign for President foregrounded the question of what makes someone a true American, while also pushing an agenda of "America First."

At this juncture of the play Washburn moves from curator to co-author, as she adds four pages of dialogue to the episode (according to the published play script). In the process she changes the focus of the episode from an examination of the breakdown of neighborhood friendships to a more specific indictment of those who parrot Trumpian rhetoric of what makes one a true American. In addressing this change of tone to the piece, she also switches the characters' positions in the argument about being a true American. Rather than Henderson spewing his anti–American rhetoric, it is now the previously put upon Weiss and his wife who challenge Henderson's suggestion of drawing lots. Their ire is driven by three aspects of Henderson's identity: living in the neighborhood for only five years; being black; and being a naturalized citizen. Henderson argues that because of his studies of American history in order to pass the citizenship test, he knows far more about the intricacies, details, and history of his new country than those born into it. Henderson: "I know more about your country ... than you do. More about your constitution, laws" (82). Weiss counters: "I don't know all of the *things* about being an American, the same way as a guy who has been *studying* them but what I know is that I have them in my *heart*, in my *soul*.... I have Democracy in my *blood*" (82). The distinct difference in their definition of what makes one an American echoes the same sentiments expressed by Trump and his political foes. While Trump, like Weiss, relies upon what he feels inside his body to make decisions, proudly proclaiming that the accuracy of his gut rather than expertise or facts, his foes have expressed counterarguments grounded in the realm that he dismisses: facts, history, and the words of the Constitution. And similarly, to the result of real world political disagreements in America, both Henderson and Weiss remain entrenched in their position, unwilling to cede any quarter to the opposing side. While Weiss echoes Trump's "feeling" about what is right and what makes one American, he also shares a similar philosophy when it comes to immigration and the changing dynamics of the American populace. Weiss parrots a familiar conservative complaint that Trump aimed against asylum seekers crossing the border with Mexico seeking safety in the United States: "I'm sick of me saying we have a problem here and then it's I'm a racist let me tell you I don't have a problem with your race I have a problem with there are too many of you ... taking up more than your fair share and you're taking it away from my kids!" (83). Another fight then breaks out as Martin, an African American, joins the conversation and he and Henderson squabble over the role of slavery in the history of the United States. After Weiss attempts to claim a leg up in terms of his American lineage by claiming ancestors who arrived in 1856, Martin reminds him that slave ships first docked in 1619 and that the American Indian was present before any settlers arrived in the country. As with Weiss and Henderson, Martin and Henderson's argument goes nowhere as well. Instead, Mrs. Weiss turns the discussion of colonial oppression back to how she is viewed by others, complaining that "I'm sick and tired of black people you can't say anything, anything you don't mean anything by it it gets construed and me I don't have a racist bone in my body I am sick and *tired*, of being construed" (85). The dispute finally winds down, as an off-stage noise, a siren, reminds them of the greater danger present than their political perspectives. Like their television cohorts, they put aside their differences and search for a way to break down the door of the bomb shelter.

The dialogue that Washburn crafted accurately captures the tone of anger, hatred, xenophobia, racism, self-interest and frustration that was happening in the United States throughout 2016 and 2017 (and the ensuing years as well). And yet, the new pages are highly problematic when considered within the narrative frame of the episode itself. Once the announcement of the incoming missiles occurs citizens only have fifteen minutes before the first missile strikes. With the possibility of death inching closer every second how likely would it be for the couples, who want to save themselves and, more importantly, their children, to argue for ten minutes about what makes one an American? While Washburn echoes Serling's belief in inserting political issues into his work, she fails to acknowledge how he also effectively subsumed it underneath his science-fiction stories of alternative universes, worlds, and aliens while maintaining a narrative plausibility in the world's he created. Washburn's attempts to update Serling's script into the political discussions of the time runs afoul of one of the tenets that Serling kept close, namely "A Martian can say things that a Republican or Democrat can't" (qtd. in Gilbert). Here Washburn clearly demarcates her Democrats from her Republicans, anti–Trumpers from pro–Trumpers, and to create such a direct link between *The Twilight Zone* and our own world was a rule that Washburn broke in her rewriting of "The Shelter."

As with her disruption to the narrative flow of the episodes, the politicization of "The Shelter" was noticed by the London reviewers. A few appreciated her tinkering with Serling's script. Dominic Cavendish found it to be "exactly on the right terrain between macabre humour and mind-spinning provocation, a relic of Cold War paranoia that speaks to today's anxieties" (33), while Paul Taylor acknowledged how the various episodes "tap into our own neuroses or flicker with current political concerns." Most, though, did not share the same opinion. Even though Washburn pointed out the "tense set-up" of the episode and how "plausible" the scenario was, the critics felt that her additional dialogue actually halted the tension and, as mentioned above, removed the story from Serling's world and into our own. Theater critics remarked upon the sudden shift in the dynamic of the show when Washburn's new dialogue appeared. Matt Wolf honed in on the new elements of the script: "As tweaked by the playwright to chime with our own grievous times, the discussion widens to fold racism and xenophobia into the mix: a laudable impulse, in principle, that has the paradoxical effect of stopping the production dead in its tracks in favor of the sort of heavy-going debate that one might find in the comments section of many an article online." Claire Allfree opined that this segment of the play reminded her of "a direct dispatch from Trump's America" (28). While Susannah Clapp thought the decision to run "The Shelter" almost in its entirety was impressive, she felt that the final product "underlines too heavily the political content" (28).

Despite the inherent difficulties of the additional material, one can offer an alternative perspective on Washburn's decision to infuse Trump into the play, especially if we consider a speech Serling made in 1968, where he addressed the important role a writer plays beyond the creation of successfully fictional worlds. He remarked: "The writer's role is to menace the public's conscience.... He must see the art as a vehicle of social criticism and he must focus on the issues of his time" (qtd. in Boulton 1227). If we consider her addition to "The Shelter" in this light, we see that Washburn did exactly that by focusing "on the issues of [her] time." Nowhere is that more apparent than in the final coda offered by The Narrator, a recurring figure throughout the play that mimics the role Serling played throughout the series. Rather than having the Serling stand-in recite the words from the end of the episode: "No moral, no message, no prophetic tract, just a simple statement of fact: for civilization to survive, the human race has to remain civilized" ("The Shelter"), Washburn has added a new coda as a direct piece of advice to the audience of today, especially apt since the concept of behaving civilized was already under attack in the political venues and confrontations between supporters. The Narrator tells us "our civilization is in peril" because "all that is good and right in mankind can be obliterated by no more than an image formed in the darkest recesses of the frail human mind" (90), which has proven to be true since Trump first made his way down the Trump Tower escalator to announce his candidacy. While purists of *The Twilight Zone* as well as London theater critics will find and have found fault with Washburn's choices of disrupting the narrative of and adding contemporary politics to the iconic series, her movement into the political realm of theater, which is something absent from her plays previous to *The Twilight Zone*, places her as a writer after Serling's own heart. Washburn's sojourn, as initially a curator and then as a co-author, in *The Twilight Zone* shows how Serling's influence continues to inspire writers and the role of politics in their works well into a new century.

Works Cited

Allfree, Claire. "One of TV's Greatest Creations Transformed into Pure Sci-fi Kitsch." Review of *The Twilight Zone*, by Anne Washburn. *The Daily Telegraph*, 14 March 2019, p. 28. *NewsBank*. Accessed 6 April 2020.

"And When the Sky Was Opened," *The Twilight Zone*, written by Rod Serling, directed by Douglas Heyes, Image Entertainment, 2010.

Appleyard, Bryan. "Lost in the Zone." *The Sunday Times*, 19 November 2017, pp. 28–9. *NewsBank*. Accessed 6 April 2020.

Boulton, Mark. "Sending the Extremists to the Cornfield: Rod Serling's Crusade Against Radical Conservatism," *Journal of Popular Culture*, vol. 47, no. 6, 2014, pp. 1226–1244.

Cavendish, Dominic "A Vortex of Diminishing Returns." Review of *The Twilight Zone*, by

Anne Washburn. *The Daily Telegraph*, 14 December 2017, p. 33. *Lexis-Nexis*. Accessed 6 April 2020.

Clapp, Susannah. "Retro Anxieties from Another Dimension." Review of *The Twilight Zone*, by Anne Washburn. *The Observer*, 17 December 2017, p. 28. *NewsBank*. Accessed 6 April 2020.

"Eye of the Beholder," *The Twilight Zone*, written by Rod Serling, directed by Douglas Heyes, Image Entertainment, 2011.

Gilbert, Sophie. "Reimagining The Twilight Zone for the 21st Century." *The Atlantic*, 20 December 2017. *NewsBank*. Accessed 6 April 2020.

Hitchings, Henry. "Spooky TV Tribute Could Do with an Extra Dimension." Review of *The Twilight Zone*, by Anne Washburn. *Evening Standard*, 14 March 2019, p. 33. *NewsBank*. Accessed 6 April 2020.

"Little Girl Lost," *The Twilight Zone*, written by Richard Matheson, directed by Paul Stewart, Image Entertainment, 2011.

"The Long Morrow," *The Twilight Zone*, written by Rod Serling, directed by Robert Florey, Image Entertainment, 2011.

Longo, Chris. "*The Twilight Zone* Play: How The Stories Were Selected." *Denofgeek.com*, 17 March 2019. Web. Accessed 12 May 2020.

Mortenson, Erik. "A Journey into the Shadows: *The Twilight Zone*'s Visual Critique of the Cold War," *Science Fiction Film and Television*, vol. 7, no. 1, 2014, pp. 55–76.

Murray, Brian "The Enduring Legacy of *The Twilight Zone*." *New Atlantis*, vol. 48, Winter, 2016, pp. 90–112. *Lexis-Nexis*. Accessed 6 April 2020.

Nightingale, Benedict. "The Alien Feeling of Watching *The Twilight Zone* on Stage." Review of *The Twilight Zone*, by Anne Washburn. *The Daily Beast*, 17 December 2017. *NewsBank*. Accessed 6 April 2020.

"Nightmare as a Child," *The Twilight Zone*, written by Rod Serling, directed by Alvin Ganzer, Image Entertainment, 2011.

"Perchance to Dream," *The Twilight Zone*, written by Charles Beaumont, directed by Robert Florey, Image Entertainment, 2010.

"The Shelter," *The Twilight Zone*, written by Rod Serling, directed by Lamont Johnson, CBS, 1961.

Taylor, Paul. "A Witty and Piquant Alternative to Forced Jollity." Review of *The Twilight Zone*, by Anne Washburn. *The Independent*, 13 December 2017. *NewsBank*. Accessed 6 April 2020.

"Time Enough at Last," *The Twilight Zone*, written by Rod Serling, directed by John Brahm, Image Entertainment, 2010.

Trueman, Matt. "The Drama of Division." *Financial Times*, 16 February 2019, p.14. *NewsBank*. Accessed 6 April 2020.

Washburn, Anne. *The Twilight Zone*. Oberon Books, 2017.

"Will the Real Martian Please Stand Up?," *The Twilight Zone*, written by Rod Serling, directed by Montgomery Pittman, Image Entertainment, 2011.

Williams, Holly. "After *Twilight Zone*, the Trump Zone." *The New York Times*, 10 February 2019, p. AR: 6. *Lexis-Nexis*. Accessed 6 April 2020.

Wolf, Matt. "The Paranormal Turns Pedantic in *The Twilight Zone* Adaptation." Review of *The Twilight Zone*, by Anne Washburn. *The New York Times*, 16 December 2017. *Lexis-Nexis*. Accessed 6 April 2020.

Zara, Christopher. "CBS Pulls the Rights for *Twilight Zone* Stage Show, but Says Don't Blame Jordan Peele." *Fast Company.com*, 14 March 2019. Web. Accessed 7 May 2020.

Zicree, Marc Scott. *The Twilight Zone Companion*, 3rd Ed. Silman-James Press, 2018.

A *Twilight Zone* of Our Own

Production Is Storytelling

Steve Krahnke *and* Michael Aronson

Introduction

In fall of 2017, a group of over one hundred undergraduate and graduate students, faculty and community members "reimagined" three episodes of *The Twilight Zone* (1959–1964) based on iconic scripts by Rod Serling: "The Monsters Are Due on Maple Street" (1959), "Will the Real Martian Please Stand Up?" (1961), and "The Shelter" (1961). The idea seemed simple: use classic stories as inspiration for new ones written by, and for, a new generation of visual storytellers. But something deeper happened; producing these fully reimagined stories taught students that writing is only part of telling the story. Production—all of the processes that make audio-visual storytelling possible—from directing, photography, scriptwriting, and acting, to discussion and planning, or even laying electrical cable and carrying bottled water. The story is not simply the script; storytelling is production.

The purpose of this essay is to describe the educational objectives of teaching with Serling's work and to describe the process of production as an integral part of storytelling. Our goal was not to improve on or copy Serling, but to use his work as an inspirational foundation to simulate realistic, collaborative, creatively successful production environments in an academic setting. In the first place, admiration of Serling oriented students to achieving high-quality production goals in order to live up to Serling's legacy. Most TV writers rarely achieve name recognition across generations—Serling did. Almost every student had seen at least one episode of *The Twilight Zone*. Many had seen every episode. Serling is so important in United States popular culture, his teleplays are even taught as literature in some school curricula. Many students, for example, had read and seen "The Monsters Are Due on Maple Street" in high school English classes. I did, too.

Also important, Serling makes his concepts and concerns in *The Twilight Zone* extremely, often painfully, clear. This owes as much to Serling's keen interest in combining biting social commentary with lucid writing, as to his opening and closing monologues that bookend each episode. This helps students, no matter their role in production, to take ownership of Serling's anxieties (often very close to their own) and find resonance that would help them produce their own episodes with similar messages based on their own experiences. This points to a third crucial aspect of organizing the course around Serling: that his concerns with social justice and profound human failings, though situated in his social context, also transcend generations. The things that bothered Serling certainly haven't gone away; we still need these stories.

Our setting wasn't exactly like a real industry production environment because we weren't concerned with distribution. We did not face issues related to network censors or commercial sponsors. But, firm deadlines to make and screen these episodes in a single semester provided a sense of urgency similar to that found in industry production and, in particular, to the fast pace of production in the late 1950s. The overarching goal was to give students an idea of how Serling told his stories through the entire production process.

Storytelling, Human Evolution and The Twilight Zone

Yuval Harari suggests that human evolution in societies required them to develop "big brains" to process and deliver information necessary to survive and thrive (Harari 27). Over time, *homo sapiens* developed the ability to keep multiple storylines ready to hand in their minds (Harari 24). Concepts including, but not limited to, who, what, when, where, why, and how became parts of human storytelling, which allows us tell stories about others *and* ourselves.

It is impossible to know when, but at some point, people started asking questions about "truth." For example: "Are they telling the truth?" "Why would they lie?" or "Can they be trusted?" These questions are stories about others, but they are valuable to us. As stories, they represent human competitive life experiences. Some scholars may consider such stories to be simple "gossip," but this is dismissive. Stories about others aren't frivolous when societies become so large and complex that individual survival *requires* other people and their stories (Harari 27). Storytelling is part of the individual and social process of making sense of the world around us, trading information, and storing memory.

Serling seems to have understood a key aspect of this: if you want to teach someone something, tell them a *useful* story. A *useful* story can be used to teach others something important about the world around them, whether or not the story is factual. But *useful* stories are also about *useful* questions. To that extent, the experience or the imagination of the storyteller doesn't matter as long as the story itself is *useful* to someone else.

Useful questions can often be about seemingly banal, yet vital, parts of life: for example, what is safe to eat and where it is safe to sleep. Socially, useful questions deal with interactions between ourselves and other people: "Which people can I trust, and how do I find out?" Questions of otherness and difference are crucial here: if a group of people looks/thinks/behaves differently from me, how can I trust them? *Trust* is a central problem in useful questions of this kind, and is a central preoccupation of Serling. Many Serling scripts deal with paranoia, and forms of *social* breakdown that occur when paranoia erodes trust. This is almost certainly due to his own experiences with McCarthyism, the red scare, and even corporate and advertiser influence (Lacy).

Useful stories can also help us survive. Stories about foods that aren't safe to eat are good examples, because they are about more than their individual subjects. They are about potentially dangerous outcomes, or what not to do. They engage homo sapiens' developed ability to simultaneously consider past, present, and future as heuristics to think about problems. Because of stories, we do not need to experience something ourselves to avoid a negative outcome. A causal story about someone else's death can be enough of a warning to keep us alive (Gigerenzer 24). Thinking about Serling's social concerns, Gigerenzer's notion of past, present, and future as heuristics reminds us of George Santayana's famous statement, "Those who cannot remember the past are condemned to repeat it" (Santayana 172).

Paranoia is a kind of story, too. We can imagine negative futures based on faulty imagined facts. But *The Twilight Zone* argues that paranoia is a cyclical cause and effect of prejudice, which Serling considered the greatest threat to society. In a 1967 interview, Serling says, "the worst aspect of our time is prejudice. In almost everything I've written, there is a thread of this—man's seemingly palpable need to dislike someone other than himself." (May 22–23). Paranoid stories about past, present, and future simultaneously generate and are generated by "man's seemingly palpable need to dislike someone other than himself" within and across all three heuristics. Paranoid fantasy destroys the social conditions necessary for healthy storytelling and society by playing on the very survival considerations that make storytelling and society work.

Storytelling Technologies

Introductory audiovisual storytelling students are often surprised when the first slide in my PowerPoint deck is of primitive cave paintings of simple handprints in France. Such paintings are obviously a form of "storytelling." These messages are not entirely clear—the medium of berry juice on stone is not precise enough. I invite students to speculate about the potential meanings of such "handprint" stories. The dozens of hand-prints may mean, "We are many, do not dare to enter this cave." They may mean, "We are together and value our society." Of course, some of my students speculate that, "We are many" could be a lie. After all, one person can make many handprints.

Many animals tell stories, but few have the technology to preserve them. We may not think of chewing berries and chalk and spitting on our hands to leave a "permanent" story on a cave wall as technological, but it is an improvement over pheromones, urine, and musk. It is also an improvement on an oral tradition. While the oral tradition can relate an event or story—say, a description of a great flood in Mesopotamia—a version in print fixes the story (as with a photographic print) and allows it to be shared without filter or alteration. Anyone who has ever played a game of "telephone" knows that it doesn't take many iterations for a story to be completely different between the beginning and the end. Several versions of a story might be combined into one; this new "meta" story then carries the weight of numbers: "Everyone says if you eat this, you will die" and requires less reliance or "trust" in a single person's story, even better if we already agree on one person's version of the story. These stories have become the scaffolding with which to build other stories. *The Qur'an*, *Holy Bible*, *The Odyssey*, *The Iliad*, *The Torah*, and countless other texts are obvious examples of the preservation of the stories of generations, but so are the *Magna Carta* and *The Declaration of Independence*. Many an argument is settled by statements like: "Well, why don't we just see what the book says about it, shall we?" or "The First Amendment says." (Of course, this essay—another form of storytelling—cites from sources.)

In the mid-nineteenth century, chemistry gave us photography (which, predictably, created ripples among painters). Photography, at first a tool of professionals and enthusiasts, in the early twentieth century became a primary form of communication for many. According to historian Daniel Czitrom, in the PBS documentary film, *American Photography: A Century of Images* (1999), "Ordinary folks begin to get a sense that if an event is not documented by photography, if you don't have a photograph to show, for example, that you were on vacation, or to show the family opening presents on Christmas morning, or to show your little infant baby, somehow it's not real." Photography, radio, film, and eventually television became, in the twentieth century, in many ways, *the* way to tell stories, at least to large groups of people. From brushes and paint, chisels and stone, to theater, books, photography, audio and visual recordings, and now digital, we are at a point where literally billions of stories of others are at our fingertips. The information-filled screens of our smart phones, referenced in the popular British television series *Black Mirror* (2011–), are ubiquitously described in the press as a "twenty-first century *Twilight Zone*."

Television was the cutting-edge communications technology of Rod Serling's time. The development of television as a communication and distribution technology in the United States was shelved during World War II and further delayed by the FCC freeze on station licenses between 1948 and 1952. When station licensing resumed, television production exploded. At first, many writers and producers considered live television the gold standard of television storytelling (Foust 584–602). Networks dedicated shows to the live transmission of "tele-plays," both adapted theater plays and drama written for television. In the *American Masters* documentary "Submitted for Your Approval," Kim Hunter describes the exciting creative environment of *Playhouse 90*, a flagship anthology drama series that aired on CBS from 1956 to 1960. Serling's own "Requiem for a Heavyweight" (1956) remains a canon example of *Playhouse 90*—and live television—at its best.

From a social perspective, television represented a low-cost technology for the broadcasting of [moving pictures] stories to America. This generated excitement and concern about the kinds of stories the new medium could be used for and how the new medium should be used and/or controlled. Serling, disturbed by the Cold War paranoia of the 1950s that often labeled social criticism of the United States as "un–American" and put critics at risk of being blacklisted—often with threatening consequences for the livelihoods of themselves and their families—intentionally pitched *The Twilight Zone* as a science-fiction show about ordinary people in strange situations, obscuring the critical, socially concerned intentions of the show behind a veil of fantasy (Lacy). The censors seemed not to recognize that Serling was working out how to tell stories about possible futures in a paranoid environment, using the new medium both to circumvent, expose, and comment on that social paranoia. Serling believed in human beings' desire for stories about what might happen (if only so as not to have to experience tragedy, dystopia, and hardship themselves), and the educational potential of this desire combined with these kinds of stories written for television. *The Twilight Zone* produced many such stories—useful stories—about how fear and ignorance lead to hatred and the destruction of society, and ultimately the individual (Lacy).

That being said, often lost in "great man histories" about Serling and *The Twilight Zone*, is the collaborative nature of television storytelling. Such histories tend to focus on Serling as an auteur, celebrating finished episodes from his oeuvre as if they had sprung from his head fully formed. But television, like Serling, comes out of theater traditions that rely on the abilities of a community of talented artists and craftspeople working in tandem to produce a performance. This involved (and involves) weaving together a diverse array of storytelling technologies (e.g., movement, sound, various kinds of visual and technical artistry) to put the finished story together. Finished stories in this tradition reflect the production process, such that the story of production is part of the finished product. The process of storytelling is, in many ways, part of the story itself. This is what is most often taught in television and film production classes: you must work with a team to achieve a common vision of the story.

Working together toward a common vision is well evidenced by the production of *The Twilight Zone* series. *The Twilight Zone* required talented actors, directors, artists, and composers, among many others who put these stories together. Serling may have written the lion's share of episodes, but the episodes themselves are the products of the production team, its creative conversation, and team storytelling.

Directors, show runners, designers, artists, editors, etc., all have a say in the production of any television show. I tell my students to be suspicious of any script they find that seems identical to a finished episode. "If we find a *script* on Ebay that is identical to the program we are watching, it is probably a *transcript*, not the original teleplay." Transcripts, which are often created to make closed captions, must be identical to final films. But they are not teleplays. Teleplays can be thought of as the instructions that the craftspeople who make television (or film, or musical recordings, or really anything) use to turn the writer's words into television. To that end, craftspeople are essential components of storytelling.

Often, it turns out that writers have little connection to the actual production of their scripts. For example, Warren Light, Executive Producer of *Law & Order: Special Victims Unit* (2011–2016, 2019) says, "You know, on *Law & Order*, before I took over the show, the writers were not supposed to be on set. Dick [Wolf] doesn't want the writers interfering with production and he doesn't want production interfering with editing" (Kallas, 47–48). That said, creatives must respect the vision of writers, even if the process of mediated storytelling adds distance between the writer and craftspeople. Of course, students of film and television production need to learn that production is not simply the rote construction of a writer's story, as if it were a building constructed from a set of blueprints. The process may begin with the writer, but production continues the complex process of storytelling. Because in film and television—without production—and the diverse skill-sets different people bring to the table in production—would there be any story at all?

A Twilight Zone *of Our Own*

In 2016, Professor Jane McLeod, an Associate Dean in the College of Arts and Sciences at Indiana University, mentioned, "We are creating a semester of connected courses all wrapped around a single idea. This semester the idea is 'Diversity-Difference-Otherness.' Can you think of any courses or projects the Media School might offer?"

The Media School was a new venture in the college, which combined the former Journalism School with two college departments, Telecommunications and Communications and Culture. As a way to involve all sorts of students with diverse academic backgrounds, I had already been noodling with the idea of a big project involving several courses and independent studies. I decided that a workable project might be to reimagine three *The Twilight Zone* episodes in a single semester. Such a course would use virtually every resource of the Media School, from multi-camera studios to on-location film equipment. At least one hundred students would be involved, filling every possible position necessary to produce the episodes. Our proposal was titled: *A 21st Century Twilight Zone.* In her notes in the project study guide, Dean McLeod states:

> The 2017 Themester faculty advisors proposed the theme of diversity, difference, and otherness … because we believe that investigating these concepts will help prepare you and other students to make a positive contribution to our increasingly multicultural, multiethnic, multinational world, and to the future of a planet that is rapidly exceeding its capacity to sustain human life. What does *The Twilight Zone* contribute to our investigation of these concepts? Difference and otherness reverberate through every episode.

The idea was fairly simple: use three iconic episodes of *The Twilight Zone* as the inspiration for new stories written by student writers that would be entirely created by undergraduate and graduate students.

Three iconic scripts by Rod Serling were chosen to be "reimagined" for the *21st Century Twilight Zone* project: "The Monsters Are Due on Maple Street," "Will the Real Martian Please Stand Up?" and "The Shelter." The stories are similar to each other. In each, the suggestion that an individual or group does not belong drives one or more characters to extreme action. In each script an external force provides the framework for the tension, paranoia, and mistrust, largely due to the themes of otherness.

Although inspired and guided by Serling, each writer's script is original: The cast of characters, design, direction, production, editing, and musical scoring were all students' original expressions under the supervision of faculty. Over one hundred people spent hundreds of hours on these episodes. Such work included shoots at four o'clock in the morning, or midnight; on weekdays and weekends; shoots in rain and snow, heat and cold; days editing footage that took hours to shoot, but represents seconds on screen; weeks designing sets; days searching for props and set pieces like sinks and doorknobs, rugs and chairs; weeks in the scene shop putting everything together and building everything else; days writing and revising scripts; days learning lines or camera techniques; endless meetings; and more. All of this to tell three thirty-minute stories.

Most of the people involved would agree that telling a useful story is reason enough to begin the hard journey of production. Most felt we honored Serling's legacy when we asked: "What would Serling say, now?" As the narrator says in the 1964 episode of *The Twilight Zone*, "I Am the Night—Color Me Black," (1964) "a sickness known as hate; not a virus, not a microbe, not a germ—but a sickness nonetheless, highly contagious, deadly in its effects. Don't look for it in the Twilight Zone—look for it in a mirror. Look for it before the light goes out altogether." Over sixty years later, he may have said or written the same thing. Serling wanted to use the medium of television and the genre of science-fiction (for the most part) to tell stories about possible futures at a time when the future was deeply troubling. While the Cold War is now largely behind us, in 2016 a surprising Presidential election result caused many students to feel trepidation about their own futures. The issues raised in the election about immigration, international responsibility, space, climate change, social and racial inequity, #metoo, etc., gave them plenty to think about. They were motivated to tell stories about the futures they imagined both as reflections of where they were, but also as warnings about where we might be headed.

Everyone involved in the *21st Century Twilight Zone* project committed to the theme of the *Themester: Difference-Diversity-Otherness.* But this was an academic exercise. Many of the students who worked on these episodes had never seen the inside of a television studio or worked on a film set. Terminology, responsibilities, workflow, equipment—much of this was unfamiliar. This required us to agree to a common mantra: Everyone is doing their best, and everyone can do better, even me. Freshmen, many who knew literally nothing, had to work with seniors and graduate students, who, in some cases, thought they knew everything. Students who had only learned the term "art director" in the previous semester suddenly found themselves in charge of the "looks" of an entire production. That was the point: production is storytelling, and the way we learn to tell stories is by telling stories.

The Episodes

Production of these episodes served several educational functions:

- each is an interesting thought experiment for liberal arts students aligned with the theme of the semester
- each reflects and pays homage to the mission of Rod Serling and the original series production team
- each addresses the collective vision of new writers, directors, and craftspeople
- each compares mid-twentieth-century Cold War anxieties and Red Scare politics to contemporary problems of religion, race, technology and ideology.

Although paranoia and fear of the unknown are thematically at the heart of "Monsters" and "Martian," the plots are basically about aliens from space. It is obvious—largely because Serling tells us—that the "aliens" are a metaphor for "people who are not like us." In his epilogue to "Monsters" Serling says, "Prejudices can kill and suspicions can destroy," but we felt it important to also include ideas about "otherness" that did not involve suspicions about "people not from around here"; we did not want the conversation to completely be about immigration. We chose "Shelter," because it deals with the consequences of choices we make about ourselves and how we live with other people. Serling (as narrator) says in the epilogue to "The Shelter": "For civilization to survive, the human race has to remain civilized."

I will discuss each reimagined episode in turn, and, when possible, use the words of students who created each episode. Episode writers were given the opportunity to rename their episodes, but each chose—independently of each other—to retain the original titles. To that end, the titles of the original scripts will be identified by Serling and the date of production; similarly, our reimagined episodes will also be identified by writer and date.

Reimagining "The Shelter" (Reed, Teleplay, 2017)

"In a near dystopian future, the United States has been transformed. Replaced by a totalitarian form of government that works to control all space and thought, a group of intellectuals united in opposition are caught between their hopes for the future and their personal survival." This was the preface to Cara Reed's script for "The Shelter"; Reed was a graduate student at Indiana University at the time of production. While Serling's original script was about a family man trying to keep his family safe during a nuclear exchange, Reed felt that those sorts of ideas were no longer first and foremost in the public mind. She felt that story had been told.

It is ironic that our remake of "The Shelter" is arguably the closest to speculative science fiction than either the original teleplays for "The Monsters Are Due on Maple Street" or "Will the Real Martian Please Stand Up?" because the original "Shelter" isn't really science fiction. It's a social drama and morality play and is the most exposed in its subject matter of these Serling teleplays. Reed's script addresses our anxieties about religious totalitarianism and intellectual control by showing us a world ours could become. The threat is no longer a foreign government, but a domestic, totalitarian religious regime. The shelter, rather than a safe house from nuclear bombardment built in someone's basement, is a secret library in a house in the woods, purposely far from civilization. The library preserves books banned by the religious government. It is a place of intellectual survival with only room enough for one or two people. It only becomes a human safe house when a threat of attack seems imminent. Although the remade "Shelter" is more speculative science fiction than the original, there are no ray guns or flying cars. The characters look like us, their technology is contemporary; there are no aliens. The speculative elements concern the totalitarian religious government, and what happens to people living within its regime of fear. "Monsters" and "Martian" are concerned with fear of infiltration and subversion, but "Shelter" deals with a different kind of invasive fear. Producer Emily Ward explains that this fear is best understood through a short scene in which government military police called "acolytes" execute their prisoners by strangulation: "Originally, the police shot their prisoners. But 'Maple Street' [uses guns] so we wanted to do something a little different. Director Jaeson Jackson suggested execution by garrote, a length of wire, as seen in [spy and mafia] movies. This makes the threat and the fear more barbaric, but also more immediate, more real." Jackson adds that:

> the idea of the garrote means a more intimate kind of fear. Here you have people hiding out in the middle of the woods, watching an execution take place on [closed-circuit] camera. The message is that, even with the imposed distance from civilization implied by being in the wilderness, even watching all of this play out from the "safety" of your own living room, this government still has its hands around your throat.

Coercive fear is a pervasive element in the remade "Shelter" and central to its commentary, as the presence of the regime is evident in the measures the protagonists employ to defend themselves against it. The house features extensive surveillance equipment to provide advance warning not only of attack, but of enemy surveillance itself. These elements are not passive, but proactive, and suggest the appropriation of the methods of the enemy for use against them. The theme of the appropriation of the enemy's methods becomes central to the destabilization of the community when personal survival is threatened. When Will, the homeowner, takes refuge in the library vault, James and Leah demand refuge as well. But Will argues that they and the beloved books cannot all survive the invasion. James and Leah will simply have to run from the authorities. Everyone must take their chances as the secret police approach.

But James and Leah make common cause in setting the house on fire to "smoke Will out," which obviously denies the shelter to anyone, moralizing the decision as a matter of mutual survival or mutual destruction. Were the shelter opened, we would expect the alliance between these two characters to be temporary, given James' anti-religious sentiments and Leah's implied status as a Jewish woman practicing in secret. But it is closer to the mark to view this less as a marriage of convenience than as evidence of the effacement of the duo's humanity. They set Will's house on fire to get into the shelter, becoming an invasive presence of fear not dissimilar to the totalitarian government. Any viewer will understand the absurdity of their panicked logic—should the shelter survive, it will no longer be hidden and they eventually must emerge. All the authorities have to do is wait them out. This is similar to the ridiculously simple way that the neighbors beat down the door of Dr. Stockton's shelter in the original—if you can knock down the door with a board, you can do it with an atomic bomb. Although no one will be safe once the door is knocked down, they weren't actually safe in the first place.

Appropriating the enemy's methods also reflects appropriation of the enemy's logic. The enemy, by definition, wants control of all space and thought, and, therefore, desires access to all shelters that prevent this control. This desire is instinctive and compulsive, expressing the regime's all-consuming interest in its own long-term survival. James and Leah, in the name of their own compulsive desires for survival, ignore the books they have worked so hard with Will to protect and assume the stark binary categories of the government: those who have shelters, and those people who don't. Much like the regime might rationalize its own actions against people who resist it, Leah remarks, "Will's made up his mind. There's nothing else I can do." In the end, Leah and James destroy the same knowledge the regime wants destroyed, securing its victory. The books are central to the discussion of the remade "Shelter" insofar as they symbolize the diverse perspectives and points of view that manifest our shared humanity, and indicate the potential for a rehabilitated human civilization. They lose all value when animal survival instincts take over, coopting human reason to rationalize terrible actions. The books' thematic disappearance precedes their physical destruction, paralleling the characters' own loss of their human solidarity, and their social credentials as educated, civilized people. To remain civilized, we have to retain ownership of ourselves, our humanity, and our knowledge of who we are. How can we remain in control of ourselves when so many forces seek to persuade us of their interpretation of the truth? How do we avoid binary reasoning and false dichotomies? How do we avoid appropriating destructive tools and logic in pursuit of inclusive society and truth? What does utopia look like?

The challenges of producing this episode were immense. First, an exterior house location (which could be "set on fire") had to be arranged for. Second, an interior (where most of the teleplay takes place) had to be created in a television multi-camera studio. Third, a realistic "secret library" had to be created in the wall of the studio set. In some ways, the toughest decisions were related to, "What books would be in the library?" In the words of Art Director Riley Dismore, "Choosing which books would exist in the library was an all-team effort. We pooled all of our collective books together and asked ourselves: what books would you die for?"

Reimagining "Will the Real Martian Please Stand Up?" (Munro, Teleplay, 2017)

"A freak encounter with a UFO forces a Chicago-bound flight to land at a remote airport. Following this unexpected landing, passengers and personnel realize they have one more passenger than they should, and a witch hunt ensues." Production director Russell McGee says in his study guide notes, "My main aim with this production was to focus on the characters—on their humanity—then slowly build the suspense and paranoia and watch the characters fall apart. Who is an alien, extraterrestrial, or otherwise, and what makes one a monster?"

To fans of *The Twilight Zone*, this may sound like the description of dozens of episodes. Yet "Martian" is at once more sinister and, frankly, goofier, than many of Serling's scripts. In Serling's teleplay for "Martian," one alien has an eye in the middle of his forehead; another has three arms. Yet these features have a theatrical reveal at the end. For most of the episode everyone looks basically "normal." Other than age, gender, economic or marital status, there is little to distinguish anyone. How one behaves is basically the only distinguishing factor. No one has a name—they merely exist as "types." Businessman, housewife, counter attendant, drunkard, floozy—Serling is careful enough not to use race or ethnicity as a red-herring. Near the end of the episode, after the central mystery has not been solved, we find out that the "businessman" is a malevolent alien. He has murdered all of the characters but one, "the counterman." He turns out to be an alien too—but he is benevolent; he simply runs the diner. He is powerful enough to be the businessman, but he chooses to wait tables in a diner in the middle of nowhere. More important, the coincidence of two aliens happening to meet in this unlikely location suggests there must be alien countermen everywhere. That said, the counterman himself says, "a colony is coming. But it's from Venus." Somehow the counterman is in the right place at the right time (though not for the unfortunate cops and bus passengers) but this is not explained.

"The middle of nowhere" was the central problem faced by writer Kali Munro. In early conversations with the senior production team, it was clear we could not stick too close to Serling's original premise. The original involves a bus, a bridge, a river, and a diner. While we could, and did, find abandoned diners near Bloomington, Indiana, the students couldn't figure out why, in 2017, such a diverse group would be stranded in a small diner in the "middle of nowhere." Why would the bus be there? Why couldn't they call for help? Where were they going? Instead, based on a personal experience, the team decided to set the episode in a remote airfield where a small commuter plane has been forced to land through an encounter with a UFO. Fortunately, Bloomington, Indiana, has such an airport, and the script and art direction became tied to this location. The cast of characters, and storyline, were altered significantly from the original. Race, religious intolerance, sexual orientation, and age all become key factors in the investigation.

Pervasive attitudes and failures of reasoning come together in our remake of "Martian," producing subtle but important differences. These differences function within and maintain Serling's original structure while suggesting new meanings relevant to our concerns. Grandma, who replaces Grandpa, is similarly sidelined by *ad hominem* reasoning, but resetting the character as a woman makes it necessary to read her character through the lens of gender, and to consider how her portrayal and treatment reflects how women are viewed and treated. We have the foresight of the original episode to know things don't work out too differently, but the new character prompts the question: would Grandma have been taken more seriously today if she were still Grandpa? Like Serling's version, the ironic twist is that perhaps the passengers would have found the alien had they listened to the reasonable positions of the socially defined Other, who was one of them all along. Prejudice later arrests the process of reasoning meant to locate the alien completely. When the middle-aged husband accuses a Muslim teenager, Fatima, of being a terrorist, the pilot's care for the teenager and anger at the husband's baseless accusation towards her, causes him to cut the Gordian knot in the wrong way: he declares that perhaps he did miscount the number of passengers who boarded the plane. The passengers get on their way and, unlike the original, presumably make it home safely.

The closing of our episode plays out somewhat differently from Serling's. Aliens are revealed, but their behavior in the remake leaves us even less certain of their intentions than Serling did. These aliens know about each other, and their respective planets are clearly at war. The "Martian" is in his dire situation because the "Venusian" has shot down his spacecraft, which in turn forces our commuter plane to land. The Venusian kills the Martian and the clock is reset, but there has been damage done: a girl has been accused of being a terrorist, simply because of her headscarf; an elderly woman has been utterly discounted; a young woman is repeatedly shut down by the misogynistic businessman (who turns out to be Venusian). We aren't sad when he "gets what's coming to him," but we also find it somewhat ridiculous. The humans remain entirely unaware of what might have happened to them. They are simply happy to be on their way to Chicago. They probably don't even notice that the annoying businessman is not on the plane with them. Our version adds apathy as a necessary catalyst to prejudice. We have not learned the lesson Serling was trying to provide, and, in fact, we have added a layer of resignation: this is the way things are.

Reimagining "The Monsters Are Due on Maple Street" (Dhncke, Teleplay, 2017)

"Strange occurrences transform the peaceful 38th floor of Maple Street Apartments into a community on the brink of disaster. Deprived of air conditioning, water, electricity, and any way to leave the building, tensions boil over as residents clash over keeping the peace or giving in to suspicion." In the words of undergraduate student writer, Jonah Dahncke:

> Serling could take a peaceful suburb of people and get them at each other's throats with a little bit of suspicion, or he could ruin someone's dream with a simple pair of broken glasses. For a kid who still thought good writing was equal to the number of pages you could crank out, they were powerful lessons in simplicity. When I signed on for "Maple Street," I did my best to remember those lessons. We reeled in the scope a bit, and focused on just a few small changes we could throw at our characters. We treated the story like a good experiment; one variable, close the system, and let our players react.

Much of the conversation that proceeded the writing of this episode had to do with a central tenet of television production (actually any production):

you make what you can make with what you have. Time, money, resources, personal availability—these are all factors that can make or break a show. What makes Serling so amazing to a professional producer/director is that he worked under so many restraints, yet still churned out an enormous and enormously successful body of work.

This was an important learning objective for the students. In our first discussions, we made clear we would not be able to build an entire neighborhood on a soundstage; we would not be able to block off an entire street on location; and we would not be interested in simply recreating Serling's script. Our mission was to "reimagine," not to "reproduce"; further, we had a limited budget and time—sixteen weeks is not a long time to create a complicated episode, let alone three.

An inspiration was Lars Von Trier's *Dogville* (2003). The setting for this film is essentially a map, drawn out in lines, doorways, and furniture in a soundstage. The theatrical quality felt true to Serling's roots (after all, Serling spent many years writing scripts for live television). Because of the nature of the academic schedule, this episode would have to be shot entirely in the multi-camera studio, with no exterior or location footage. To that end, the writer proposed that his episode take place in a high-rise apartment building in a big, un-named, city. He suggested that the "idyllic neighborhood" depicted in the original is less common now; it is more likely that people in your neighborhood (or apartment floor) are simply the people you see every day, but don't necessarily know. His solution was elegant, because it allowed the director and designers to create a valid setting for the morality play, but with a twist.

Serling's "The Monsters Are Due on Maple Street" is a tale of human fear and social collapse. David Melbye, in his exploration of pervasive forms of irony in *The Twilight Zone*, addresses the episode as a critique of Cold War paranoia:

> [T]he triumph of the alien invaders is implied, although in this case their methods make the ironic point that humans (Americans) defining themselves against "otherness" are their own worst enemy. And, again, *The Twilight Zone*'s moral universe is less concerned with restoring national security in this context than with eradicating anyone prone to either paranoia or prejudice [91].

Tony Albarella, in his commentary on the episode, tells us that "Monsters" is about what happens to human beings when pitted against elusive or hidden opponents: "It focuses not on the external threat of invasion but instead on one of the curiously disturbing facets of human nature: We are capable of banding together to fight a common enemy, but when our opponent is not conspicuous or clearly defined, we often allow our fears and animal instincts to strip away the very humanity we seek to protect"

(126). Our reimagined episode follows a similar trajectory as does the original, in which a mid-twentieth-century American suburb is destroyed by wild suspicions of alien infiltration. Both episodes open with normalized views of a community, show us the destabilizing effects of runaway paranoia and fear on the community, and end with a revelation that this is all part of alien activities.

Although similar, it is important to understand the differences between the two versions to appreciate what the remake brings to the table. Serling's suburban Maple Street is replaced by Maple Street Apartments, exchanging the open outdoor spaces of the original for a claustrophobic indoor setting. Streets in the neighborhood are hallways in the apartment complex, and an elevator and emergency stair become the main access points to the outside. People are different too. Playing with cellphones replaces cleaning cars and watering lawns. At least a few people on Serling's Maple Street seem handy enough to fix their own appliances, but in Dahncke's apartment building, people rely on professional fixit people to keep their appliances and services in working order. This includes the elevator or the door to the stairs, making handymen the guardians of the inhabitants' physical freedom.

Other modes of contact with the outside world, like cellphones, are even further outside the control of the people who use them, relying on maintenance and service provided by distant service providers. If Serling's "Monsters" "invokes a critique of suburban dependence on modern appliances when ... the neighbors congregate on the sidewalk to complain of power and telephone failures" (91), as Melbye argues, convenience has been largely outsourced in the remade Monsters. The further surrender of control that comes with apartment life becomes the main vehicle for the problems that plague the community. In Serling's "Monsters," the greatest emphasis is laid on cars that will not start, or that start and stop on their own, a loss of control over an appliance that, in the 1950s, was easier to maintain on your own, or with help from a knowledgeable neighbor. In the remake, all problems have a significant service component: Loss of water, electricity, and cellular service reflects the loss of conveniences provided by professionals uniquely capable of maintaining them. The exit signs, replacements for the candles in Serling's original when the lights go out and the people find themselves trapped, reflect a tragic dependence on systems and infrastructures beyond the peoples' control. Even leaving the building is beyond their control. In Maple Street Apartments, the people's freedom is a far greater source of tension, resting less with rights than with professionals keeping things in good working order.

The remake's set design reflects these circumstances aesthetically. Producer Peter Gianakakis emphasizes how "invisible barriers lend form to the peoples' lives in the apartment complex, and how these barriers further develop and define the characters: our art director, Julia Telthorst, came up with the brilliant idea to color-code the apartments, to tell us more about who these people are (e.g., green represents science, so a scientist's room is green)." Gianakakis also relates how red is the color of exit: The longer exit is denied to the apartment dwellers, the more intense the light from the red exit signs grows. Director Jared Smith reflects that these changes enhance the tensions of the original "Maple Street": "[b]y visually representing architecture as compartmentalization, by emphasizing the layout of the apartments over the architecture of the apartments, the cage-like atmosphere of the place becomes more pronounced, and the status of the apartment dwellers as prisoners becomes clearer." The floor in the updated Maple Street Apartments is immediately a more primed powder-keg than the original, with harrowing consequences.

In both the original episode and the remake, the original destabilizing premise of aliens is introduced by children. In Serling's original, Tommy, a neighborhood boy, introduces the notion of aliens and how they infiltrate communities, but, in the remake, Nora, Chris' granddaughter, introduces only the idea that "someone, even aliens" is behind what people are experiencing. An adult, Alex, theorizes about how the aliens, or rather terrorists, infiltrate the community. We don't know much about the mental state of Charlie, the main antagonist and agitator in Serling's "Monsters," although he is a fairly transparent allegory for Joe McCarthy (identified by Albarella), a man with a taste for the power granted him by riling people up into a mob. We know a bit more about Alex, a high-strung young professional who slips alcohol into his coffee and, perhaps lacking self-confidence, defines himself by his work and by his place in his own fantasy of terrorist infiltration. When Charlie mistakenly shoots a handyman, becoming a murderer, he retains enough of himself to express some human shock and remorse. When Alex shoots Nora, all he can say, over and over again, is "I got them." Whether from shell shock or madness, Alex's loss of humanity is associated with his insistence on a fantasy of the other as justification for his actions. This fantasy helps bring about the apartment floor's final unraveling.

Meanwhile, we learn the aliens disguised themselves as handymen, and this is all part of their education. The humans are simply rats in the maze of their class experiment. The humans were never in control, but the aliens didn't necessarily know what they were doing either. Instead of slowing down and asking "why is this happening," the humans leap to more and more rash conclusions, largely based on film aliens and television terrorists. While they could never have guessed that they were simply "test subjects," they simply react in predictable ways based on little actual knowledge. The alien children, pushing buttons and flipping switches, are simply "seeing what happens."

In many ways, as apathy was added to Serling's ideas about prejudice, this reimagined episode of Monsters suggests that technology exacerbates ideas about otherness. We do not have to know people if we have their "number." We do not have to talk to people in person; we can text them. To that end, technology, which is intended to connect us, actually serves to separate us. So, it is entirely plausible the people who are separated by a thin wall actually do not know each other. In that environment, it is also easy to let ubiquitous images of terrorists, aliens, and other "evil-doers" rise quickly to the forefront of the possible reasons for any negatively charged situation. This is an example of the "*CSI*-effect," first referred to as such in *USA Today* in an article by Richard Willing (*USA Today*, 2004). We tend to believe that the world is actually like what we see on television and in film, and we adjust our expectations accordingly. As I explain in an art direction course: if every car actually exploded when it was in an accident, there would be far fewer accident survivors, no need for seatbelts and airbags, and almost everyone would have actually seen such an explosion.

We are left to ask: how strong can our human bonds be in a world where people increasingly live simultaneously together and apart from each other? How can we get to know our neighbors in an ever-shrinking world, where information of varying quality is so readily available? Especially in light of notions of fake news and alternative facts in our society, how can we overcome these challenges when various actors can so easily disrupt conversation with a little well-placed spectacle and fantasy?

Conclusion

Experiential learning is tough. A key purpose of storytelling is to allow us to know about a challenging world without necessarily having to experience it ourselves, but sometimes the experience itself is part of the story. Every student and faculty member who helped produce these three reimagined episodes has a story *about the creation of the story*. Students were evaluated on their level of participation, their professionalism, and the number of roles they filled. Some students directed one episode, shot another, and edited yet another. Others simply wrote. But each contributed in their own way, and now has their own story.

The first draft of Cara Reed's script for "The Shelter" required five settings and a large soundstage. We could not accommodate that, so she and her assistants went back to the "writer's room." They came back with a script in which much of the action would have taken place in an overturned fishing boat on a lake. Impossible. We were not going to take expensive digital filmmaking equipment out onto an actual lake in the middle of November. Ultimately, however, the final draft made the right choice. Reed set her story in a remote house in the woods with an unusual library vault. Her choice was made in service of the realities of production.

Jonah Dahncke faced the challenge of how to put a community into the pressure cooker of a realistic community in his version of "Monsters." He chose an apartment building. That, of course, created its own challenges for the production team. The key component of apartment buildings is walls. Most of the conversations in the original episode take place on the street, but in this case an apartment hallway is just too restrictive, so the art director, Julia Telthorst, working with the production designer, decided to take out the walls and virtually color-code each apartment.

In Kali Munro's version of "The Shelter," a house is literally burnt down. Figuring out how to burn down a house without actual flame (and, to be honest, the house was my sister's in rural Brown County) was a challenge that involved mirrors, fog, fans, lighting—virtually anything but flame.

Of course, one of the most iconic elements of the original series was the presence of "The Narrator" (as he is named in every episode). Obviously, we did not want to cast a Serling lookalike in the "Narrator" role. What we did want was a storyteller, and we were lucky that a gifted storyteller was available. Gladys DeVane, a professor in the Department of Speech and Hearing Sciences at Indiana University, became our "Narrator." She is revealed at the beginning and end of each episode, in homage to Serling, as she steps into the shot or is revealed by clever camera movement or lighting.

Every student who worked on the project faced multiple successes and tragedies. Good choices, bad choices, poor decisions, good decisions, successful outcomes, poor outcomes. These are the realities of the creative industry. One can learn, in a fashion, about these things vicariously, but doing the thing is what creates the story.

Works Cited

Albarella, Tony. "NEIGHBORHOOD WATCH: Commentary on the 'Monsters Are Due on Maple Street.'" *The Best of Rod Serling's Twilight Zone Scripts*, Tony Albarella, editor. Gauntlet Press, 2014, pp.125–130.

American Photography: A Century of Images. Interview with Daniel Czitrom. Directed by Ellen Hovde and Muffie Meyer, PBS, 1999.

Foust, J.C. "The Paternalistic Eye: Senator Edwin Johnson and the US Television Freeze." *Historical Journal of Film, Radio and Television*, vol. 38, no. 3, 2017, pp. 584–602.

Gigerenzer, Gerd, and Peter M. Todd, et al. *Simple Heuristics That Make Us Smart.* Oxford University Press, 1999, p. 24.

Harari, Yuval N. *Sapiens: A Brief History of Humankind.* HarperCollins Publishers, 2015.

"I Am the Night—Color Me Black," *The Twilight Zone*, written by Rod Serling, directed by Abner Biberman, Image Entertainment, 2013.

May, Ellen Cameron. "Serling in Creative Mainstream." *Los Angeles Times*, June 25, 1967, p. C22–23.

Melbye, David. *Irony in The Twilight Zone: How the Series Critiqued Postwar American Culture.* Rowman & Littlefield Publishers, 2016.

Meyers, Lawrence. *Inside the TV Writer's Room: Practical Advice for Succeeding in Television.* Syracuse University Press, 2010.

"The Monsters Are Due on Maple Street," *The Twilight Zone*, written by Rod Serling, directed by Ronald Winston, Image Entertainment, 2003.

Plantinga, Carl. "Frame Shifters, Surprise Endings and Spectator Imagination in *The Twilight Zone*." *Philosophy in the Twilight Zone*, edited by Noël Carroll and Lester H. Hunt. Wiley-Blackwell, 2009, pp. 39–57.

Santayana, George. *The Life of Reason or, The Phases of Human Progress, vol. 1 Reason in Common Sense*, edited by Marianne S. Wokeck and Martin A. Coleman, critical ed. MIT Press, 2011, p. 172.

"The Shelter." *21st Century Twilight Zone*, written by Cara Reed, directed by Jaeson Jackson. Indiana University, 2017.

"The Shelter," *The Twilight Zone*, written by Rod Serling, directed by Lamont Johnson, Image Entertainment, 2011.

Sirridge, Mary. "The Treachery of the Commonplace." *Philosophy in the Twilight Zone*, edited by Noël Carroll and Lester H. Hunt. Wiley-Blackwell, 2009, pp. 58–76.

"Submitted for Your Approval." *American Masters,* directed by Susan Lacy, performance by Kim Hunter, et al., PBS Home Video, DVD, 2003.

21st Century Twilight Zone, written by Jonah Dahncke, directed by Peter Gianakakis. Indiana University, 2017.

"Will the Real Martian Please Stand Up?" *21st Century Twilight Zone*, written by Kali Munro, directed by Russell McGee. Indiana University, 2017.

"Will the Real Martian Please Stand Up?" *The Twilight Zone*, written by Rod Serling, directed by Montgomery Pittman, Image Entertainment, 2011.

Willing, Richard. "CSI Effect Has Juries Wanting More Evidence." *USA Today*, 5 August 2004.

About the Contributors

Michael **Aronson** is a doctoral student at the Indiana University Media School. He studies the intersection of media and religion, with a particular interest in media histories of the twentieth- and twenty-first centuries. His favorite episode is "The Shelter."

Simon **Bacon** is an independent scholar based in Poznan, Poland. He has authored and edited more than 20 books on vampires, monsters, and horror, including *Eco-Vampires* (2020), *The Anthropocene and the Undead* (2022), and *The Undead in the 21st Century* (2022). His favorite episode is "Monster!" from the second incarnation of the series.

William C. **Boles** holds the Hugh F. and Jeannette G. McKean Chair of English at Rollins College. Among his publications are *Understanding David Henry Hwang* (2013) and *After In-Yer-Face Theatre* (2020). Prior to attending a performance of Anne Washburn's *The Twilight Zone*, he had never watched an episode of Serling's series.

Kevin **Bolinger** is a professor of education at Indiana State University. His published works focus on developing critical thinking in secondary and post-secondary classrooms. He teaches "Philosophy in *The Twilight Zone*," which uses the classic series to explore the human condition. His favorite episodes are "Walking Distance" and "The Changing of the Guard."

Jimmy **Butts** teaches composition and rhetoric. He has worked at various universities and received his Ph.D. from the Rhetorics, Communication, and Information Design program at Clemson University. His interests include rhetorical strangeness, media studies, and writing pedagogy. His favorite episodes are "Time Enough at Last" and "It's a Good Life."

David Bennett **Carren** is a professor at the University of Texas Rio Grande Valley. He earned his MFA in screenwriting at Spalding University and has over two hundred credits in TV and film. His work has earned a Writers Guild Award nomination and a Silver Palm Award. He is the author of *Next Level Screenwriting* (2019), and his favorite episodes are "Eye of the Beholder" and "To Serve Man."

Elsa M. **Carruthers** is a speculative fiction writer, academic, and poet. She earned an MFA in writing popular fiction from Seton Hill University. Her work has been published in several anthologies, magazines, and e-zines including *Amazing Stories*

Magazine and *Space & Time Magazine*. Her favorite episodes include "Dust" and "The Trade-ins."

Paul **Chitlik** teaches screenwriting at Loyola Marymount University. He is the author of *39 Steps to Better Screenwriting* (2014), and the novels *Berns with an "E"* (1996) and *Rug Berns* (2011). His latest film is *The Wedding Dress* (2014). His favorite episode (other than his own) is "To Serve Man."

Nicholas **Diak** is a pop-culture scholar. He is the editor of *The New Peplum* (2018) and coeditor (with Michele Brittany) of *Horror Literature from Gothic to Post-Modern* (2020). He is a co-host of the H.P. Lovecast Podcast and co-creator of the Ann Radcliffe Academic Conference. "To Serve Man" is his favorite episode.

Erin **Giannini** is an independent scholar. She has served as an editor and contributor at PopMatters and her work has focused on portrayals of corporate culture on television, as well as religion, socioeconomics, production culture, and technology. Her favorite episodes are "Time Enough at Last" and "Twenty Two."

Brandon R. **Grafius** is an assistant professor of biblical studies at Ecumenical Theological Seminary. His second book, *Reading the Bible with Horror* (2019) has been nominated for the Grawemeyer Prize in Religion. He is a coeditor (with John W. Morehead) of *Theology and Horror* (2020). His favorite episodes are "Twenty Two" and "It's a Good Life."

Valerie L. **Guyant** teaches at Montana State University–Northern. She received her Ph.D. in literature from Northern Illinois University. She studies folklore, popular culture, and speculative fiction and is the author of "Deadites vs. Adaptation" (2019) and "What or Who Is 'Matska' in *Carmilla*?" (2014). Her favorite episodes include "Five Characters in Search of an Exit" and "Night Call."

Alexander E. **Hooke** is a professor of philosophy at Stevenson University in Baltimore County, Maryland. He is a coeditor of *The Twilight Zone and Philosophy* (2018) and the author of *Philosophy Sketches* (2018). In addition to the classic episodes, he enjoys "The Masks" and "The Trade-Ins."

Melissa A. **Kaufler** enjoys writing about Gothic pop culture, hauntology, and the many iterations of Frankenstein in film and literature through a feminist-Marxist lens. She earned an MA in gothic culture from St. Mary's University and works for the California legislature. Her favorite episodes include "The Last Flight" and "Once Upon a Time."

Dawn **Keetley** is a professor of English, teaching horror and the gothic at Lehigh University. She is the author of *Making a Monster* (2017), editor of *Jordan Peele's Get Out* (2020), and coeditor (with Matthew Wynn Sivils) of *The Ecogothic in Nineteenth-Century American Literature* (2017). Her favorite episodes include "Mirror Image" and "Number 12 Looks Just Like You."

Steve **Krahnke** received an MA in theater from the University of Michigan and is a senior lecturer in the Indiana University Media School. He is also an accomplished manager or producer of films for PBS, and has won two Emmys and three CINE Golden Eagle Awards. His teaching has earned the Provost's Award for student mentorship, the Trustees Teaching Award, and the Career Distinguished Teaching Award.

David **Melbye** is a professor of film and media studies in the School of Advanced Studies at the University of Tyumen in Russia. He received his Ph.D. from the University of Southern California's School of Cinematic Arts. His research interests include modernist visual media and social critique. He is the author of *Irony in The Twilight Zone* (2015). His favorite episode is "Living Doll."

Michael **Meyerhofer** received an MFA in poetry from Southern Illinois University. He is the author of five books of poetry, including *Ragged Eden* (2019), as well as two fantasy trilogies. His work has appeared in *Asimov's Science Fiction, Rattle*, and *DIAGRAM*, among other journals. His favorite episodes include "The Shelter" and "Shadow Play."

Paul **Popiel** is a writer, photographer and gamer. He earned an MFA in popular fiction from Seton Hill University. He has published short stories in *Fantastic Futures 13* and *Vampires Suck*. His favorite episodes include "An Occurrence at Owl Creek Bridge" and "The Incredible World of Horace Ford."

Ron **Riekki** is an author whose books include *Niiji* (2020), *My Ancestors Are Reindeer Herders and I Am Melting in Extinction* (2019), and *Posttraumatic* (2019). He has coedited numerous collections of essays, including *Undocumented* (2019) and *The Many Lives of* It (2020). His favorite episodes are "It's a Good Life" and "The Silence."

Molly A. **Schneider** is an assistant professor at Columbia College Chicago. She received a Ph.D. in the screen cultures program at Northwestern University. Her work focuses on cultural histories of the midcentury television anthology drama in the United States. Her favorite episodes include "The Monsters Are Due on Maple Street" and "I Am the Night—Color Me Black."

Kevin J. **Wetmore**, Jr., is a professor at Loyola Marymount University, the author of 10 books and the editor of another 17, including the Bram Stoker Award–nominated *Uncovering Stranger Things* (2018) and *The Streaming of Hill House* (2020), as well as the author of more than 75 book chapters and journal articles. His favorite episodes include "Mr. Garrity and the Graves" and "Will the Real Martian Please Stand Up?"

Index